The Tiger Project

THE TIGER PROJECT

A SERIES DEVOTED TO GERMANY'S WORLD WAR II TIGER TANK CREWS

ALFRED RUBBEL

SCHWERE PANZER (TIGER) ABTEILUNG 503

Series edited by Dale Richard Ritter

Schiffer Military History
Atglen, PA

Main translation: Peter Schlosser
Other translation assistance from Claudia Kühn, Edward Ritter, and Conrad Weck

Thanks to my wife, Lisa, and my three little girls Brittani, Mackenzie, and Gabriella for supporting my hobby, and to my dad for the encouragement and support in more ways than one!

Book Design by Ian Robertson.

Library of Congress Control Number: 2003116011

Printed in China.
ISBN: 0-7643-2000-9

Published by Schiffer Publishing Ltd.
4880 Lower Valley Road
Atglen, PA 19310
Phone: (610) 593-1777
FAX: (610) 593-2002
E-mail: Info@schifferbooks.com.
Visit our web site at: www.schifferbooks.com
Please write for a free catalog.
This book may be purchased from the publisher.
Please include $3.95 postage.
Try your bookstore first.

In Europe, Schiffer books are distributed by:
Bushwood Books
6 Marksbury Avenue
Kew Gardens
Surrey TW9 4JF
England
Phone: 44 (0) 20 8392-8585
FAX: 44 (0) 20 8392-9876
E-mail: info@bushwoodbooks.co.uk.
Free postage in the UK. Europe: air mail at cost.
Try your bookstore first.

CONTENTS

PREFACE

Unfortunately I failed to take advantage of a wonderful opportunity that was in front of me as a young soldier in a foreign land. Spending four years in Germany provided me with the perfect setting in which to conduct interviews of the soldiers who had once served in the highly regarded Panzerwaffe. Instead, my interests developed more after I had returned home and found a focus for my curiosity.

I began by writing to veterans, German veterans, of the Second World War. My first focus was on quantity. I wanted to write to as many veterans as possible and seek contacts who were willing to answer some of my questions. Admittedly, I only sought out the Knight's Cross recipients in my initial correspondence. Their addresses were available and their experiences were typically documented.

From that mass of correspondence with some extremely fascinating individuals I began to focus my growing interests on the Panzerwaffe and particularly on the Tiger abteilungs of the Wehrmacht. The few, still-living, Knight's Cross recipients who had served in the Tigerwaffe were very helpful and kind and helped me tremendously with contacting other individuals from their old units. Men like Clemens-Heinrich Graf von Kageneck, Walter Scherf and Werner Freiherr von Beschwitz took the time to introduce me to their comrades and from that point the list of contacts snowballed and I found myself writing to many old Tiger soldiers who previously had little or no contact with outsiders seeking their personal stories.

True gentlemen like Martin Burmester, Ulrich Koppe, Horst Krönke, Dr. Günther Polzin, Richard Freiherr von Rosen, Alfred Rubbel, and many, many more were extremely kind and accommodating in responding to my persistent mails. I was invited to visit with them in their homes and allowed a personal look into their lives. For their courtesy I am extremely grateful because without such receptive individuals I would never have been able to have the success that I am in contacting and corresponding with so many veterans of Germany's vaunted Tigerwaffe.

Thanks to the many veterans, and their widows, wives and families with whom I have had contact, I am able to present some of the information shared with me in what promises to be a series of unique books that present biographical and anecdotal information of individual veterans of the *Heeres Tiger abteilungen*.

For a couple individuals there were adequate materials to fill their own books, and for others I will combine several Tiger veterans to form a single book. Whenever possible I used unpublished photographs and documents but there will also be some more familiar pictures and even a story or two, which the veteran had shared previously.

All of the credit for the information goes to the individuals and their families; I was simply a catalyst for many to get the information out to an interested public.

Dale R. Ritter
September 2003

FOREWORD

I met Dale R. Ritter a few years ago and we had been exchanging many letters. They mostly contained insistent questions regarding certain events during the war, which seemed to me a bit peripheral and sort of beside the point. Then, in December of 2000, he had written to me that he was very much interested in the personal observations and impressions of one involved in war. Because I happened to be one of the few surviving Panzer officers with many years of combat experience (out of five years in the military, I spent 3 years in a tank battling on the front lines), I was in a position to answer many, many questions and to relate my experiences and impressions of those times. This was a new, inquisitive direction that Dale was taking. These types of themes were unfortunately also missing in large part from the literature known to me. It has always been a matter of great personal importance to adhere to the realizations that also in war, there is a tremendous human aspect that never loses its meaning and that the spirit of brotherhood and humanity amongst men never dies.

When Mr. Ritter paid me a visit in Germany in June of 2001 there then took place, in addition to getting to know one another on a personal level, a very lively and stimulating exchange of ideas, in which the human aspects of combat experience were the focus of the conversation. When I then showed him my "Personal Combat Diary 1939-1945", he asked if I might leave this document with him for his perusal. I must admit, I agreed to this request with some apprehension, as this document was a unique copy. His determination to actually attempt to publish this piece of work surprised me greatly because I had assembled this for my family and myself. Inside were conveyed the most striking and lasting impressions of my entire life! I also agreed to disclose this because my "experience of war" was emblematic in many a way of the experience of millions of young Germans who, although barely 20 years of age, were involved in this titanic struggle. Of those boys born in 1920, 34% paid the ultimate price. An additional reason for my agreeing to all this was that I could indeed bear living witness to the events of that time, even if my personal perspective of the war was a bit narrow emanating from the lower tactical combat levels and surely not free of subjective opinions and appraisals. The German Wehrmacht as instrument of an increasingly treasonous Governing Body of State is not without its own implications of guilt and responsibility. There were 18 million German soldiers involved in the Second World War and, yes, there were atrocities. However, these were always the exception and never the rule. Until the end of the war there was always a reverent adherence amongst all good military detachments to the standards of military international law. I had the good fortune of being amongst these fine men.

Alfred Rubbel,
August 2003

INTRODUCTION

All combat troops carried a War Diary, or *Kriegstagebuch* (KTB), with them. The purpose of this was to allow one to register the day's events and back those up with documentation. This was intended to portray where, when, and how the actions of these troops took place.

In addition to this diary, which I kept, it is my further intention to complete the memoirs of my days as a soldier from 1939 to 1945 by working in additional material obtained by means of my own personal sources, memories, photos, and documents. It is a piece of history that totally consumed me. I wish this to serve as an account to those of our younger generations who, apparently all-knowing, deserve to learn just how those of us who were there actually viewed the war period and individual events, even if through one subjective and limited source. For me, this period was alive and fraught with tales of camaraderie, care, loyalty, bravery, and humanity. It took place under exceptional circumstances.

I have brought together many things to accomplish this work. I quite frequently pick up these pages I wrote. These memoirs today provide me with insights I could never imagine to have had back then. Most importantly, I was extremely lucky to have survived that war, as one third of all German soldiers lost their lives. I was a soldier for 67 months—41 of those in action inside a tank. I lived through 81 days of Panzer combat; I commemorate those comrades outside of the tank for my survival.

Alfred Rubbel
Oberstleutnant a.D.
1.5.2001

1

Recruitment into the Infantry at Braunsberg/East Prussia

Volunteer for War (December 1939)

On September 1st, 1939, the Second World War began with the march of the German Wehrmacht into Poland. The fact that war may have been imminent did not go unnoticed by those of us in East Prussia. The drafting of young men, strange detachments of various troops in the villages, blackout measures, the suspension of the right to drive

Private automobiles or the actual confiscation of vehicles, specifically aimed reports in the press and radio, and limitations on the provisioning of foods and supplies all pointed to war. The feeling amongst the people was varied. The older generation, who had experienced the First World War, was very reserved. We boys, inexperienced and therefore easily impressionable, viewed the war—at least the war against Poland—as necessary.

And so that's how it all started. I had just turned 18 when I volunteered for duty on the 3rd of September. There were basically two motives for all this: If there was war, it was only fitting and proper that I should become a soldier and, as a volunteer for war, I could then choose the branch of armed services of my liking, and that was the armored forces.

Increasingly my older friends were being drafted out of school and the Hitler Youth to the point where the entire student populations born in the years 1919 and 1920 were called up. As one attached to the News Staff, which was of interest to me, I observed the Hitler Youth as they were sent away in the most impressive of ways. This amounted to a roll call to fall into a procession, which in turn drew many into its ranks and ended up as a hysterical, unorganized march through the evening. The speeches that were given on that night were not like those we normally heard; they were thoughtful and deep. As the ones who were staying behind, we accompanied our so-called comrades striking out one last time into the local surroundings, in order to say a proper farewell to those cherished places of their youth. Nothing again would ever be the same, as England and France had declared war on Germany. The relatively easy battle for Poland would certainly be won; however, the initial euphoria would pass.

In November 1939, I too received my orders for duty. My parents did not agree with my decision. My father was very ill with cancer and died just about a year later. Because of his

condition, my mother attempted to hinder my entry into the services by reporting to the Office of Replacement Personnel that my services were required to tackle domestic farmhand duties. But this had been in vain.

I was initially quite pleased with my recruitment, as I had landed in the branch of my supposed choice. As fate would have it—I didn't really know any better—I had been called up into the 14th Panzer-Abwehr Company, Infantry Replacement Regiment 21 in Braunsberg. The abbreviation "Pz" was misleading, as I actually ended up in the infantry on the 5th of December 1939! The Infantry Ersatz Regiment 21 acted as reserve to the 21st Infantry Division, which was on the ready in the Eiffel. I must say, I was not in the best of sorts being away from home for the first time, especially as I was stuck in the infantry! It was a bitter cold, frosty December day with no snow on the ground when I got off the train in Braunsberg, along with many other young men who had been soldiers since the previous midnight. There was quite a lot of noise and commotion on the platform, as two men in gray-twined overcoats shouted at the top of their lungs: "Artillery recruits step to the left, and those in the Infantry step to the right!"

Since I had, according to my own opinion, no business in either of these detachments, I remained standing with my bags all by myself in the middle of the platform and waited to be invited to the proper Panzer unit. One of these gentlemen dressed in field-gray approached me and quite disquietingly wanted to know what the hell I was waiting for. I then held my detachment orders under his nose. This guy went completely dark-red in the face and roared: "You are not even in the Infantry!" I was to spend the next six months there.

Emil Witt (far left) , our Squad Commander; Walter Wegmann (sitting to Witt's left) from Westphalia, whose nickname was "Vulture" (*Geier*); (standing behind Wegmann) Karl-Heinz Knollmann, also from Westfalia. A particularly eloquent young man who as an officer in the 21st Infantry Division with Infantry Regiment 24 was awarded the Knight's Cross. Then later, when serving with the BGS (*Bundesgrenzschutz* - Federal Border Guard) he became embroiled in some sort of spying affair. Name I don't remember (standing to Knollmann's left), he entertained us with these unusual speeches, which he took very seriously. He also had a ravenous appetite, which expressed itself in the form of the stereotypical question: "Has anyone bread?" Also another name I don't remember (sitting, center, to Wegmann's left), he was one of the quiet ones. Heinz Behrmann from Memel (sitting, bottom row, left) with his nickname-in-tow of "Teddy." We were friends and went together into the Panzer Corps. He was killed during the first days of combat in Russia near the city of Minsk. Name I don't remember (sitting, bottom row, right). Helmut Stars from Tilsit (middle row, fourth from left), a somewhat grumpy type. Schmidt (middle row, fifth from left), I don't remember the first name. Alfred Rubbel (back row, far right). Helmut (?) Krönke (farthest right in the picture) from Braunsberg. Went into the paratroops (*Fallschirmjäger*) and was paralyzed due to a mishap during the airborne assault on Crete.

Schütze Rubbel in various military garbs, January/ February 1940 in Braunsberg.

Snow shoveling in front of our Company Block. It was March 1940, and the sun shone quite warmly then. One did not need to work up a sweat to stay warm, which the picture portrays.

Gardening was also appropriate. Because I pretended to know something about this, I limited myself to the dispensing of suggestions and let comrade Schmidt do the digging.

Our three-month recruit training was very difficult, yet we learned well. During that time, as well as the time spent in Braunsberg, I was exposed only to the best and fairest of instructors. The Company Chief (*Kompanie Chef*) was *Hauptmann* von Boddin, an excellent officer whom we revered, in military jargon also called a *Spieß*, as he was appropriately known. This person held the entire Company and staff of *Unteroffiziere* tightly in his grip. I don't remember our *Zugführer* (Platoon Commander); however, I recall quite well our *Korporalschaftsführer* (Squad Commander), *Unteroffizier* Emil Witt. Everybody liked him. He was kind-hearted and understanding, and he knew this, which is why he tried so hard to camouflage these features behind a certain air of austerity and strictness. But his lovely character shone through nevertheless.

With the formation of our squad, which with ten men occupied a barracks, one had an opportunity to gather one's thoughts. We were all students, yet the imperative in this formation was to ascertain early on just who amongst us would be suitable as new blood for positions of leadership. As a practical consequence among us, I can say that things were somewhat "cultivated" when measured with the tone of the remaining barracks, where there existed certain social strife. I remember that we all got on very well, especially since there was a considerable spread in ages, ranging from the birth years of 1918 to 1921. For me as an only child it was the first time in my life that I ever really had to find myself within a group, which I think I did successfully. I felt very comfortable. Consideration and tolerance must have abounded, as I remember neither strife, nor any individual or group laying

A Sunday excursion with the Backwater-Bank Express from Braunsberg to Tolkemit. From there we took the steamer by way of the Frische Lagoon to Kahlberg. It must have been the end of May 1940, as our group was still together. Seen here from the left: Rubbel, Knollmann, and Krönke.

"Has-anyone-Bread," Rubbel and Schmidt after obtaining a beach set-up within correct operating distance to a female beach crew. This was during the time when dancing was temporarily forbidden and one needed to find other ways to initiate relations.

claim to the majority. I believe that my upbringing at home combined with the sense of community experienced in the Hitler Youth provided me with a certain tolerance and willingness to get along with others.

After recruit training in March 1940, the group was moved along to *Unteroffizier* Applicant Training, and thereafter we all separated, as transfers and administration of various functions naturally followed.

Too Late for the French Campaign (June 1940)

The march West against France and against the British Expeditionary Force had been decided upon since the turn of the year ('39-40). Up to that point, we had all been enjoying the *drole guere*, or "phony war." Our foes in the West had been dragging their feet, considering whether to risk an attack. It became clear to us that Hitler would force the issue. Therefore, the troops were massed and made ready for a western campaign. Thus the 12th Infantry Division was set up, and to this the 286th Infantry Regiment was also attached, which consisted of personnel from the East Prussian Ersatz Infantry Regiments 1, 21, and 43(?). Those of us from Braunsberg were huddled together with the 14th Company and were assembled anew. We relocated into the base of the old, famous 1st Infantry Regiment in Königsberg on our parade route to the west. Up to now we had been training on the 3,7 cm Pak (*Panzerabwehrkanone*) and had been moving this gun around from place to place manually. The platoon's vehicles—beautiful civilian six and eight-cylinder Horchs, Mercedes, and Wanderers, which had been sitting in the garage up till now in order to save fuel—were brought back up to snuff, and we then were afforded the chance to lounge about in the cushions of these "General-Director" sleighs.

During our march further through the countryside we arrived at the *Truppenübungsplatz* (Troop Drill Grounds) at Groß Born near Neustettin in East Pommerania. On May 10th 1940 the campaign in the West had begun. In the campaign, which many felt would be an impossible accomplishment, France fell on the 17th of June. We were no longer needed in action. I admit most of us were affected, as we were denied our "probation." As a replacement for real action at the front we

On the return march of the 14th Company, Infantry Regiment 286 at rest by Marienburg. From left to right: Rubbel, and next to him Erich Derwelis. An exquisitely ambitious man, Derwelis later, although hailing from small-time roots and a very modest level of education, was promoted to the rank of *Generalmajor* in the NVA (East German Army). All the way to the right in the picture is our half-section leader Günter Schwanitz. A cultivated man, who was awarded the Knight's Cross while serving in the 21st Infantry.

In January 1940, in position on the Braunsberg drill grounds. This was located about four kilometers from our base, and we had to haul this 3,7 cm Pak gun by hand with a team of four men. The "Army Knock-Knock Device," which weighed about 400 kilograms (800 pounds), really worked up quite a sweat in deep snow.

then received "simulated" live combat training on the drill grounds, which I still consider a load of nonsense. This was undertaken to attempt to make us battle-hardened. To even things out, on the march back to East Prussia in Bütow/ Pommerania we were stationed in civilian quarters, and then enjoyed close to two weeks of festive carrying-on with excursions, evenings amongst the company, and contact with civilians who imagined us "Victors of France." We then traveled back to Braunsberg, whereupon our company was dissolved. A very generous "Labor Holiday" was to follow, of which I, as a former farmhand, took full advantage. We previously attempted many times to report for Panzer duty; our tanks had proven extremely valuable as evidenced by the French campaign, and as a result its ranks were about to be doubled in size. Teddy Behrmann, who had found no reason to put in for leave, held down the fort in Braunsberg. He, Walter Wegmann, and I all reported to the "Guys in Black" (Panzer-Corps). Hardly fourteen days later a telegram arrived: "Return at once-Relocation of Panzer Corps is in effect." I could hardly wait to get there. Next thing I knew, we were sitting in a train with our orders to report to Panzer Ersatz Abteilung 5 in Neuruppin/ Brandenburg. Departing from Braunsberg and my old friends there was easy for me. After all, I was going to "my" Panzer detachment, and with me were good comrades who had become friends.

On the 5th of December 1999, commemorating the 5th of December 1939:

On December 5th 1939 I was called up to the 14th (Panzer Abwehr) Company, Infantry Ersatz Regiment 21 in Braunsberg.

We were stationed at the Infantry Base, the peacetime location of the Infantry Regiment 24. With the beginning of the war, reserve troops were created out of active troops. The Infantry Replacement Regiment 21 consisted of the following:

Regimental staff of the Infantry Ersatz Regiment 21
Infantry Ersatz Abteilung 24
13th (Infantry. Squadron. Company) Infantry Ersatz Regiment 24
14th (Panzer Abwehr) Company, Infantry Ersatz Regiment 21

The initial troop detachments of the 21st Infantry Division were put in place for Infantry Regiments 3 and 45:

Infantry Ersatz Abteilung 3 - in Mohrungen
Infantry Ersatz Abteilung 45 - in Elbing

These three locations were the locations belonging in peacetime to the 3rd Infantry Regiment of the 21st Infantry Division. Commander of the Infantry Ersatz Regiment 21 was *Oberstleutnant* Wisotzky, affectionately known as "Papa" Wisotzky.

In my first days of combat near Leningrad I was in action with the 21st Infantry Division because the 12th Panzer Division had delegated their tanks to supporting the infantry. Unfortunately, I never encountered any of my former comrades whom I knew were in that division. The only contact I had existed all the way into the 1980s with Walter Wegmann. He lived in Oldenburg on the Oder and arranged for my first position of civilian employment after my release from captivity as a "Quality-Control Examiner" for fruits and vegetables in Bremen. Unfortunately, I later lost all contact with him.

Totally different situation in June 1940. There we had the eight cylinder Horch at our disposal, which was requisitioned as a means of transport. We enjoyed lounging about in the General director Cabriole on plush leather seats, and we set off on a small pleasure cruise to Stettin and back.

2

Panzer Training in Neuruppin/Brandenburg

"Change at the Front"

We were sitting on the express train on the way to Berlin; Walter Wegmann, Heinz Behrmann, and I were discussing what awaited us. Besides us there were a few comrades from Braunsberg who also had been deployed to the Panzer Corps. I had only positive expectations. I was not to be disappointed until the actual bitter end of the war in 1945.

We arrived at the peacetime locale of the 6th Panzer Regiment in Neuruppin; but we only stayed a few days. The barracks were overcrowded, so the 5th Company actually moved out to the countryside and into civilian quarters in the villages of Wildberg and Kerzlin, which were situated between Neuruppin and Neustadt/Dosse. The three of us were quartered in the farmers' tarpaulin in Kerzlin. In this village there were two platoons; the platoon leaders were *Leutnant* Brosco and *Feldwebel* Hornung. The Company Command and one further platoon were located at Wildberg, which is also the spot where our armor for training stood. We used the solid Panzer I and the Driving School tubs Pz I, Pz II, and the Pz 38t.

Although pushed through our operative service training in the areas of Panzer Education, Shooting, Armored Driver Ed., and Sports in a speedy way, I must also admit that the unique style of the Panzer Corps and our accommodations in a village instead of in a closed camp allowed us certain liberties that we had never known in the Infantry. Contact between superiors and subordinates were to be respected on both sides. One time the farmers, who were the ones accommodating us, had felt, in their opinion, that *Feldwebel* Hornung had been treating us a bit too harshly. On a particular evening in the village pub a riot broke out because of this, and from that day forward Hornung was forced to display the utmost respect in our presence.

A Command Tank of the Type Maybach- command Pz. I. This tank was discharged after the French Campaign because the enemy knew, quite correctly, that inside sat the unit commander, and therefore was superior in thwarting it in combat.

Vehicle Garage in the Panzer Camp at Neuruppin. Today these look very different, as the Russians were stationed there for fifty years.

Church in Neuruppin.

Panzer-Schütze Rubbel receives his pay—10,00 RM every ten days.

We were often allowed trips out to Neuruppin and weekly holidays to Berlin; however, our mobility was restricted due to the fact that we only had public transportation at our disposal, of which there really wasn't much out in the countryside.

My promotions were exceptionally laborious. On the first of June 1940 I became a *Oberschütze*, and on the first of December 1940 I became a *Gefreiter*. After completing my training I was assigned as a *Ladeschütze* and then

Service Remuneration in Kerzlin. There was a standing order that during this process the Company Command had to be on site. Here stands our Company Commander, *Hauptmann* Prinz Vollradt von Schaumburg-Lippe, and next to him the "*Spieß*"

Sporting Hour. Kneeling in the middle in the training suit is our instructor, *Unteroffizier* Kühne.

Behrmann and Rubbel doing a load of wash at our quarters in Kerzlin.

Rubbel, Wegmann, and Behrmann during a typical Sunday sun bath.

The three of us on an excursion to Berlin, Wegmann, and Wehrmann. Here in front of the Guardhouse, and in the background the Crown Prince Palace on Unter den Linden: Under the Linden Trees (Famous street in Berlin, which leads to the Brandenburg Gate). The inside of the old war-memorial guard-house on Unter den Linden.

View over "Unter den Linden" in the direction of the Brandenburg Gate. On the right are the Old Guardhouse and Humboldt University, formally the Prince Heinrich Palace.

When amongst the reserve troops we were not allowed to wear the black uniform. We got around this by going out in our field-grays and stowing our black threads in our suitcases. In the railway restroom we would change uniforms and then check our baggage afterwards. I had these photos taken during holiday in Tilsit. I could proudly ascertain that I, at least during this period of leave, was the only Panzer man in Tilsit. The uniform was not readily familiar, and people associated it with the strangest of institutions. The impossibly oversized Service Caps really distorted the features of us Panzer guys, who were mostly pretty small, at just over 5 feet tall. The silver braid on the shoulder flap demonstrates that the wearer had passed an *Unteroffizier* applicant course of training, and that he was now eligible to become an *Unteroffizier*. The officer-applicant wore 2 silver braids and led a stringent path to a junior-leader career.

Sundays at 12:00 noon the Berlin Main Guard would parade. Here was the Luftwaffe-Guard Regiment in October 1940.

Richtschütze—even though I hadn't even fired a tank gun. We were then detached to the newly organized Panzer Regiment 29 in Sagan. In Sagan was the Regimental Staff and the I.Abteilung. The II.Abteilung was in Lüben, while the III.Abteilung was in Sprotten. From Sprotten we marched together, and we became the 9th Company in the III.Abteilung—the middle company. We were equipped with Panzer IVs. Wegmann, Behrmann, and I remained together. I believe we were together in the same barracks.

View from the museum over the Pleasure Garden to the Berlin Palace.

Behrmann, Wegmann, and Rubbel in September 1940 in the private quarters in Kerzlin Kreis Neuruppin.

Behrmann during a weekend visit to Berlin in front of the Monument of Friedrich II on Unter den Linden.

3

With the 29th Panzer Regiment in Sprottau/Silesia

Location and Camp

Once again we were sitting in the train with our things. The Wehrmacht leadership was of the opinion that the individual soldier should be able to transport his personal military equipment by himself. In the infantry one employed the use of a knapsack called a "monkey," because the flap consisted of fur. The motorized troops had two bags for packing; they were utilized to put service-related materials in and looked like big briefcases with eyelets for holding. Whatever there wasn't room for we carried on our person, which meant lugging around our coats during the oppressive summer heat. If one had personal belongings he had to further those by rail or post.

The journey went by way of Berlin, Lübben, Cottbus, Forst, Sorau, and Sagan to Sprottau. Sprottau was a small country town in Lower Silesia at the confluence of the Sprotte and Bober rivers, which flowed down from the mountains. This place did not really appear all that attractive to us. We were especially disappointed with the barracks itself, which was an ugly building from the last century. All three companies were in one building, and each company had one floor. The sanitary facilities were more than just primitive. The toilets were located in an airy building far away from the barracks itself. Each barrack-room, occupied by about twenty men in three-story bunks, had four washbowls. In the hallway there were two faucets, which led to long lines waiting to cleanse ourselves, and as a result led many of us to just simply skip our daily preening duties altogether, in order to save time.

Here we were finally introduced to our gadget. It was a motley old vehicle indeed. The two light companies of the division used the Czech Pz. 38t, a very quick vehicle with a ridiculous 3,7 cm cannon on board. We had the intermediate Pz IV with a 7,5 cm "Stump-Cannon," which we believed to be more than adequate in terms of firepower.

We spent the period of time in Sprottau (from November 1940 until May 1941) enrolled in special education, after which each was then assigned his specific function and the armored crews were put together. The Company had seventeen intermediate Pz. IVs. They then sent me with a few others to a *Richtschützen Lehrgang* (Richtschützes Training Course) at the Panzer Corps Firing School in Putlos, near Oldenburg/H. Selten. Later, while in the *Bundeswehr*, I also received quality, focused instruction that lasted four weeks at that same school. Good teachers and suitable training materials, out of which were emphasized just the correct finer points for our instruction, pretty much guaranteed a successful result. In subsequent comparison to the *Richtschützes* Instructor's Course, however, which Officer Candidates and Tanker Sergeants of the *Bundeswehr* Panzer Corps had to pass, the *Bundeswehr* course mainly only scratched the surface. I also really liked my days there at that school, which account for my affection toward Putlos and Oldenburg that still holds true today.

Unfortunately, I then fell ill at the end of January 1941 with pneumonia in both my lungs. Only through the certain diagnosis of our troop physician, a reserve staff doctor named Dr. Messdorf—whom we would later encounter in a critical situation—did I end up in a quality hospital in Lübeck, where I slowly was nursed back to health. The local municipal hospital on the St. Juergen Ring had a "military wing," as there really was no actual "field care unit" there. I would like to say that in that place there were both German soldiers and French P.O.W.s. I know that people today like to portray the *Wehrmacht* as the incarnation of evil and find it hard to believe that that could

On a Sunday in November 1940 in the Camp at Sprottau there was time for a few pictures. The Pz.I was supposedly a reconstructed vehicle, on which Wegmann and I had a little fun.

Also worth showing is that we knew how to handle the motorcycle and sidecar, although neither of us had a corresponding driver's permit.

happen! We all received the exact same attention, and the French were not divided up any differently than we were. Where the barriers of speech allowed we had real contact with each other; for example, when German soldiers had—through either shopping in Lübeck of from visitors—additional things to eat, we gladly offered these to our French compatriots. It is very important for me to communicate that fact.

I then returned back to my Company around March/April and was allowed three weeks recovery holiday in Tilsit. In April I was sent to the Formation Firing School at the Troop Drill Grounds in Neuhammer. Thereafter I traveled to Putlos for sharp shooting instruction with the entire Company by way of train. I was the *Ladeschütze* (loader) in the head panzer with *Oberleutnant* Obermann. Our Company Officers were

Pictured here was our tank, the "900," the lead-tank with our driver "Charlie," who fell near Tichwin in November 1941.

Right: Although I didn't quite belong to this place atop the turret, I let myself be photographed there nevertheless. It would still be another year until I would arrive there for real.

Above and following: These photographs are memories of my recovery time in Lübeck from January-March 1941. This is the Holsten Gate.

The Cathedral

Leutnants Sommerfeld and Spiegel. It was probably the middle of May 1940 when we left Sprottau—forever! From then on I would be "on the roll" for the next five years until the end of the war, plus a couple of months thereafter until I could begin civilian life again in a fixed geographical location.

The regiment then relocated to the Wandernlager near Züllichau, and afterwards to a Regenwurmlager, both of which were situated east of Frankfurt on the Oder near the German Reich border to the province of Posen. Somehow we got through this time, which lasted about three weeks, I assume. Then

St. Maria Church

Old Lübeck

Salt Storehouses on the Trave.

Hospital of the Holy Ghost.

around the 10th of June we loaded up onto the train and steamed our way east. In the area of Allenstein we got off and marched into the supply areas by way of Nikolaiken, near the border in the area of Lyk. There, in a well-forested section, we formed up under cover. Lately it was plainly evident to the last man that there would be war soon. Whether through latrine-perpetrated scuttlebutt or through conscious misinformation, we were under the impression somehow that the Russians had granted us, as the so-called "Iran-Army," the right to march through their territory into the Caucasus, in order then to meet up with Rommel's Army, if they had indeed pushed through to Iran by way of Egypt. According to a company dispatch, we were told that shortly we would butt horns with an opponent whose tank squadrons were of a similar quality to ours. Not a word was spoken about the notorious "Commissar Order."

It was the 21st of June 1941, a beautiful summer day, which at that time of year in Masuren is almost always the rule.

A portion of 9th Company with *Leutnant* Sommerfeld at an advanced training session for non-commissioned officers (NCOs) in Sprottau, December 1940.

At a sporting event in early 1941, Sprottau. In the meantime a Reserve Officer Candidate Course had taken place in Lüben with the II.Abteilung, to which I belonged. Pictured here from the right: Brodhagen; name unknown; name unknown; Rubbel; and Stockman. The result of this training, which was not made known, didn't see me fairing especially well. It wasn't until 1943, in the Tiger-Abteilung, that I was ever thought of.

Once again pictured from the left in the foreground: name unknown, Stockmann from Würzburg and Rubbel. The personnel merry-go-'round was now turning ever faster. Out of the team from the snow piles of January 1940 in Braunsberg there were left now only Wegmann, Behrmann, and I. We learned that camaraderie grows quickly amongst ordinary soldiers, yet true friendship is a higher virtue that grows more slowly and endures longer, if not lasting forever.

Modifications in form; the mounts for the climbing bars were forged in a village blacksmith's shop because of overcapacity in the home factory. There seemed to be no shortage of Panzer recruits, however.

At the Regenwurmlager near Meserwitz there was also a Labor Service Camp, which meant women! I was successful in picking up one of these charmers, who also happened to be the one taking this picture. Unfortunately, her photo has long since gone missing.

Above and right: At a typical Sunday photo session intended for those "at home." Rubbel in the Commander's Seat, where he also didn't belong at that time, rather in the left hatchway in the unattractive *Ladeschütze* seat. The driver "Charley" sat correctly here in the Pz. IV. Above: the "Krupp-Sport" Panzer I.

9th Company squared up in formation, waiting to be divided up for daily service. In black the "battle corps," and in gray the "wheel corps," who we referred to as "baggage servants." We were soon to feel this first-hand, for without them there wouldn't be much to all this tank stuff.

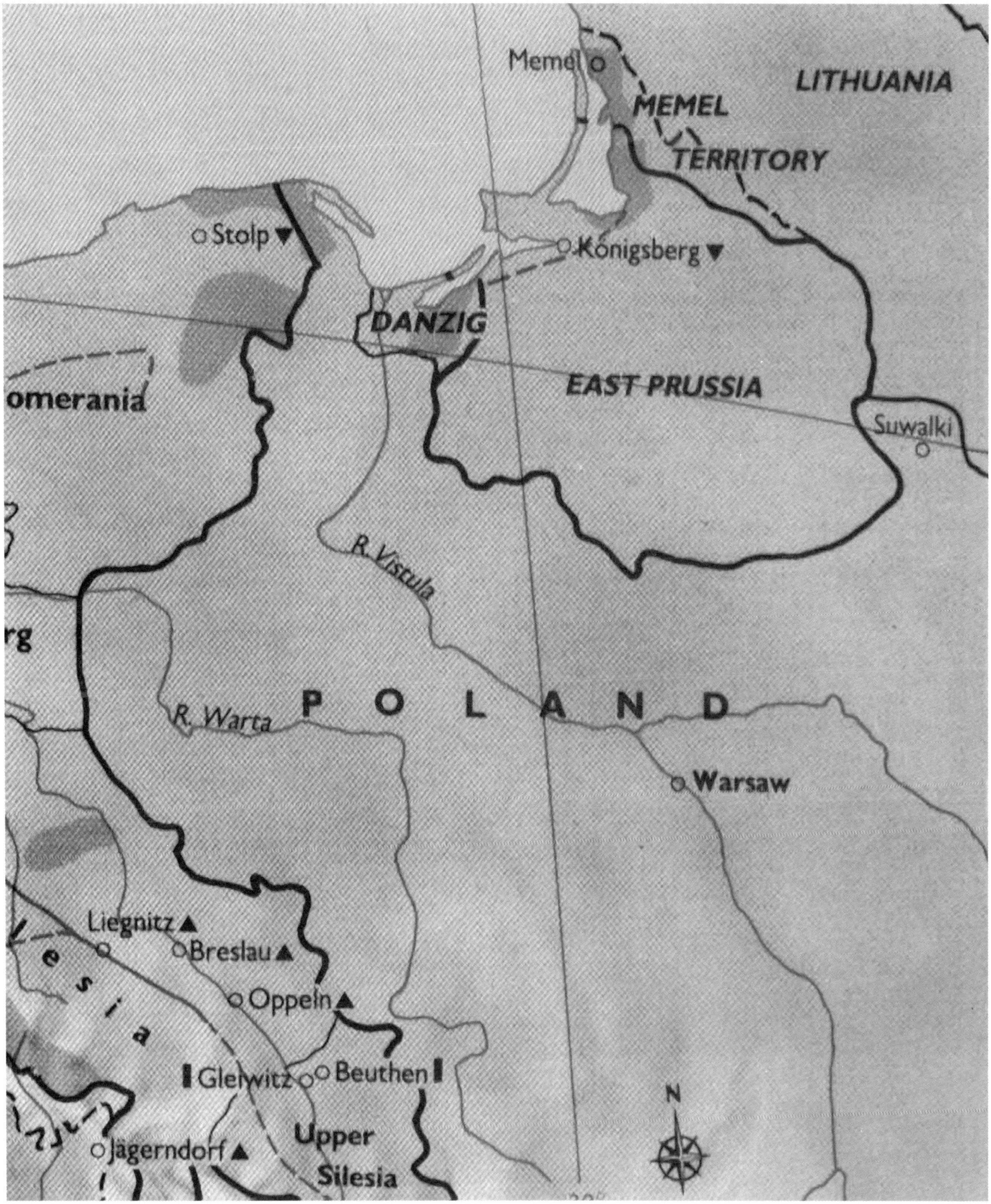
Memel
LITHUANIA
MEMEL
TERRITORY
Stolp
Königsberg
DANZIG
omerania
EAST PRUSSIA
Suwalki
R. Vistula
rg
R. Warta
P O L A N D
Warsaw
Liegnitz
Breslau
Oppeln
esia
Gleiwitz
Beuthen
Jägerndorf
Upper
Silesia
N

4

The Russian Campaign Battle Group Center

June 22nd, 1941 "Barbarossa"

Our division (the 12th Panzer Division), along with the 7th and 19th Panzer Divisions and the 4th Motorized Division, formed the 3rd Panzer Group, of which *Generaloberst* Hermann Hoth was in charge. This Panzer Group and the 9th Army under *Generaloberst* Adolf Strauss, along with the 8th Infantry Division was assigned the task of outflanking and trapping pockets of the 3rd and 10th Russian Armies gathered near the border by way of one quick thrust. The swift German formations would then win further territory to the east, stop enemy forces advancing to the west, and trap them decisively. The slower formations advancing in the rear would extinguish the entrapped enemy, and that would be that. This strategy basically went as planned.

During the evening of June 21-22 we advanced right up to the border. The advanced Suvalki Point, which had belonged since 1939 to East Prussia, was in our possession. We didn't see even a stir of the enemy until we crossed over the Memel (Nemunas) near Olita. At one point our tank fell out due to problems with the transmission, and repairs took a bit of time. We only encountered dispersed enemy resistance, and never really had any regular action until the great encirclement at Minsk. Here the encirclement was divided, and on the 11th of July we accomplished an impressive double encirclement and destruction of Bialystok and Minsk. We took about 400,000 prisoners and crossed the Beresina, where I thought about Napoleon. Through sloppiness we sustained heavy losses. In a wooded area we were carelessly lounging about outside our tanks when an artillery attack killed our Company Commander, *Leutnant* Obermann, and five other soldiers from the Company's Battle and Wheel Corps, as well as further wounded. There were a series of battles along the roads around Witebsk and Smolensk in the direction of Moscow. I was the *Ladeschütze* in the lead tank, while the *Richtschütze* was Walter Wegmann. He had been severely injured with a head wound, and I then took his place. Heinz Wehrmann was killed. The regiment had a reconnaissance platoon outfitted with the light Panzer II, which was headed up by *Leutnant* Brosko, with whom we were quite familiar since the days at Neuruppin. He had assembled his own crew and employed the services of Wehrmann as the

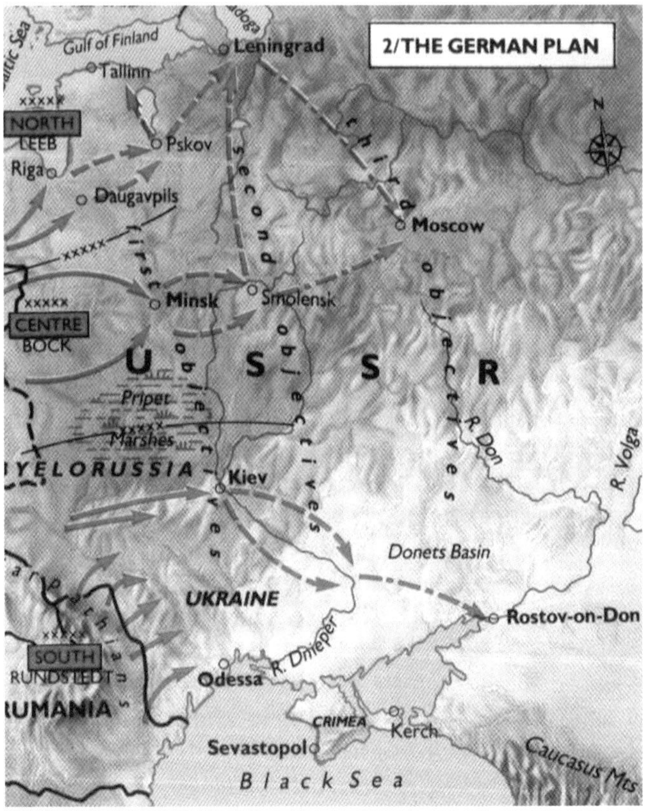

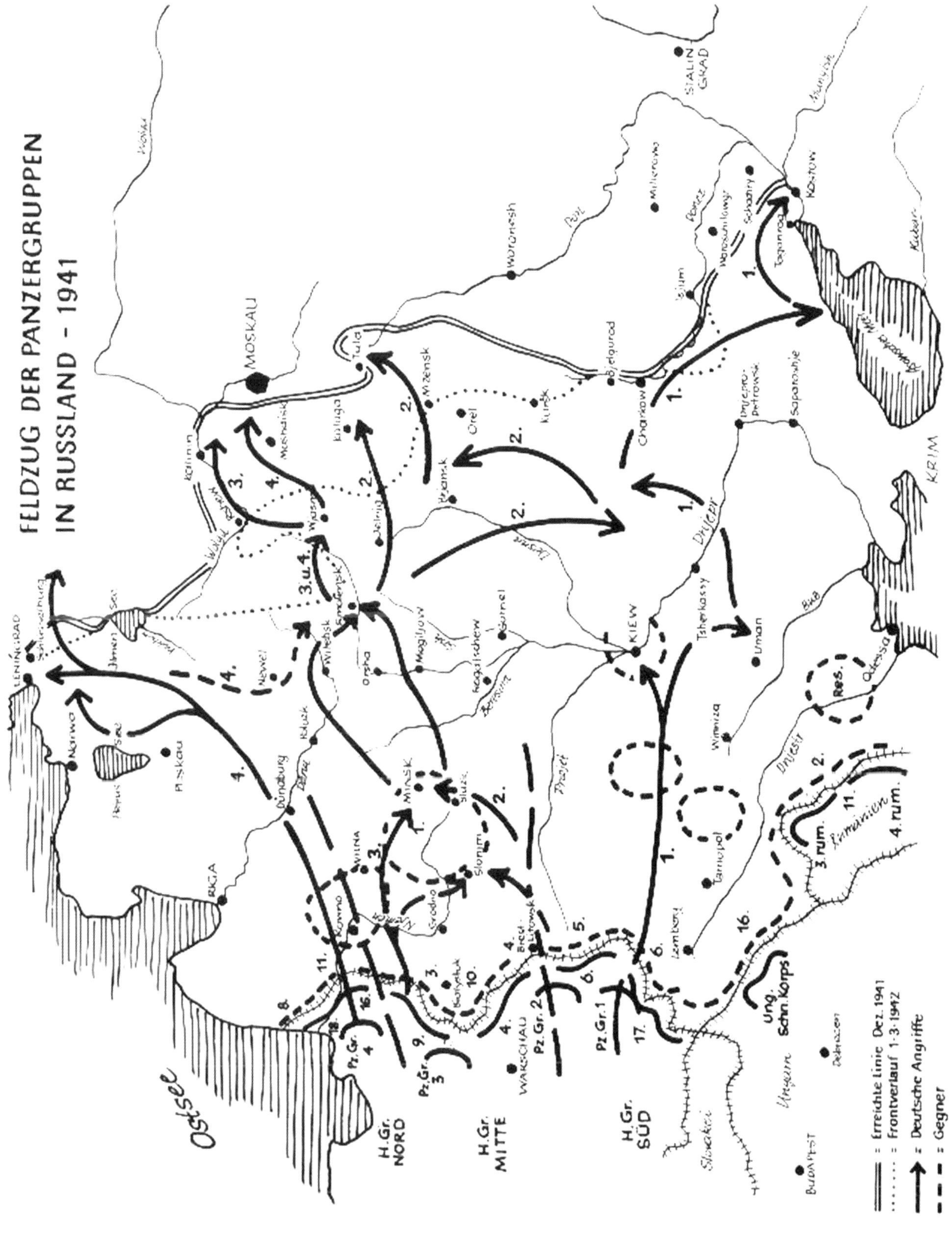
FELDZUG DER PANZERGRUPPEN
IN RUSSLAND - 1941
Ostsee
H.Gr. NORD
H.Gr. MITTE
H.Gr. SÜD
Pz.Gr. 4
Pz.Gr. 3
Pz.Gr. 2
Pz.Gr. 1
Ung. Schn.Korps
3. rum.
4. rum.
Rumänien
Ungarn
Slowakei
LENINGRAD
MOSKAU
KIEW
MINSK
RIGA
WILNA
WARSCHAU
BUDAPEST
STALINGRAD
Smolensk
Tula
Charkow
Rostow
Odessa
KRIM
Dnjepr
Uman
Lemberg
Tarnopol
Dünaburg
Pleskau
Orel
Kursk
Woronesh
Kalinin
Res.
= : Erreichte Linie Dez. 1941
..... : Frontverlauf 1.3.1942
→ : Deutsche Angriffe
- - : Gegner

Funker. His grave and the shot-out Panzer lay near a road in the area of Orscha. I had the opportunity to seek out both of them and take pictures; however, these photos unfortunately have been lost.

On the 18th of August in the area of Wjesma the 12th Panzer Division was halted, redirected, and betook to marching toward the northern front.

Overall German Political and Strategic Condition

With the invasion of the Soviet Union at the latest, the actions of the Reich Government are deserving of analysis. Qualified scholars have surely accomplished this in the post-war years; however, due to the National Socialist crimes committed against humanity, these studies have always been accompanied by a certain ideological bias, which tends to distort a truly objective viewpoint.

Having said that, we recall the following: On September 1st, 1939, Germany declared war on Poland. Through the Treaty of Versailles East Prussia had been cut off from the Reich. During the 1920s, when Germany was virtually incapable of action, Poland had been arrogantly provoking Germany in many ways. Negotiations during the 1930s, which Germany had organized, did not bring any relief due to Polish failure to accurately read the situation. On the contrary, the Polish did not actually comprehend that Germany, in the meantime, was no longer an insignificant second-rate power. With unabashed arrogance and complete trust in the Franco-Anglo guarantee for Poland, the Poles continued to defy and provoke Germany. The upshot was that in Poland, as well as in Germany, the attitude of the peoples slipped into chauvinistic waters. Bromberg Bloody Sunday took place in August 1939, where hundreds of Germans were killed. The Reich felt it had to act. Now the Poles realized the gravity of the situation; however, they still felt they didn't have to make any concessions due to their false recognition of the attitudes of their protective allies, whereby Poland considered herself in a safe harbor. In this instance, Hitler wanted to solve the dilemma with war, in order to achieve a lasting solution. The concessions of the western powers with the re-militarization of the Rhineland, the annexation of Austria, and the dissolving of Czechoslovakia could only be fortified, according to Hitler, by leaving it implicitly up to Germany herself to correct the injustices of Versailles.

France and England declared war on the Reich on the 3rd of September 1939. Whether Hitler had reckoned this eventuality remains doubtful. Primarily England, but also France, had no other choice. It was not as much a matter of defending Poland as it was defending its (England's) reputation in the world, especially given the task of holding together its colonial possessions, in which things were really brewing. One is not bound to take the peace offering made by Hitler very seriously, which occurred after the Polish Campaign ended in victory for Germany on the 17th of September. But Hitler did hold the English and French in high esteem. Pronouncements and actions (the halting of German troops at Dunkirk 1940) document this conviction. Hitler's vision was to jointly combat Communism, which stood as a permanent threat to the West, and to render it harmless. The post-war years legitimized his view on this. Unfortunately, he never realized that the goal of the West, from Richelieu to Margaret Thatcher, was to maintain a policy of assuring there would no longer exist a strong powerful state in the middle of Europe (Germany). It was only after his offers for peace went repeatedly unanswered that he ordered preparations for the Western Campaign. The fact that the order to attack had been delayed no less than twenty-nine times also serves as evidence of Hitler's indecisiveness to this armed course of action.

On the 23rd of August 1939, Germany and the Soviet Union shocked the world with the signing of the non-aggression pact and the secret internal clause that divided their control interests. On the basis of this pact the Soviet Union occupied eastern Poland and later the Baltic States. The buffer states envisioned by the Treaty of Versailles were now dissolved; Germany now shared a common border through East Prussia and occupied Poland with the Soviet Union. This was an extremely beguiling fact, especially for the Western Allies.

The fact that both sides had intended to cheat the other was in fact a done deal. In his book *Mein Kampf*, Hitler had repeatedly stated that the two front war was the worst mistake Imperial Germany could have made in terms of its policy. Therefore, Hitler wanted to employ every means necessary to avoiding this calamity again. And from this point on begins Hitler's illusive thinking, which he subordinated to the fact, real or imagined, that he could do nothing else. In addition, he had reacted to the conditions imposed upon Germany by the West, responsible for the Polish situation before September 1st, 1939. As the emerging hero on the world's stage since 1935, this policy did not sit well with Hitler. Stalin was able to plan in other ways. He had assumed that the Western Allies, including the USA and Germany, would become decimated in a long, draining conflict, and that the peoples of these lands followed the directives of the Communist Internationals, as there already were strong Communist Parties there. It was then assumed that Communism, or Socialism, would soon follow in its wake. Whether they might become satellites or Soviet Republics was really of secondary importance. To understand how such a state of affairs could have transpired we need look no further than the post-war era at the Eastern-Bloc nations comprising the Warsaw Pact. As an example, in Czechoslovakia the population of actual Communist Party members exceeded no more than 5%! A fundamental mistake on Stalin's part was underestimating the strength of the German *Wehrmacht*. And because he never liked to admit fault, he blamed the disaster in the West (1940) on the inability of Western Allied troops instead.

On April 9th, 1940, the English began landing troops in Norway. Germany reacted immediately, although engaged in the Western Campaign, and occupied Denmark and Norway. To speak of Germany's violation of neutrality in the case of Norway is indeed incorrect.

On June 10th, 1940, the Western Campaign against France and the British Expeditionary Force began with the violation of neutrality for two countries: Holland and Belgium. It seems to be a fact that Belgium had already cast its lot with the Western Allies, as Germany encountered French soldiers there. By the 24th of the same month, the French campaign had already ended in victory for Germany. Belgium, Holland, and France had all capitulated, and the English Expeditionary Forces were virtually decimated, although a large contingent was able to escape ultimate catastrophe by being ferried across the Channel.

From this point hence there would be no turning back for those countries engaged in war. Indeed, there was no other way out than to see absolute victory straight through to the bitter end, even at the expense of many lives. The map of Europe then portrayed a dramatic situation. Even Africa was drawn into the fray, and all of this had come about as a direct result of the war. England was growing ever more confident and emboldened through the support she was receiving from the USA as the war drew on. Hitler had grossly underestimated this situation. Also, the crimes against both the Jews and the Poles had sullied Germany's reputation amongst the world's onlookers.

On November 12th, 1940, Molotov had demanded further German concessions with respect to Soviet spheres of influence in Finland, the Balkans, and Turkey. The Reich had been blackmailed. As a demonstration of further power after these demands, the Soviets had gathered 100-150 divisions along the western borders. The craftiness of the Georgian Stalin was no match for Hitler. On the first of May 1941 the Soviet decision to march West had in fact been made. Due to the threatening presence of troops along its flanks, the Soviets had placed a strategic heavy force of troops in the middle. It is still debated today whether this had been a preventive measure, as the Germans made no secret out of revealing their own troop positions along the western border. And perhaps Stalin considered war inevitable and was looking for measures to prevent such a course of action.

On June 22nd, 1941, Germany declared war on the Soviet Union, and thus began the Eastern Campaign. It is an absolute mockery if modern-day thinking assumes that Germany had invaded a peace loving Soviet Union. The post-war subjugation of the Eastern Bloc and the continued Soviet threat to the rest of Europe throughout the Cold War only precipitated a small number of historians to question whether Germany had indeed anticipated an imminent invasion by the Russians. But, having said all this, we Germans are of the opinion that we had indeed conducted an unnecessary and treasonous war of aggression.

It must have been recognized from the outset that Germany would never have won this two-front war. The resolutions agreed upon at Yalta called for the unconditional surrender of Germany and for the country to be fully occupied after the war. This offered the Reich leadership no other alternative than to fight to the end. The hope that the Western Alliance with the Soviet Union would disintegrate, which it did only too late, turned out to be an illusion. As German foreign policy was totally incapable of creating an atmosphere attenuating the absolute worst of consequences, the path to ruin was lain.

Enemy Behavior During the Summer Offensive

In my paybook I had registered the following battles:

Army Group Center

June 22- 23rd, 1941:	Breakthrough of the border positions
June 24- 27th, 1941:	Encirclement of Bialystok-Slonim
June 27th- July 3rd, 1941:	Seek and destroy to Düna
July 6- July 16th, 1941:	Breakthrough of Düna positions
July 11th- July 16th, 1941:	Battles for Witebsk- Smolensk
July 17th- August 18th 1941:	Defensive Battles at Jarzevo and Wop

According to recollection and the tempo with which this attack was carried out against an enemy vastly superior in numbers leads one to determine that we were dealing with an enemy who had not been ready to defend itself. There were no defensive fortresses, no field positions, no tank traps, no echelons of defense, and no shock troops in reserve. There was not even any air cover, which a defender would normally plan ahead of time. There can only be two possibilities for all this:

- Bad defensive planning and leadership or, and this is quite probable,
- The Soviet Army was actually on the march to attack west.

Most of the troops we took prisoner were either fleeing or completely demoralized. We encountered only sporadic local pockets of resistance and hardly any counter-attacks. The Stalin Line, which was of real concern to us, I hardly noticed, as it turned out to be of no hindrance at all. This can only signify that the Red Army had completely counted on its offensive, and therefore had totally neglected defensive measures.

An analysis of these events requires complete objectivity to arrive at the truth. Unfortunately, I do not have any pictures from this period of time.

On Sunday, the 22nd of June 1941, the days before and after:

It is the 22nd of June 1941. The media had occupied themselves during that time, just as in days prior, with the start of the Russian Campaign, Operation *Barbarossa*. Increasingly, the widely accepted explanation that Germany deviously attacked her peaceful neighbor (USSR) was called into doubt by credible historians, and the question posed as to whether this notion indeed corresponded with the truth. The Ribbentrop-Molotov Agreement, which was incomprehensible to most of the world, has proved today to be an alliance between two thugs with which each tried to hoodwink the other. Hitler wanted to win time until he could risk an invasion of the USSR because he thought their ideological differences would propel the two nations to inevitable conflict. Stalin thought that after the Communist Manifesto, with its theories of just and unjust wars, the expansion of Communism to the West was necessary. He wanted to bide his time until Germany and the Western Europeans had so worn themselves down that resistance to this expansion would have been useless. This background cannot be revised any further. As Molotov placed further demands on Germany to concede further geographical spheres of influence, Hitler's position became one of necessity to wage a pre-emptive war, which was unavoidable at this point. In this case, the aggressor also would have the advantage of determining when and where this would take place. Conclusive evidence that Hitler had preceded Stalin's attack on Germany and her neighbors by only a few weeks is still missing today. The events of the first weeks of the invasion in Army Group Center; however, do seem to confirm this theory. Although the Russians had been aware of the German troop movements up to and along its borders for months, the Russians chose not to take up any defensive positions, but chose instead to mobilize their troops for an invasion. This is evident to us today; but back then it was not. There were rumors, misinformation, and assumptions that emanated from our own very limited point of view.

We of the 29th Panzer Regiment from the 12th (Pomeranian) Panzer Division had spent a few weeks at the Training and Military Exercise Facilities in the area of Landsberg-Meseritz. Afterwards, around the middle of June, we arrived in East Prussia by rail transport and unloaded at Sensburg. Because there were no proper quarters there, we immediately moved into positions in the forested areas under camouflage and were forbidden to move, which we stringently obeyed. We marched on wheel and chain (truck, bike, and tank) by way of Nikolaiken-Arys-Lyck to the old East Prussian border mostly at night, although after the 20th of June we also moved by day. On the other side lay Augustovo. The resting area for the Third Regiment also was situated in the forest, and we occupied it during the early morning hours of the 21st of June. This would become the Preparation Area for the attack of the 22nd of June; but we first became aware of this on the evening of the 21st.

Naturally we had been asking ourselves what was going on ever since we left our garrison at Sprottau, and we spun the wildest stories in our attempts to answer these questions. Everybody knew, both soldiers and the civilian population, that the German army was involved in a massive relocation to the East. It was also quite obvious that this was not undertaken on behalf of entertaining the people; rather, this meant war. Only against whom would this war be directed, our new allies? It could hardly be the Russians, about whom only positive things were now being written in both the *Völkischer Beobachter* (People's Observer), as well as in *Der Stürmer* (The Striker). The theme of reports coming out of the media had taken a 180° turn. The sworn enemies of Communism and Fascism had struck a mutual deal. Could this mean we would combine our forces in a joint attack against the Anglo-American threat? Otherwise, there really was no one else on the map of Europe we could think of as a viable target. Even the most naïve of people did not wish such a scenario. And bullheaded Nazis, who parroted Goebbels, were absent amongst us young warriors, as far as I can recall.

The Company Commander, *Leutnant* Obermann, dispensed commands for the 9th Company. Obermann was an officer who was fairly well regarded and assiduously went about his work. He also had to suffer greatly at the hands of the Regimental Commander, *Oberst* Stegelein, because of a harsh Company inspection in November 1940 that had gone awry. It is to his honor that he did not drag the entire Company down with him by taking idiotic measures, which would have also created a reputation for himself amongst his superiors as being somewhat of a "loose cannon." Through the intentional communication of mis-information to the outside world our plans to invade the USSR were hidden: the German East Army had marching rights granted by the Russians to traverse their territory to get to Iran. In Northern Africa Rommel was simultaneously advancing, and the two armies were supposed to form a great pincer formation to capture the British in Egypt and Palestine and destroy any other remaining pockets of Anglo resistance. As a byproduct of all this we would also capture the Persian oil! I'm still not sure I really believed it. It sounded too fantastic; however, hadn't we just witnessed this unimaginable consolidation of German and Russian troops? Alas, we decided

Besitzzeugnis

Dem Gefreiten

(Dienstgrad)

Alfred R u b b e l ,

(Vor- und Zuname)

9./Panzer - Regiment 29

(Truppenteil)

wurde das

Panzerkampfabzeichen

— Silber —

verliehen.

Im Felde, den 21.7. 1941.

(Ort und Datum)

Harpe

(Unterschrift)

Generalmajor u. Kdr. d. 12 Pz.-Div.

(Dienstgrad und Dienststellung)

(Für die Richtigkeit)

(Dienstgrad und Dienststellung)

to call ourselves the "Iran-Army" as a counterpart to the Afrika Korps. A few of the soldiers even tried to estimate how much their "Asian- Bonuses" might be when reflected in their normal service pay.

As was not the customary routine when receiving our orders, we sat around our Commander on the grounds of the forest under the trees in a circle of about 120 men. What I knew for sure was that the following morning, on Sunday the 22nd of June, we would attack. We were told that the enemy—the words Russians or Soviets were not actually uttered, I believe—have an armored division which is almost the equal to ours. The I.Abteilung will make up the spearhead of the attack. This is about all I remember having been said, and I am especially aware that we still didn't hear anything about the famous "Commissar Order." I believe that after so much uncertainty, given the noteworthiness of the situation, any word that came across as part of the message or as a clarification of this situation could not be easily forgotten. And how did I feel about all this? I was aggrieved, as it was evident to me that we would be attacking the Russians. Geography and history had always been favorite subjects of mine when I was in school. I was painfully aware of the awesome expanses of land between Moscow and us, then to the Urals, and then that's where Russia really started, as it stretched out all the way to its Siberian territory and the Pacific Ocean. I was also aware of the Beresina, the Battle at Borodino, the burning of Moscow in 1812, and the eventual destruction of the "Grand Armee" (Napoleon's French Army). The stark realization of the unending vastness of Russia and the inability of man and his armies to capture this territory, at least up till now, weighed heavily on me then and still does today. The expanses of the East in my mind start with the Tucheler Heath, through which I traveled ten years ago in the direction of East Prussia. And East Prussia, once a manageable piece of land, now seems to me to have grown into a bleak, alien, and depressing landscape.

Having said this, I'd like to refer back to the events of the 22nd of June. We spent the prior evening either on or in our tanks with the appropriate cover, correctly positioned field posts and loaded weapons ready for action. The Company was divided by columns of wheeled vehicles into Battle Groups and Equipment Units 1 and 2. The morning came; at 3:30 AM the attack commenced. We could barely make out the artillery barrage, as it must have been a long way from our positions. However, we did see small squadrons of our airplanes flying east. The war seemed to be moving ahead without us for now. During the first few days, I'm not certain how many, our Panzers did not see any enemy action whatsoever.

To Army Group Center, in which the 9th Army belonged to the LVII Army Corps (motorized), along with our 12th Panzer Division, the 19th Panzer Division, and the 18th Infantry Division (motorized), our division was originally held in reserve. We in this Regiment, really the III.Abteilung, followed closely on the heels of the spearhead division, which supposedly was the 19th Panzer Division. Our path led through the Suvalki-Point and on toward the North, swinging round in the territory of Lithuania, which the USSR had occupied. There we encountered only border skirmishes. I was the *Ladeschütze* in the lead-tank. Unfortunately, our tank fell out on the second or third day due to transmission difficulties. As was customary amongst the Panzer Corps, the Company Commander would get into another tank and leave us standing there alone. We hoped that help would arrive soon to carry us off to the maintenance facilities; however, this actually took some time. We were alone in a wide meadow and feared the worst. Perhaps a band of dispersed Russians might stumble across us, and we knew they wouldn't exactly be too kind. Finally a flatbed truck arrived on the scene and snapped us up. We were then towed across the Memel, the Nemunas, and the Nyemen near Merkena, and then finally arrived at the repair stations, which I believe were in the area of Lida. The regiment was far off toward the front and involved in fighting. These areas were still very dangerous, as dispersed Russians, not only fleeing but also ready to fight, were everywhere around us. The village where the repair stations were located had to be secured at great cost. Our patrols were constantly searching for Russian soldiers. There I was eyewitness to a horrible scene—the shooting of three "partisans" on a churchyard wall. Shortly thereafter our tank was back on the mend, and we rolled out in the direction of our Company to the East. Our detachment to the Company, to which I felt forced at least, had been delayed again and again by a certain CO, actually a Junior NCO, whom we didn't exactly hold in the highest esteem. He liked to instill a sense of fear and told us all manner of stories concerning his experiences in the French Campaign and the general horrors of war. Detrimental to his leadership position, he tried afresh to convince us he was one of the boys. We (the *Fahrer*, *Richtschütze*, and *Ladeschütze*), were really adversely affected by his plaintiveness and decided not to join in. And so we eventually did get to our Company, which must have been just outside of Minsk, where the breakthrough of the former Russian western borders followed shortly after. These positions were really of little value in terms of holding us back. The battles that took place were basically meaningless, as the Russian forces were in full disarray. The upshot of all this was the generation of the great encirclement formations in and around Bialystok and Minsk.

Our Company was employed in many an aggressive way toward dividing the encirclements. It was here that Walter

Wegmann had been severely wounded and I took his place. After completing the encirclements and subsequent capitulations of Minsk-Bialystok, we continued to advance forward by way of Smolensk to Wjasma. The 12th Panzer Division was held up at this point and, together with the LVII Army Corps (motorized), redirected north toward the capture of Leningrad in August 1941. We marched north for over a week through all kinds of marshland and finally arrived at our destination in the beginning of September. We were thrown immediately into the fight, and I was wounded on the third of September near Mga and was transferred to the field hospital.

In June I received the Panzer-Combat Badge in silver for having served three times in battle.

The following is the English translation of the orders for Operation Barbarossa (*seen below and on following pages*):

The German Armed Forces must be prepared, even before the conclusion of the war against England, *to crush Soviet Russia in a rapid campaign* ("Operation Barbarossa").

The *Army* will have to employ all available formations to this end, with the reservation that occupied territories must be insured against surprise attacks.

The *Luftwaffe* will have to make available for this Eastern campaign supporting forces of such strength that the Army will be able to bring land operations to a speedy conclusion and that eastern Germany will be as little damaged as possible by enemy air attack. This build-up of a focal point in the East will be limited only by the need to protect from air attack the whole combat and arsenal area which we control, and to ensure that attacks on England, and especially upon her imports, are not allowed to lapse.

The main efforts of the *Navy* will continue to be directed against *England* even during the Eastern campaign.

In certain circumstances I shall issue orders for the *deployment* against Soviet Russia eight weeks before the operation is timed to begin.

Preparations which require more time than this will be put in hand now, in so far as this has not already been done, and will be concluded by 15th May 1941.

It is of decisive importance that our intention to attack should not be known.

The preparations of the High Commands will be made on the following basis:

36 C 162 211 8

\- 3 -

Die Vorbereitungen der Oberkommandos sind auf folgender Grundlage zu treffen:

I. Allgemeine Absicht:

(Die im westlichen Russland stehende Masse des russischen Heeres soll in kühnen Operationen unter weitem Vortreiben von Panzerkeilen vernichtet, der Abzug kampfkräftiger Teile in die Weite des russischen Raumes verhindert werden.)

In rascher Verfolgung ist dann eine Linie zu erreichen, aus der die russische Luftwaffe reichsdeutsches Gebiet nicht mehr angreifen kann. Das Endziel der Operation ist die Abschirmung gegen das asiatische Russland aus der allgemeinen Linie Wolga - Archangelsk. So kann erforderlichenfalls das letzte Russland verbleibende Industriegebiet am Ural durch die Luftwaffe ausgeschaltet werden.

(Im Zuge dieser Operationen wird die russische Ostseeflotte schnell ihre Stützpunkte verlieren und damit nicht mehr kampffähig sein.

Wirksames Eingreifen der russischen Luftwaffe ist schon bei Beginn der Operation durch kraftvolle Schläge zu verhindern.)

37 C 162 212 9

\- 4 -

II. Voraussichtliche Verbündete und deren Aufgaben:

1.) (Auf den Flügeln unserer Operation ist mit der aktiven Teilnahme Rumäniens und Finnlands am Kriege gegen Sowjetrussland zu rechnen.

In welcher Form die Streitkräfte beider Länder bei ihrem Eingreifen deutschem Befehl unterstellt werden, wird das Oberkommando der Wehrmacht zeitgerecht vereinbaren und festlegen.)

2.) Rumäniens Aufgabe wird es sein, den Angriff des deutschen Südflügels, wenigstens in seinen Anfängen, mit ausgesuchten Kräften zu unterstützen, den Gegner dort, wo deutsche Kräfte nicht angesetzt sind, zu fesseln und im übrigen Hilfsdienste im rückwärtigen Gebiet zu leisten.

3.) Finnland wird den Aufmarsch der aus Norwegen kommenden abgesetzten deutschen Nordgruppe (Teile der Gruppe XXI) zu decken und mit ihr gemeinsam zu operieren haben. Daneben wird Finnland die Ausschaltung von Hangö zufallen.

4.) (Mit der Möglichkeit, dass schwedische Bahnen und Strassen für den Aufmarsch der deutschen Nordgruppe spätestens von Operationsbeginn an zur Verfügung stehen, kann gerechnet werden.)

I. *General Intention*

The bulk of the Russian Army stationed in western Russia will be destroyed by daring operations led by deeply penetrating armored spearheads. Russian forces still capable of giving battle will be prevented from withdrawing into the depths of Russia.

The enemy will then be energetically pursued and a line will be reached from which the Russian Air Force can no longer attack German territory. The final objective of the operation is to erect a barrier against Asiatic Russia on the general line Volga-Archangel.

The last surviving industrial area of Russia in the Urals can then, if necessary, be eliminated by the Luftwaffe.

In the course of these operations the Russian *Baltic Fleet* will quickly lose its bases and will then no longer be capable of action.

The effective operation of the Russian *Air Force* is to be prevented from the beginning of the attack by powerful blows.

II. *Probable Allies and their Tasks*

1. On the flanks of our operations we can count on the active support of *Romania* and *Finland* in the war against Soviet Russia.

The High Command of the Armed Forces will decide and lay down in due time the manner in which the forces of these two countries will be brought under German command.

2. It will be the task of *Romania* to support the attack of the German southern flank, at least at the outset, with its best troops; to hold down the enemy where German forces are not engaged; and to provide auxiliary services in the rear areas.

3. *Finland* will cover the advance of the *Northern Group* of German forces moving from Norway (detachments of Group XXI) and will operate in conjunction with them. Finland will also be responsible for eliminating Hango.

4. It is possible that *Swedish* railways and roads may be available for the movement of the German Northern Group, by the beginning of the operation at the latest.

38

- 5 -

C162 ~~10~~ 213

III. Die Führung der Operationen:

1.) Heer (in Genehmigung der mir vorgetragenen Absichten):

In dem durch die Pripetsümpfe in eine südliche und eine nördliche Hälfte getrennten Operationsraum ist der Schwerpunkt nördlich dieses Gebietes zu bilden. Hier sind 2 Heeresgruppen vorzusehen.

Der südlichen dieser beiden Heeresgruppen - Mitte der Gesamtfront - fällt die Aufgabe zu, mit besonders starken Panzer- und mot. Verbänden aus dem Raum um und nördlich Warschau vorbrechend die feindlichen Kräfte in Weissrussland zu zersprengen. Dadurch muss die Voraussetzung geschaffen werden für das Eindrehen von starken Teilen der schnellen Truppen nach Norden, um im Zusammenwirken mit der aus Ostpreussen in allgemeiner Richtung Leningrad operierenden nördlichen Heeresgruppe die im Baltikum kämpfenden feindlichen Kräfte zu vernichten. Erst nach ~~Erledigung~~ Sicherstellung dieser vordringlichsten Aufgabe, welcher die Besetzung von Leningrad und Kronstadt folgen muss, sind die Angriffsoperationen zur Besitznahme des wichtigen Verkehrs- und Rüstungszentrums Moskau fortzuführen.

Nur ein überraschend schnell eintretender Zusammenbruch der russischen Widerstandskraft könnte es rechtfertigen, beide Ziele gleichzeitig anzustreben.

Die wichtigste Aufgabe der Gruppe XXI bleibt auch während der Ostoperationen der Schutz Norwegens. Die darüber hinaus verfügbaren Kräfte sind im Norden (Geb.-Korps) zunächst zur Sicherung des Petsamo-Gebietes und seiner Erzgruben sowie der Eismeerstrasse einzusetzen, um dann gemeinsam mit finnischen Kräften gegen die Murmansk-Bahn

- 6 -

39

- 6 -

C162 ~~11~~ 214

vorzustossen und die Versorgung des Murmansk-Gebietes auf dem Landwege zu unterbinden.

Ob eine derartige Operation mit stärkeren deutschen Kräften (2 - 3 Div.) aus dem Raum von Rovaniemi und südlich geführt werden kann, hängt von der Bereitwilligkeit Schwedens ab, seine Eisenbahnen für einen solchen Aufmarsch zur Verfügung zu stellen.

Der Masse des finnischen Heeres wird die Aufgabe zufallen, in Übereinstimmung mit den Fortschritten des deutschen Nordflügels möglichst starke russische Kräfte durch Angriff westlich oder beiderseits des Ladoga-Sees zu fesseln und sich in den Besitz von Hangö zu setzen.

Auch bei der südlich der Pripetsümpfe angesetzten Heeresgruppe ist in konzentrischer Operation und mit starken Flügeln die vollständige Vernichtung der in der Ukraine stehenden russischen Kräfte noch westlich des Dnjepr anzustreben. Hierzu ist der Schwerpunkt aus dem Raum von Lublin in allgemeiner Richtung Kiew zu bilden, während die in Rumänien befindlichen Kräfte über den unteren Pruth hinweg einen weit abgesetzten Umfassungsarm bilden. Der rumänischen Armee wird die Fesselung der dazwischen befindlichen russischen Kräfte zufallen.

Sind die Schlachten südlich bezw. nördlich der Pripetsümpfe geschlagen, ist im Rahmen der Verfolgung anzustreben:

im Süden die frühzeitige Besitznahme des wehrwirtschaftlich wichtigen Donez-Beckens,

- 7 -

III. *Conduct of Operations*

A. Army (in accordance with plans submitted to me)!

In the theater of operations, which is divided by the Pripet Marshes into a Southern and a Northern sector, the main weight of attack will be delivered in the *Northern* area. Two Army Groups will be employed here.

The more southerly of these two Army Groups (in the center of the whole front) will have the task of advancing with powerful armored and motorized formations from the area about and north of Warsaw, and routing the enemy forces in White Russia. This will make it possible for strong mobile forces to advance northwards and, in conjunction with the Northern Army Group operating out of East Prussia in the general direction of Leningrad, to destroy the enemy forces operating in the Baltic area. Only after the fulfilment of this first essential task, which must include the occupation of Leningrad and Kronstadt, will the attack be continued with the intention of occupying Moscow, an important center of communications and of the armaments industry.

40

C 162

- 7 -

215

im Norden das schnelle Erreichen von Moskau. Die Einnahme dieser Stadt bedeutet politisch und wirtschaftlich einen entscheidenden Erfolg, darüber hinaus den Ausfall des wichtigsten Eisenbahnknotenpunktes.

B.) Luftwaffe:

Ihre Aufgabe wird es sein, die Einwirkung der russischen Luftwaffe soweit wie möglich zu lähmen und auszuschalten sowie die Operationen des Heeres in ihren Schwerpunkten, namentlich bei der mittleren Heeresgruppe und auf dem Schwerpunktflügel der südlichen Heeresgruppe, zu unterstützen. Die russischen Bahnen werden je nach ihrer Bedeutung für die Operationen zu unterbrechen bzw. in ihren wichtigsten nahegelegenen Objekten (Flussübergänge!) durch kühnen Einsatz von Fallschirm- und Luftlandetruppen in Besitz zu nehmen sein.

Um alle Kräfte gegen die feindliche Luftwaffe und zur unmittelbaren Unterstützung des Heeres zusammenfassen zu können, ist die Rüstungsindustrie während der Hauptoperationen nicht anzugreifen. Erst nach dem Abschluss der Bewegungsoperationen kommen derartige Angriffe, in erster Linie gegen das Uralgebiet, in Frage.

41

C 162

- 8 -

216

C.) Kriegsmarine:

Der Kriegsmarine fällt gegen Sowjetrussland die Aufgabe zu, unter Sicherung der eigenen Küste ein Ausbrechen feindlicher Seestreitkräfte aus der Ostsee zu verhindern. Da nach dem Erreichen von Leningrad der russischen Ostseeflotte der letzte Stützpunkt genommen und diese dann in hoffnungsloser Lage sein wird, sind vorher grössere Seeoperationen zu vermeiden.

Nach dem Ausschalten der russischen Flotte wird es darauf ankommen, den vollen Seeverkehr in der Ostsee, dabei auch den Nachschub für den nördlichen Heeresflügel über See, sicherzustellen (Minenräumung!)

IV. Alle von den Herren Oberbefehlshabern auf Grund dieser Weisung zu treffenden Anordnungen müssen eindeutig dahin abgestimmt sein, dass es sich um Vorsichtsmassnahmen handelt für den Fall, dass Russland seine bisherige Haltung gegen uns ändern sollte. Die Zahl der frühzeitig zu den Vorarbeiten heranzuziehenden Offiziere ist so klein wie möglich zu halten, weitere Mitarbeiter sind so spät wie möglich und nur in dem für die Tätigkeit jedes Einzelnen erforderlichen Umfang einzuweisen. Sonst besteht die Gefahr, dass durch ein Bekanntwerden unserer Vorbereitungen, deren Durchführung zeitlich noch garnicht festliegt, schwerste politische und militärische Nachteile entstehen.

42

- 9 -

217

V. Vorträgen der Herren Oberbefehlshaber über ihre weiteren Absichten auf Grund dieser Weisung sehe ich entgegen.

Die beabsichtigten Vorbereitungen aller Wehrmachtteile sind mir, auch in ihrem zeitlichen Ablauf, über das Oberkommando der Wehrmacht zu melden.

Only a surprisingly rapid collapse of Russian resistance could justify the simultaneous pursuit of both objectives.

The most important task of Group XXI, even during these eastern operations, remains the protection of Norway. Any forces available after carrying out this task will be employed in the North (Mountain Corps), at first to protect the Petsamo area and its iron ore mines and the Arctic highway, then to advance with Finnish forces against the Murmansk railway and thus prevent the passage of supplies to Murmansk by land.

The question whether an operation of this kind can be carried out with *stronger* German forces (two or three divisions) from the Rovaniemi area and south of it will depend on the willingness of Sweden to make its railways available for troop transport.

It will be the duty of the main body of the Finnish Army, in conjunction with the advance of the German North flank, to hold down the strongest possible Russian forces by an attack to the West, or on both sides of Lake Ladoga, and to occupy Hango.

The Army Group operating *South* of the Pripet Marshes will also seek, in a concentric operation with strong forces on either flank, to destroy all Russian forces west of the Dnieper in the Ukraine. The *main attack* will be carried out from the Lublin area in the general direction of Kiev, while forces in Romania will carry out a wide enclosing movement across the lower Pruth. It will be the task of the Romanian Army to hold down Russian forces in the intervening area.

When the battles north and south of the Pripet Marshes are ended the pursuit of the enemy will have the following aims:

In the *South* the early capture of the Donets Basin, important for war industry.

In the *North* a quick advance to Moscow. The capture of this city would represent a decisive political and economic success and would also bring about the capture of the most important railway junctions.

B. *Luftwaffe*

It will be the duty of the Luftwaffe to paralyze and eliminate the effectiveness of the Russian Air Force as far as possible. It will also support the main operations of the Army, i.e. those of the central Army Group and of the vital flank of the Southern Army Group. Russian railways will either be destroyed or, in accordance with operational requirements, captured at their most important points (river crossings) by the bold employment of parachute and airborne troops.

In order that we may concentrate all our strength against the enemy Air Force and for the immediate support of land operations, the Russian armaments industry will not be attacked during the main operations. Such attacks will be made only after the conclusion of mobile warfare, and they will be concentrated first on the Urals area.

C. *Navy*

It will be the duty of the Navy during the attack on Soviet Russia to protect our own coasts and to prevent the breakout of enemy naval units from the Baltic. As the Russian Baltic fleet will, with the capture of Leningrad, lose its last base and will then be in a hopeless position, major naval action will be avoided until this occurs.

After the elimination of the Russian fleet the duty of the Navy will be to protect the entire maritime traffic in the Baltic and the transport of supplies by sea to the Northern flank (clearing of minefields!).

IV. All steps taken by Commanders-in-Chief on the basis of this directive must be phrased on the unambiguous assumption that they are *precautionary measures* undertaken in case Russia should alter its present attitude towards us. The number of officers employed on preliminary preparations will be kept as small as possible and further staffs will be designated as late as possible and only to the extent required for the duties of each individual. Otherwise there is a danger that premature knowledge of our preparations, whose execution cannot yet be timed with any certainty, might entail the gravest political and military disadvantages.

V. I await submission of the plans of Commanders-in-Chief on the basis of this directive.

The preparations made by all branches of the Armed Forces, together with timetables, are to be reported to me through the High Command of the Armed Forces.

Signed: ADOLF HITLER

5

The Russian Campaign Battle Group North

Leaving the Central Front and Marching to the Northern Front

On the 18th of August 1941, our regiment was situated in the area of Wjasma engaged in defensive battles on the Wop and Jarzevo rivers, which are tributaries of the Oka. We then disengaged from the front and, together with the XXXIX Army Corps (motorized) under Schmidt; we marched off toward the area of Leningrad. The momentum of attack, with the main thrust being Army Group Center, was now brought to a standstill near the gates of Moscow after initial success. The strategic objective of seizing the capital before the winter months had not been realized. Hitler had changed his strategy and decided to win the battle by shifting the emphasis of attack to his flanks. To this end the mouth to the Don River and Rostow were to be captured in the South in 1941. With this capture the industrial areas around Krementshug and Dniepropetrovsk would be safely in German hands, and would also serve as the staging area for the seizing of the Caspian oil fields. In the North all eyes were on Leningrad and the prestige its fall would bring about at the hands of the Finns and Germans. Therefore, reinforcements to Army Group North with the XXXIX Army Corps (motorized) were demanded at once to force the capture of Leningrad. The forest and swamplands, criss-crossed by a number of rivers, hampered the successful approach of motorized and armored forces.

After a long march of 900 km, which we accomplished in about a week's time from Wjasma by way of Smolensk, Witebsk, Nevel, Dno, Novograd, and to the southern outskirts of Leningrad near Kolpino and Mga, we broke off our march and formed up for attack along the main road from Tossno to Kolpino. Besides the unforgiving landscape we had to contend with bitter defenses in the southern ring of the city. Increasingly inclement weather and the Soviet Air Force were combining to make life harsh for us. At the time I was the *Richtschütze* in a Panzer IV belonging to *Oberfeldwebel* Wolf. The regiment, which up to then had consisted of three abteilungs, was shrunk down to two because of heavy losses and destruction of armor while engaged in battle with Army Group South. Our entire III.Abteilung was dissolved and divided into the I. and II.Abteilungs. We then landed in the 3rd Company.

The fighting on the city borders, from whose southern area we could see the streetcars running, took place for me from August 25th to September 3rd, 1941. On September 3rd, during a lull in hostilities, I opened the hatch and sat upright with my head exposed to the outside. An impact in the immediate area of our tank caused by a grenade launcher had caught me by surprise, which fortunately later turned out to be only minor injuries. The words: "Multiple fragments in the head, back, and rear-end" were scripted onto my "Injury Tag," which was then pinned upon me. It was a typical "Get-to-Go Home" type of injury. Inside a JU52 I was flown from Tossno to Tchudovo, and then loaded into a hospital train after a few days, which then delivered me after a week's journey to Bad Kissingen. Indelible memories of this time are still with me today. On September 3rd the ground was already lightly frozen. Mud, rain, lice, and danger were all things we relatively inexperienced-in-combat, Russian-front soldiers had to surmount. We traveled through a mild early springtime, peaceful Germany, and arrived as "honored citizens of the nation," at that time, in Franconia during the first days of the grape gathering season. I stayed there almost three months, and it was a wonderful experience. To this day the attraction of Bad Kissingen lives on, and a return visit at least once a year is an absolute must.

Around Christmas time 1941 I found myself attached to the Panzer Reserve Abteilung 10 in Gr. Glienicke near Potsdam. An as of yet unscathed Berlin had put me under its spell. I traveled there whenever possible. Theatres, cabarets, and museums were always open to us. Then came our marching orders to head east again to our old bunch, the 29th Panzer Regiment, with quarters in Narwa. Almost like in September of '41, we traveled the way back to the regiment in January 1942 in an empty hospital train on about the same exact stretch of countryside in harsh winter weather. I was so happy to come back to the same detachment of troops. Something had indeed developed which I had not formally been aware of: it was great to come back to my good old comrades.

Though some were now missing, many of these soldiers had experienced a lot of things in the meantime: the encirclement of Oranienbaum; the road battles between Tossno and Tchudovo; the capture of Schlüsselburg and Tichvin; and the withdrawal and bloody battles at Wolchow. The regiment was now situated in the area near Narwa in order to gather its strength, and was detached to various battle units of the infantry close to enemy positions, those being the 1st Infantry Division, the 21st Infantry Division, and the Schützen Regiments of the 12th, 5th, and 25th Panzer Divisions. Those of us in the I.Abteilung were situated in the Hermann Fortification, while the II.Abteilung in the castle of Ivangorod. This establishment was almost like a garrison, as on Sundays we even attended church services. With Regimental Commander *Oberst* Vahl at our head, we moved into the Estonian-Lutheran church. Our duties consisted exclusively of maintaining the operational capacity of the tanks. It was bitter cold at this time. Then came our call to action, and it became clear to old well and rested *Gefreiter* Rubbel that I would be in service as a *Richtschütze* in the tank belonging to *Oberfeldwebel* Fendesack. Then began the first of two personal winter campaigns spent in and around Wolchow.

In the Field Hospital in Bad Kissingen, and in the 10th Panzer Reserve Abteilung, Gr. Glienicke

It must have been around the 10th of September 1941, when the hospital train had disposed of the rest of its patients in Schweinfurt after unloading those inflicted with head wounds at the University Clinic at Würzburg. I accompanied the others to a so-called "reserve hospital," which was set up in a Catholic nursing home. My bed was situated in a large sleeping hall. With the help of a cane I could run around a bit, and we were indeed encouraged to do so. Because we had not yet been deloused, which was an "Entry Permit to the Reich," so to say, this procedure was made up for here. My beautiful, black Panzer uniform with grenade shrapnel holes in it was taken away from me and replaced with a field-gray outfit. My first course was down into the cellar, where our requisitioned uniforms lay in a great big pile for disinfecting and cleansing purposes. Because I knew that afterwards this pile would end up in a small room somewhere and that I would be without my normal threads, which I liked to wear a lot, I fished my uniform out, wrapped it into a newspaper, and hid it. Then I discovered a seemingly trustworthy cleaning lady who was ready and willing to wash my uniform and stitch it up. In a week I was once again milling about dressed in black!

We had settled in to Schweinfurt quite nicely and, above all, had obtained the right to leave, and were only required to be present during ward rounds and meals. At that time (in the fall of 1941), severely wounded soldiers in western and southern Germany were somewhat of a rarity. One was generally passed

Bad Kissingen, view from the ground alcove.

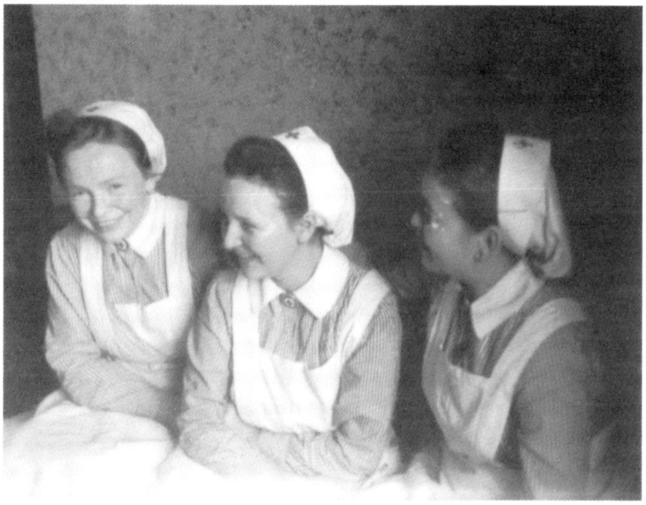

The three nicest nurses, from left to right: Anny from Stockheim; Maria from Kronach; and Tina from Lichtenfels.

on from one station of medical care to the next. After about fourteen days, the less-severely wounded and more able-bodied patients were transferred to Bad Kissingen, probably due to the fact that they would soon recover and be in fighting shape again. Therefore, it seemed only fitting that they would be allowed to experience the wonderful flair and appeal of this health resort before returning to the front. This was not okay with me, as I had met a nice female shortly before I had to leave.

I arrived in the Rhön Sanitarium, a medium-sized home of the Security Establishment, and now the Reserve Hospital II of Kissingen. After only a few days I realized it had been a mistake to stay in Schweinfurt. I was housed in a room for two, and my roommate was a nice chap named Helmut Quednau from Ragnit. We were surrounded by young nurses and had quite a nice time of it. In Schweinfurt we had a "dragoon" as head nurse, who had taken up with the worst "*Spieß*" of one of the companies. In Kissingen everything was freewheeling and pleasant. In one of the "paltry wine taverns" I became familiar with the Kissingen-Frankish wine. Cinemas, theatres, and

During our daily strolls. Above: Maria and Helmut. Right: Ruth from Sonneberg and Helmut. The main duties of photographer seemed to have landed on me.

When the nurses weren't walking us around, they tended to the fox terrier belonging to the head field doctor, who ran the hospital as well as a practice in Bad Kissingen. Kissingen was stock full of illustrious visitors who tried to overcome the travails of war in their own particular way here.

events in the regents building all ensured we never had a dull moment. Then one day, shortly before Christmas, I received my marching orders for the Reserve Abteilung in Gr. Glienicke near Potsdam. I admit that I would have rather spent the winter, which appeared with the first snows in the Rhön, in Kissingen. But I would again be on consignment. My little "regimen holiday" was officially over. However, life was not bad in the Reserve Abteilung either, as almost every evening there would be an excursion to Berlin or Potsdam. There was a deep sense of peace in both cities. In the first ten days of January 1942 I ended up by pure coincidence in Tilsit at the front control station. I was allowed to actually live at home until transportation to the northern armies on the eastern front could be arranged. The most important thing here was that we were lucky enough to be able to cover ourselves with sufficient winter clothing for the Russian front, which were mostly civilian pieces obtained through the "Winter Donation" program. With every kilometer that the train chugged away toward the northeast it became ever more apparent what this winter would have in store for us. Faster than I had wished, I found myself with my old bunch back in Narwa.

Narwa, on the Narwa, situated as an outlet of the Peipussee, is an establishment of the Livonian Order of the Sword-brotherhood, which was later incorporated into the Germanic Order (Germanic Knights Order). Narwa and Estonia belonged

at one time or another to Denmark, Sweden, and Russia, and was heavily influenced by German eastern colonization during the Middle Ages. In the 13th Century Narwa was the border between the principality of Novgorod and the Realm of Order. This political boundary was also a cultural one, which is quite noticeable by looking at the buildings comprising the fortifications. The Hermann Fortification, named after the land master of the Order Hermann Balk, stands as the so-called eastern border post of Western Europe, and directly across from it sits the Castle Ivangorod, viewed as a symbol of Eastern Europe and its push toward the west. In both of the fortification's buildings one encounters sentiments of both cultural and everyday life, which is a style hardly found on our continent. The Hermann Fortification is a modified form of the type of castle found in eastern Germany belonging to the Germanic Order. Quadruple-winged construction stretches from a narrow foundation sharply to its heights. Decorations are lacking. This is quite different from the Castle of Ivangorod. Wide courtyards are fanned by rings of walls. Inside stand churches, living quarters, defensive installations, and a fortification landscape, which is wide and flat. Today Narwa is again the border between Estonia and Russia, but from 1920 to 1944 the border was situated further east on the Luga.

Balk, Hermann, died 1239; the Land master of the Germanic Order. Balk had supposedly hailed from a family from Brandenburg-Lower Saxony and became Head Master of the Germanic Order. Hermann von Salza was named as first Land Master of the Order and charged with the assignment to fight the heathen Prussians, after which the Polish Duke Konrad von Masowien called for help to the Order, and Friedrich II had assured the German Knights Order all land to be conquered. In the year 1230 he crossed the Vistula River with a band of Knights of the Order, and with the zeal of crusade driving him on spent the next several years campaigning hand in hand with Christianization, political acquisition, and Germanic settling of the Kulmlands and Ermlands, as well as the establishment of the cities of Thorn (1231), Kulm (1233), Marienwerder, and Elbing (1237). In 1237 Balk conducted the unification of the Germanic Order with the Swordbrotherhood's Order and, with the assistance of the Danish King Valdemar Livland, conquered the territories of Kurland and parts of Estonia; additionally, he became master of those territories he won in this manner. Even though parts of these lands had to be ceded to King Valedemar, Balk, during the 8 years of his reign and who later died in Germany in 1239, still managed to lay the cornerstone for the State of the Germanic Order on the Baltic Sea and was responsible for its magnificent cultural achievements.

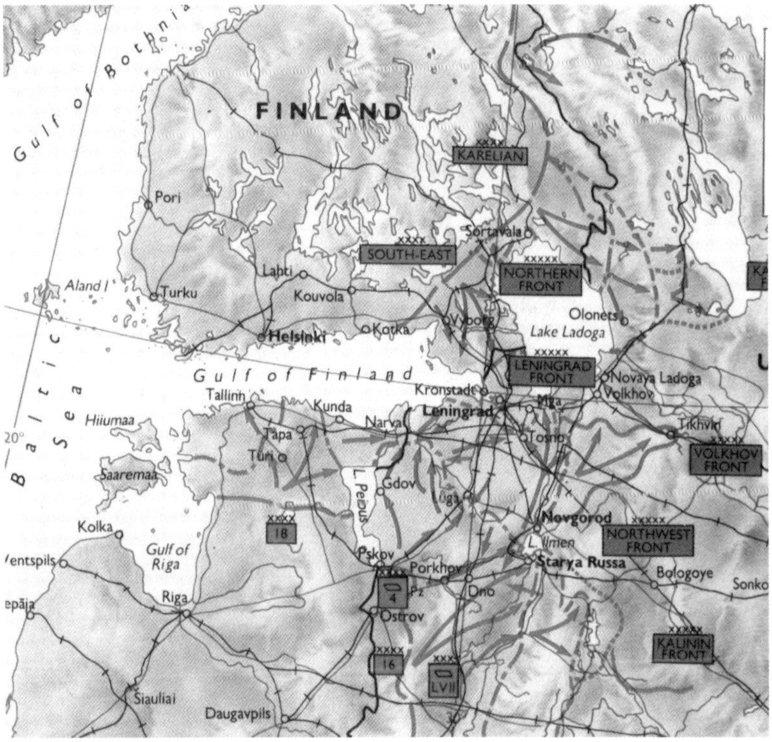

Above and following: The "quarters" of the Panzer-Regiment 29 in the winter of 1941 to the middle of 1942. I.Abteilung in the Hermann Fortification, II.Abteilung and Regimental Staff in the Castle of Ivangorod. Above: Hermann Fortification and the Castle of Ivangorod, January 1941.

Corner Tower at Ivangorod with disposal facility facing the river.

Our quarters in the Hermann Fortification, January 1941—an Estonian camp. *Leutnant* Thiele, Company Officer in 3./29.

Both fortifications' construction originate from the 13th century.

First Action by Wolchow from January 11th, 1942 to around February 10th, 1942

With the 3rd Pz IV on the march from the train station after unloading to Kingissepp on the road by way of Gatshina in the area south of Narwa. *Oberfeldwebel* Hans Fendesack headed our Battle group; I was the *Richtschütze* in his tank. In spite of immense snowfall, the road had been cleared. Although I hailed from a "cold homeland," I had no idea how my first combat action in the winter of'41 would play out. I was in action four times.

We are at our destination. Fendesack returns from the combat briefing. However, our Panzers are still dark-gray in color and therefore dangerously easy to spot in a snowy landscape. There is no white paint to be found, and the usual replacement for such (limewater) does not work well in hard, frosty conditions.

We overnighted and refueled on the grounds of the Czars' Castle Krasnovardeisk, near Gatschina. The new name originated from the Soviet days. In the fully intact palace were situated the Corps Staff and a Fighter Squadron, where "Bubi" Hartmann was the Group Commodore.

When there were canteen wares to be found we hoped to get hold of handouts of alcohol, chocolate, and tobacco ware. But these always seemed to go missing in a strange way, which only increased the closer one got to the front. This time we still had some toothpaste, which we despised. Who the hell ever brushes their teeth in -20° C weather anyway? But, our driver "Gobby" Tost had an idea. Because there was so much of this scorned toothpaste around, he thought this should at least increase our level of security. We warmed the tubes up and proceeded to spread the contents for reasons of camouflage all over the surfaces of the tanks. In this manner we invented our own brand of "*Countfiti.*"

Here is the discoverer Gobby Tost from Hildesheim with the exemplary snow-like camouflage. One never asked how long it took us, yet we did indeed have some time and, above all, we had fun doing it.

Fendesack's crew with *Ladeschütze* above left. *Funker* Kurth above right. *Fahrer* Tost bottom left. *Richtschütze* Rubbel bottom right. We were well equipped with our "Winter-Donation Clothes." We just didn't look much like soldiers.

Oberfeldwebel Fendesack on his way back from dissemination of orders. Soon it would all go off!

Riflemen are quickly on the scene atop the *Panzerspähwagen*.

This is a *Panzerspähwagen* (armored personnel carrier) with DO Cast Frame. This weapon, which the Russians feared quite a bit, was nicknamed the "Roaring Cow." It was shot by means of rocket propulsion, could reach a distance of 6 km, and had 38 cm worth of shattering effect. It also shot incendiary explosives. The DO projectile had surface-impact capability, also killing by air pressure.

We had to "shoot our way forward" through an infantry attack with our tank. I took this picture through the rear slot for the machine gun. There were two riflemen on the heavy machine gun. A little later we caught our first Russian tank, a KW I, who had probably been sleeping on the job, as it was 9:00. We couldn't penetrate its armor with our ridiculous 7,5 cm stump cannon. The *Ladeschütze* was blown to bits in front of the tank, as he was standing in the bushes. The crew bolted out of there and left their vehicle standing. A destruction-brigade from the *Schützen* of the 12th Panzer Division came by and scuttled it. But then we would be polished off as well. On this Russian supply route the enemy knew we'd be coming, as our Panzers could not advance either in the forest or in the snow. They hid a mine in one of the tracks and rrrrrrrrummmmms! The tank blew up, the hatches blew open, and everybody was screaming: "we've been hit, we've been hit!" The *Kommandant* was hanging on the cannon. I waited, knowing that something else would have to happen. Then I saw a piece of the tank tread lying behind us. At some point we all got out. The infantry went back, as did we; but the tank stayed in enemy hands after we had salvaged the secret munitions.

On the march from Mga to the battle areas near Pogostye.

After we had spent a few days and nights in the bitter cold out in the open, we were then allowed to head back into a "forest and warmth camp." Here we took up in a bunker. We waited for a counter-attack so we could then recapture our tank and mend it together again. Then the positional detachments reported that the Russians had in fact blown the thing up!

With a *Panje* sled, somewhat lacking in style for us Panzer guys, the five of us returned back to Narwa safely.

The Second Action at Wolchow from the End of February 1942-May 5th, 1942

We didn't have to wait long. Narwa was situated over 100 km behind the front. Here I became used to all the things which I would never again enjoy in Russia all the way out to 1945. Namely, we had winter proof living quarters, a stove, our own sleeping quarters, regular meals, and sufficient security. It was during this time that something began to emerge, which to this day impressed me deeply. That was the contact I shared with my dear comrades and sensible commanding officers. Only, this was not quite the probationary period which I had imagined for myself as a volunteer for combat. As the next withdrawal from service of Panzers on the Wolchow front took place I was there. In the meantime, I had achieved the rank of *Gefreiten* and was given the responsibility of *Panzerkommander* in a Type IV, of which I was immensely proud. With a very difficult crew at that time—names like Pauers, Beloch, and Knispel if memory serves me—we rolled our way to the front. On slippery, icy snow, there were no studs on the tank tracks; we attempted to climb the eastern banks of the river behind the Narwa Bridge. The tank kept sliding backwards. Finally we reached the consignment railroad station. We unloaded directly onto the rail platform in Kingissepp because there were no ramps available. My artistry at instructing how to turn the wagon sideways was not sufficient in this case. The *Fahrer*, a *Unteroffizier* named Westernhage, had been patiently following my hand signals, and now even he could not save the situation from the fact that the tank became stuck and could not budge. The whole train had to be displaced in one direction or the other for the unloading to take place. My self-confidence had been reduced to nil. From the railway station we traveled on the winter road Leningrad-Moscow to Yuban for three months into wooded and muddy areas with the 21st Infantry Division. This was a very strange way to wage war for us Panzer troops. Names of places like Dubovik, Lipovik, Berosovka, and Tigoda were etched deeply in my memory. The war was literally frozen during these winter months, with temperatures of minus 40° Celsius. Both sides were engaged in a struggle just to survive. The Russians were better at this than the Germans, I might add. They were most used to the cold and were better equipped for these winter conditions; therefore their difficulties were not quite so bad as ours. Our MG 34 didn't work at all because the German weapons oil had frozen solid. Our tank batteries lost their power capacity in such cold, and in turn could not function when attempting the process to start the motors. We actually dismantled the heavier batteries and warmed them up by fire. The Russians started their tank diesel motors, in comparison, by using pressured air—and they ran! For both sides the battle against the cold really was the main concern. The consequence of this was that the front remained unchanged until the summer of 1942. What we soldiers had to endure and the ways in which we were forced to improvise remain unimaginable, even today.

The front from Wolchow to the west was carried forward during the early months of 1942 and was situated in a line along

During this action we had no snow camouflage. With one Panzer IV we were in combat with the 24th Infantry regiment, *Oberst* Sattlet at the helm, in the area of Dubovik. If I had not reported to the Panzer Corps I would have been an infantryman in this regiment, which happened to be my original field regiment, just like these soldiers to the right of the tank, as they stood in wonderment of it.

"All clear for combat"–The *Funker* Knispel—he turned out to be the most successful Panzer combatant in the *Wehrmacht*, credited with 162 enemy tanks destroyed. Here he is removing the muzzle cap from the cannon.

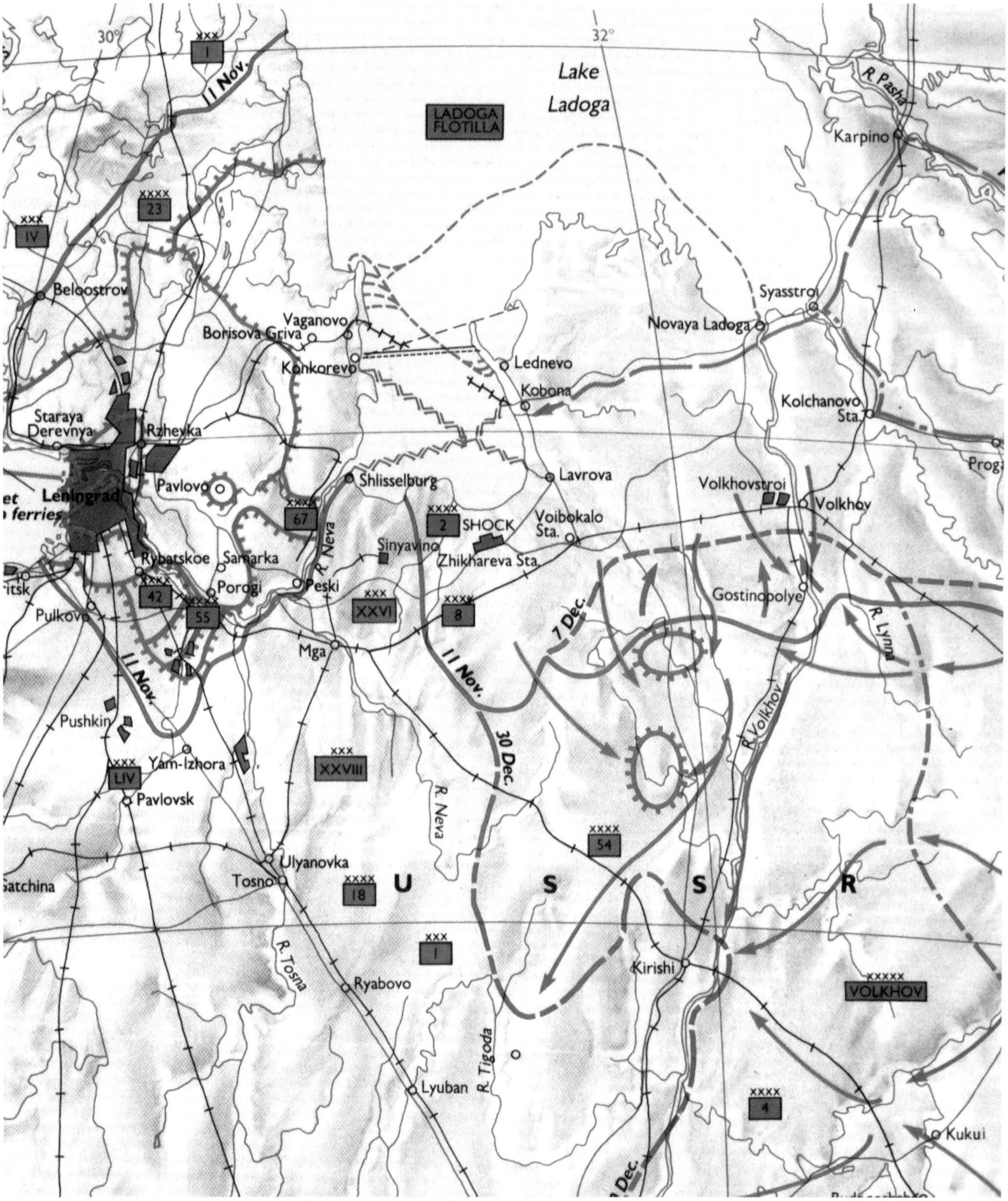
30°
32°
Lake Ladoga
LADOGA FLOTILLA
11 Nov.
XXX I
XXXX 23
XXX IV
Beloostrov
Vaganovo
Borisova Griva
Konkorevo
Lednevo
Kobona
Staraya Derevnya
Rzhevka
Pavlovo
Leningrad
Shlisselburg
Lavrova
XXXX 67
XXXX 2 SHOCK
Voibokalo Sta.
Rybatskoe
Samarka
Sinyavino
Zhikhareva Sta.
R. Neva
Porogi
Peski
XXXX 42
XXX 55
XXX XXVI
XXXX 8
Pulkovo
Mga
Pushkin
Yam-Izhora
XXX LIV
Pavlovsk
XXX XXVIII
Gatchina
Ulyanovka
Tosno
XXXX 18
U S S R
XXX I
R. Tosna
Ryabovo
Kirishi
R. Tigoda
Lyuban
XXXX 54
XXXX 4
XXXXX VOLKHOV
Kukui
7 Dec.
30 Dec.
Novaya Ladoga
Syasstroi
Karpino
R. Pasha
Kolchanovo Sta.
Volkhovstroi
Volkhov
Gostinopolye
R. Lynna
R. Volkhov

In March 1942, near Dubowik. It was still very cold. Noteworthy is how the infantry would make it through the winter with coats on like those worn at home, head gear worn under the helmets and gloves. The Russians were in a different situation. They wore felt boots, padded jackets and pants, and fur caps. Here we're getting two Panzers ready for a small-scale attack in a forested area.

the cities of Pogostje, Dubowik, Lipowik, and Tschudowo. The map (Leningrad area) shows the status of the front in December 1941.

The methods we employed here in our tanks amounted to nothing more than us wandering around like fortified bunkers, whereas in our massive land grab in the earlier center thrust into Russia we employed various armored movements, attacks, and munitions fire. We didn't like this bit of wandering about; however, we realized that the tank was a weapon that could be used more successfully in almost any situation than any other form of weaponry.

The infantry sits up in order to make the difficult advance through the snow easier. Nobody has any idea where the enemy could be hiding. The object of such attacks would normally be the improvement of the local system of strategic positions.

The tanks oversee the advance of the riflemen. The enemy occupied the forest line; therefore, the riflemen lay down. About an hour later we arrived in the forest without enemy resistance. We were in good spirits and a bit too unperturbed. Then, from a short distance away—hardly 200 m—we sustained a sudden burst of shellfire, one of which happened to strike our tank. The turret was thrust to the left, and the riflemen who had been escorting us were now lying in the snow. I then recognized that a KW I had disappeared between the trees. Next our attack stalled out. Without resistance or enemy fire we advanced slowly through the heavily snowed forest. We were on the highest lookout for tanks. Then, under the cover of fir trees, we discovered our adversary. We started shooting at it like mad (see p. 53); however, he didn't react at all. We carefully approached the tank. I got out and climbed up onto the KW under cover of the infantry. The crew had left, as it had become stuck in place fully intact. We were told before the start of our attack that the Russians had run out of tank busters. However, in the munitions bunker of this tank I counted over twenty armor-piercing shells. We were very lucky, as he had shot at us with an incendiary shell, which had left behind only a flat dent on our turret. I could hardly conceive of this: an incendiary shell. If it had been something else, I would not be writing this today.

On the Tigoda near the train station German Stukas, which we saw occasionally, had caught out this KW I with a direct hit.

This assault gun was the favorite weapon of the infantry. Unfortunately there weren't enough of them. This weapon belonged to the artillery regiments, and in times of ever decreasing availability of materials they were more worried about their own needs than those of the infantry.

Anti-aircraft gunnery also was helpful in offering defense and cover for infantry engaged in major battles. This 2 cm AA gun was positioned and employed for ground-to-ground use near Lipowik.

Between Dubowik and Lipowik sits the stranded KW I in a depression, which also served as a guide in the dark or by heavy snowfall. The tank became stuck and frozen in place.

This KW I had been shot out. In the photo on the left, a tank shell had left behind no more than a dent. In the photo on the right one sees four holes shot through the armor by means of hollow-tipped shells. These had brought about the detonation of the tank turret itself.

March or April 1942, in a small Russian city up north. It could have been Tossno or Tschudowo. I didn't get to know any other cities around there. I visited the church and was quite impressed with the deep religious faith of the Russians. I was amazed that other than myself there were more German soldiers in this church, and not just out of curiosity.

Bazaar in a small town; there wasn't much to be found there.

Life in a small northern town in the occupied zone.

From Panzer Regiment 29 to Panzer Regiment 4

Narwa in May 1942. Spring displaces winter only in the most difficult of ways. The Narwa River still flows with chunks of ice. Narwa had become somewhat of a garrison for the 29th Panzer Regiment, which was an opportunity not afforded many times to other regiments during the war in Russia.

Feldwebel Günter Herder, 3./Pz. Regiment 29.

The I. Abteilung. Commander *Hauptmann* Niedick left the regimental formation on the 20th of May 1942 for some R&R in Germany before being assigned to action in the Caucasus with the III.Abteilung of Panzer Regiment 4. The regimental music corps sees us off with a melodic performance.

Our fallen were left behind. We had fond memories of this regiment, to which we belonged since October 1940, as well as fond memories of the city of Narwa. We then left the formations of the 12th Panzer Division, which would later be destroyed in the encirclement of Kurland in 1945.

We now sat on a transport train and were traveling toward the west. For top secret reasons we were not made aware of our destination. We had a lot of time to ponder, however. Contrary to the two months we spent with Army Group Center after the start of hostilities, the war up north had a tougher face to it. The enemy and the climate didn't grant us any favors. I had a lot of luck though. From January to May 1942 I sat inside a tank on the cutting-edge of the front with the infantry. This was in no way like any sort of armored combat we had learned. Alone with one to two tanks, we were often exposed to the whims of battle-inexperienced commanders and were charged with the duty of bringing both tank and crew through all of this in one piece. Twice we lost our tanks through enemy actions; however, our crews remained intact. This is where the following rumor got its start: In Rubbel's tank you'll always be safe. I admit that things could easily have turned out differently on at least three rather dicey occasions. When I was wounded the giant piece of shrapnel, which lodged in my behind, could have landed in my head for starters. Also we were shot at plenty of times when bailing out of the tank during our experience with the explosion of the mine. The hit we sustained on the tank turret could have severely altered the "architecture" of our tank, but the loader in the Russian tank had reached for an incendiary shell instead. The most lasting impression was the following incident: Once I climbed out of the rear of the tank and over onto the left tread, when at the same time the tank began to roll and my right leg became lodged in the tread. With every ounce of energy I fought against the churning and pulling of my leg into this mass of jagged steel. Somehow I came through okay. In the meantime I was twenty years of age and I had been promoted to *Unteroffizier*. I was also awarded with the Wound Badge, the Tank Combat Badge, and the Iron Cross Second Class. I now willfully accepted every new challenge and entered into battle with morale and expectations flying high, which are contrary to what those of our younger generations would try and have us believe today.

In Narwa the fallen soldiers of the 29th Panzer Regiment are buried. They fell in combat on the Wolchow Front, the encirclement of Oranienbaum, and on the various roads and tarmacs.

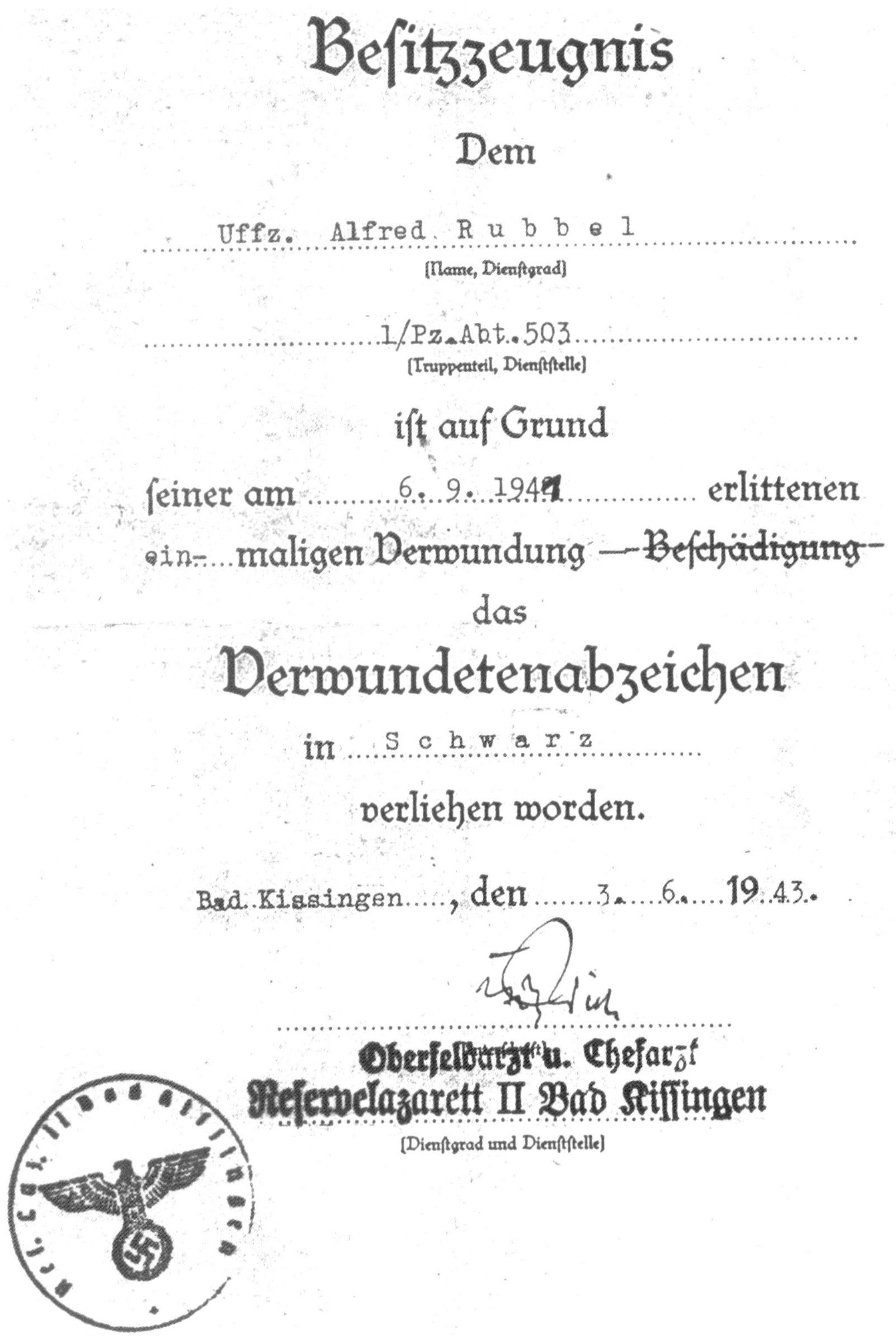

Besitzzeugnis

Dem

Uffz. Alfred Rubbel

(Name, Dienstgrad)

1/Pz.Abt.503

(Truppenteil, Dienststelle)

ist auf Grund

seiner am 6.9.1941 erlittenen

ein-maligen Verwundung ~~Beschädigung~~

das

Verwundetenabzeichen

in Schwarz

verliehen worden.

Bad Kissingen, den 3.6.1943.

(Unterschrift)

Oberfeldarzt u. Chefarzt
Reservelazarett II Bad Kissingen

(Dienstgrad und Dienststelle)

Wound Badge Document

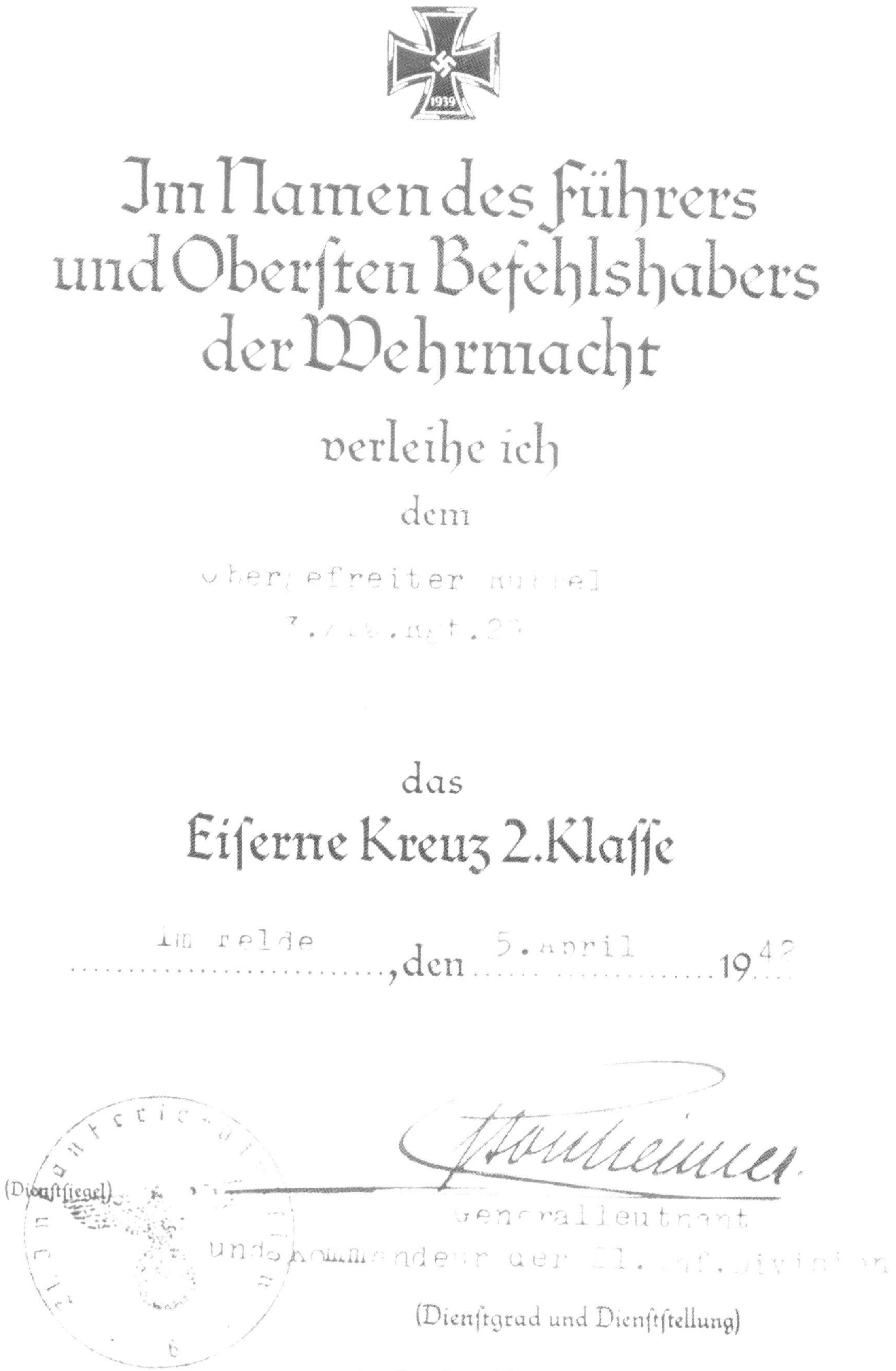

Im Namen des Führers
und Obersten Befehlshabers
der Wehrmacht

verleihe ich

dem

Obergefreiter [illegible]
7./[illegible].Rgt.[illegible]

das

Eiserne Kreuz 2. Klasse

Im Felde, den 5. April 194[illegible]

(Dienstsiegel)

Generalleutnant
und Kommandeur der 21. Inf.Division

(Dienstgrad und Dienststellung)

Iron Cross Second Class

Order of Battle: 21st Infantry Division December 1st, 1941

Infantry Regiment 45
Infantry Regiment 24 with 3rd Jäger Battalion
Infantry Regiment 3
Artillery Regiment 21
Panzer-Jäger Abteilung 21
Nachtrichten Abteilung 21
Pioneer Battalion 21
Sanitäts Battalion 21
Nachschub Dienste
Feldpost
Ordung Dienst
Veternärdienst

Nachschub (= resupply)
Ordung (= order/office)
Dienst (= service)
Dienste (=services)

Order of Battle: 12th Infantry Division December 1st, 1941

Panzer Regiment 29 with III. Abteilung
Schützen Regiment 5 with 2nd Jäger Battalion
Schützen Regiment 25
Krad-Schützen Battalion 22
Panzer Aufklärungs Abteilung 2
Panzer Artillery Regiment 2
Panzer Jäger Abteilung 2
Panzer Nachtrichten Abteilung 2
Panzer Pioneer Battalion 32
Heeres Flak Abteilung 303
Nachschub Dienste

6

With the 4th Panzer Regiment in the Caucasus

R&R In Silesia

It took about three days time by train to travel from Narwa by way of Dorpat, Riga, Schaulen, Tilsit, Marienburg, and Frankfurt on the Oder. Now all the speculating began: where are we headed? The "Führer Directive Nr. 1" stated, " nobody would be informed of any more than he absolutely had to in order to carry out his orders." This was adhered to with ironclad conviction. Of course, this then also became a breeding ground for "scuttlebutt." Would we then travel further out past Berlin to France, like several optimists had estimated? Or, would we turn south, and if so, whereto? We steamed past Guben-Sagan. The next destination on the map would be our old garrison in Sprottau. We then traveled through Sprottau and the train never stopped. However, after twenty km we came to rest at the small railway station at Neuhammer/Queis, which was the old drill ground that we knew very well. We were somewhat disappointed that we had been shunted out into the boondocks in whose soil we had left behind many a bead of sweat, as one can see.

Panzer troopers in black uniforms with steel helmets and carbines in full stride. *Oberleutnant* Süßmann (left), because of this outrageous training we were forced to do, looks on in a most repining way, whilst *Unteroffizier* Krefting completely averts his gaze.

But it wasn't so bad after a while. Although first, before we could move into our accommodations, we had to submit ourselves to the one thing that couldn't be changed, in order to obtain our "entry permits into the Reich"—delousing. This otherwise took place before crossing the Reich's borders. Our accommodations, quite differently than a year ago, found us in massive, comfortable buildings and not in a bunch of barracks.

We arrived in Neuhammer with only our personal gear and our hand-operated weapons, those being pistols and carbines. We left the rest of our equipment back in Narwa with the regiment, and were now waiting on our brand new supplies of tanks, motor vehicles, and other special equipment, which we needed to properly continue waging an effective war. It was a beautiful eastern German early summer. We were very involved in the process of picking up the motor vehicles and equipment. An especially pleasurable assignment was the try-

And not to forget a moment's rest in the shade.

The *Gefreiten* Hanjo Thaysen, left, and Kurt Knispel. I was together with both of them until war's end. Knispel fell during the last days of the war. Thaysen was with me from start to finish in the same company, and also happened to be the one who first tended to my wounds when I was struck outside Leningrad/Mga—he and I may have been the last ones remaining from 9th Company Panzer Regiment 29. We still see each other today at the annual "veterans' reunions." These two in the picture were the most diametrically opposite of characters, the likes of which would seldom be found in any community again.

When we had to patrol the terrain again by foot—the new Panzers were still not around—one had to be very cautious!

Ernst Beloch, left, Hanjo Thaysen, and Georg Tost, who would end up driving my tank for quite a long time.

out of the vehicles, as we were never asked about the number of kilometers needed to break them in. We often sped off to Sprottau in order to revive old female acquaintances. We familiarized ourselves with the large mountain ranges surrounding the area (Breslau and Lower Silesia). I experienced a very stressful event before our orders came to march off again. We had traveled to Sprottau in a truck, and it had been arranged that at midnight that evening our transportation would leave back off again from the church. I came too late and the truck was gone. It happened to be a wonderful, mild summer night; but my bed was unfortunately located about twenty km away, and there was no other alternative than simply humping it all the way back by foot along the Bober River, which was a tributary of the Oder. In the underwood the nightingales were rustling and singing, which east of the Elbe are actually called thrush-nightingales. Now, I can honestly tell you that twenty km for one of us Panzer chaps is an awfully extraordinary thing! However, once the aggravation of it all had worn away, I almost felt I was walking with wings, and feelings of euphoria swelled over me as I began thinking about Russia on the way home to my bed. It then began to get brighter; the morning's dawn broke, and then finally came the sun on its tail. I finally got back to shelter around 6:00 in the morning and fell straight away into bed. I didn't even deign to think about getting up until lunchtime. But then the unthinkable happened. At 7:00 AM the service *Gefreiter* stood at the foot of my bed and relayed to me the orders from the Spieß, which were the following: at 9:00 AM that morning I was to lead the Company in that Sunday's church service! This geezer had really contrived quite the effective counter-measure for my late arrival back home that morning.

At some point we finally scraped together our tank crews, and we then marched off to the Panzer depot in a castle near Magdeburg to receive our new Panzer Mark IV with the long-barreled 7,5 cm cannon. Time was really limited, as the 13th Panzer Division, along with the 4th Panzer Regiment—to which we as the III. Abteilung were soon to link up—had undertaken an attack on the 23rd of July across the Don toward the south and the Caucasus. Our tanks were loaded up onto a freight train and whisked off to the east on a special "rush-delivery" transport. With 17 Panzer Mark IVs we formed the old 3rd Company, Panzer Regiment 29 and the new 9th Company,

Dust and heat every day. Yes, all week long. Dust in your mouth, dust in the uniforms, dust everywhere inside the tank. The engines would get rid of all this dirt by depending solely on the air filters. Each evening they were dismantled and cleaned. Here is the crew of the "924." From left to right: *Funker* (name forgotten), *Panzerkommander* Rubbel, *Ladeschütze* Lad, *Richtschütze* (name forgotten), and *Fahrer* Tost. It was August on the Kalmücken Steppe.

We rearmed ourselves as soon as we hooked up with our regiment.

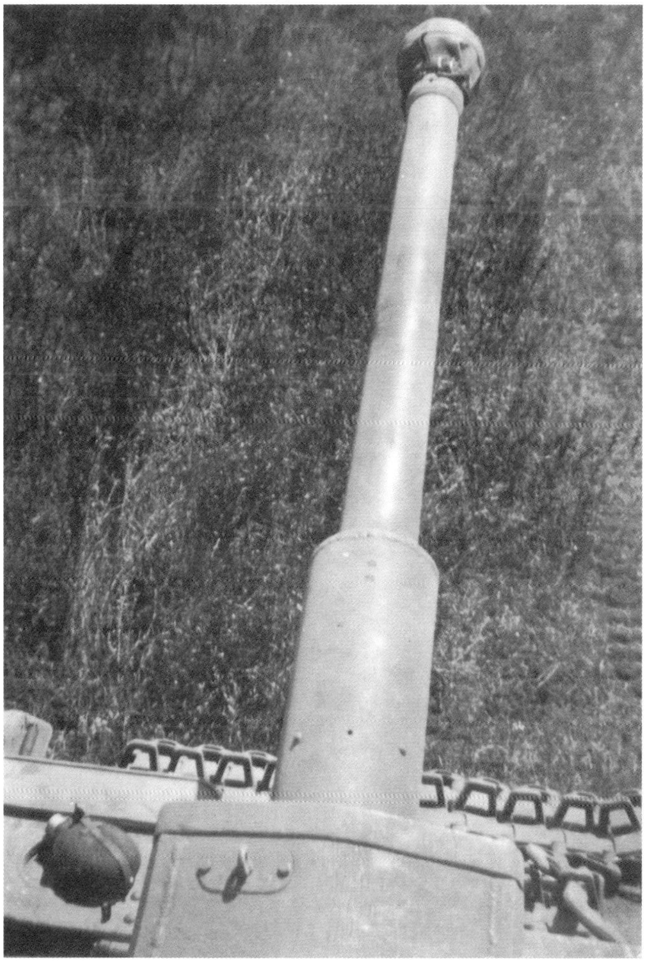

This was the long, beautiful new KwK (cannon) 7,5 cm L 48. We hadn't fired it yet; however, we were very impressed by its penetrative performance compared to the 7,5 cm short version.

Panzer Regiment 4. The train was really whipping along as it passed the stations of Dresden, Breslau, Kattowitz, Krakau, Przemmysl, and Lemberg without stopping. The Polish rail workers, who were tending to the stretches of tracks, did nothing more than loaf about on the job in hopes of possibly hindering the enemy in his attempt to wage war. We finally arrived in Stalino at the train station for unloading. There we were afforded a lasting impression of the Italian army, which was represented there with detachments of the 6th Italian AOK. They were exhibition troops, with crackling motorcycles ridden by highly polished operetta soldiers with great big tufts of feathers on their headwear. We had always wished for "imitation soldiers" when facing our enemies, yet to have them for allies was a real nightmare. We hadn't expected much out of them, and they in fact were guilty of leaving their winter positions along the flanks leading to Stalingrad, and thereby contributing to the awful catastrophe that would follow.

In our march through the country by way of Rostow-Bataisk we tried to catch up with our regiment, who were storming ever southward and facing virtually no opposition. Near Koroptokin on the Kuban we had caught up with them, and we then continued without respite through the Vogian Steppe southward. It was the most adventurous and interesting campaign of the war for me, and I believe also for my comrades.

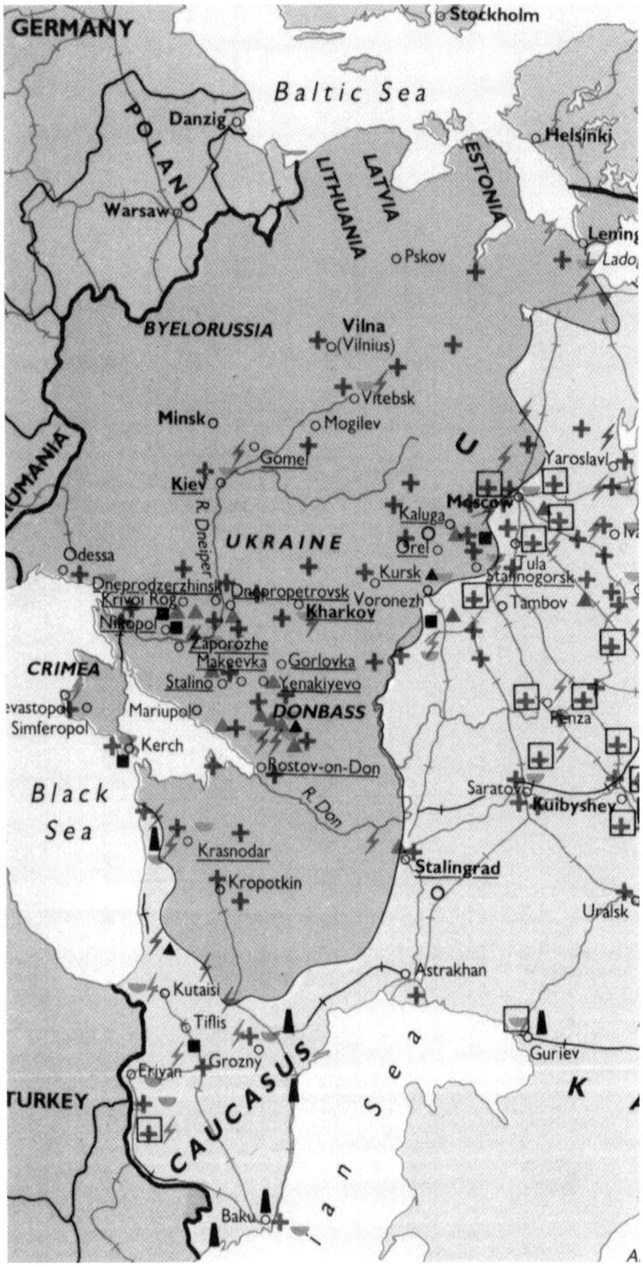

On our march south in the direction of Maikop in the Caucasus Forest. Here it was nothing but unending wideness and flat as a table, without any trees, bushes, or houses on this steppe. Here is the maintenance crew of the 9th Company on a half-track 1,5 ton. We wore sunglasses for the glaring sunlight, which made your eyes ache. We also wore scarves around the neck and goggles designed to keep out the dust, plus we always had plenty to drink.

Above: During a break from marching south of the Kuban sometime around the beginning of August 1942. *Fahrer* Tost (left) and *Panzerkommander* Rubbel. Left: Such was the sight we beheld early mornings in the Central Caucasus of Mt. Elbrus, standing 5,633 meters high. Light armored cars from the 13th Panzer Recon Abteilung lined up for night positions. On the borders of the steppe of the Wald Caucasus with the massive mountains in the background. When the sun was higher in the sky the clouds would roll in and obscure the mountains.

Oil wells in Maikop were set on fire by the Russians. The capture of the oil had been foiled.

We secured the area in Maikop, which was taken on the 9th of August 1942. Here we sit on the undestroyed bridge over the Belega River, which passes straight on through to Suchum on the Black Sea. These guys seem a bit too happy for their current assignment, as the Russians were squatting on the opposite bank. The answer to this puzzle: we didn't have any oil; however, we did manage to lay our hands on a big wooden container full of luscious Mira belle schnapps, and of course we tried some out!

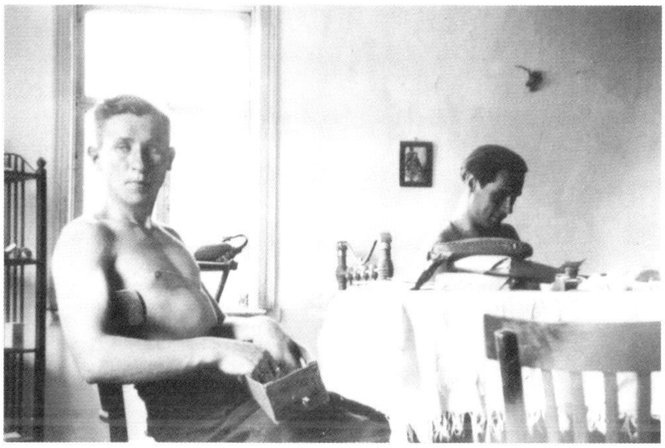

Left: In our quarters in Maikop, where we remained until the 14th of August 1942. Here we even got a bed. My roommate was Günter Herder.

Our Panzer "924" in front of our quarters after the conclusion of the battle for Maikop.

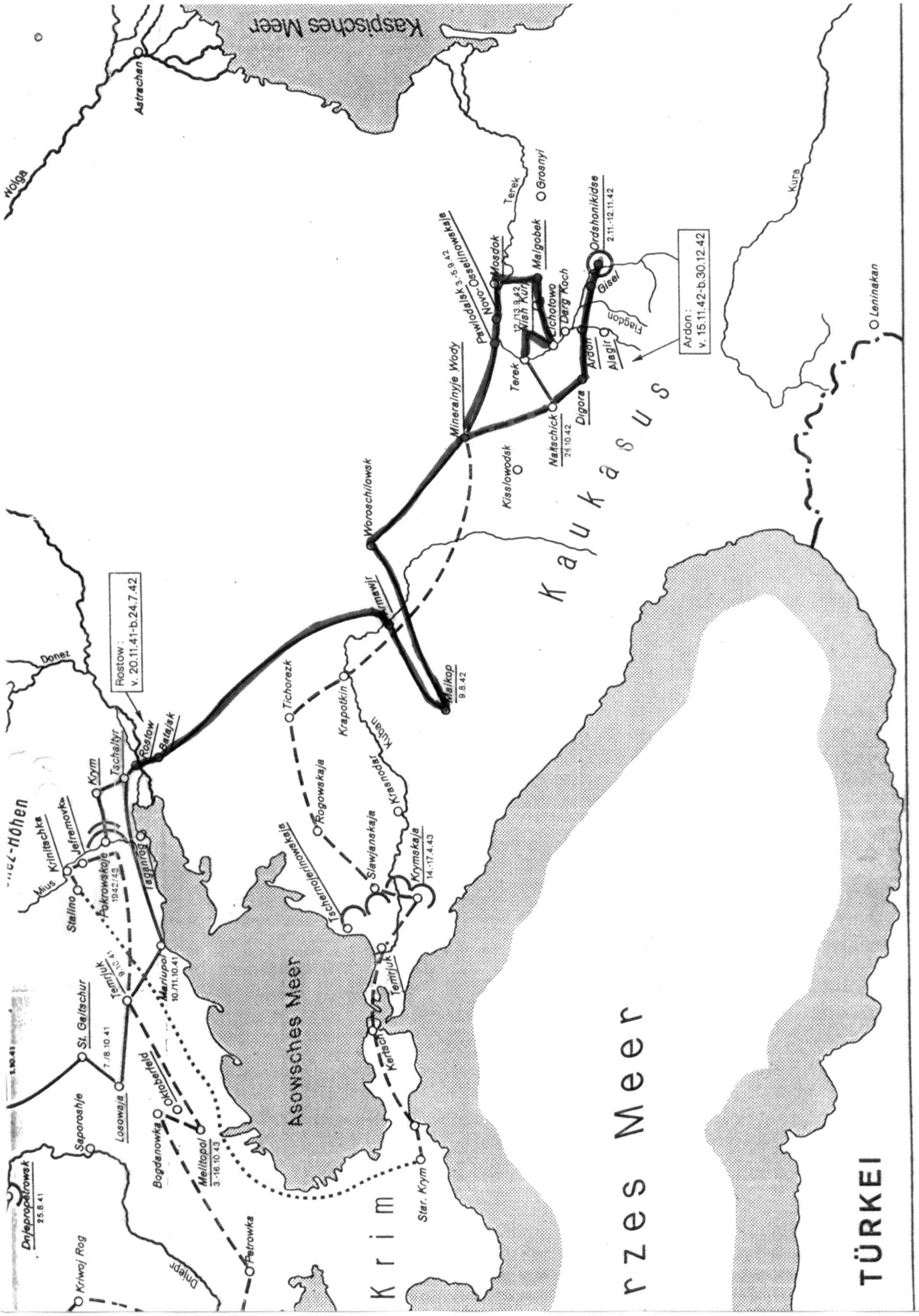
Kaspisches Meer
Astrachan
Wolga
Terek
Grosnyi
Ordshonikidse
2.11.-12.11.42
Mosdok
Malgobek
Pawlodalsk 3.-5.9.42
Novo-Osselinowskaja
Gisel
Ardon :
v. 15.11.42-b.30.12.42
Ardon
Alagir
Flagdon
Digora
Naltschick
24.10.42
Mineralnyje Wody
Kisslowodsk
Woroschilowsk
Kura
Leninakan
Kaukasus
Rostow :
v. 20.11.41-b.24.7.42
Donez
Rostow
Batajsk
Tschaltyr
Maikop
9.8.42
Tichorezk
Krapotkin
Kuban
Rogowskaja
Krasnodar
Slawjanskaja
Krymskaja
14.-17.4.43
Tschernojerinowskaja
Temrjuk
Kertsch
Krim
Star. Krym
Asowsches Meer
Taganrog
Mius
Krinitschka
Jefremowka
Krym
Stalino
Pokrowskoje
1942/43
Mariupol
10./11.10.41
St. Geitschur
7./8.10.41
Losowaja
Saporoshje
Oktoberfeld
Bogdanowka
Melitopol
3.-16.10.43
Dnjepropetrowsk
25.8.41
Kriwoj Rog
Dnjepr
Petrowka
rzes Meer
TÜRKEI

Battles in the Eastern Caucasus

This was a very unusual campaign, as almost everything was different from what we were used to in central and northern Russia.

Enemy Behavior

After Rostow had been taken there had hardly been any resistance all the way to the northern edge of the Caucasus. Even surmounting the Kuban brought hardly a skirmish. All the way to Maikop our "924" hadn't fired so much as a shot with that great big cannon, even though we had been switched into the spearhead. We all pretty much were of the opinion that this dodging tactic employed by the enemy was actually a clever strategy of the Red Army leadership to bait us further into hostile territory. We were certainly a pretty strong opponent ourselves with three Panzer divisions: the 3rd, 23rd, and 13th Panzer Divisions had great powers of penetration in this open landscape, which was absolutely ideal for armored warfare. 300 km of steppe and barenness had taken a horrible toll on the tanks themselves. We were also drawing dangerously far from our provisions base on the Don and our railway supplies. In addition, we now had a completely open left flank, which was left unprotected for a distance of over 600 km. A recon plane for the depths of these areas, plus some roving bands of Cossacks who were fighting along with us, oversaw our flanks and provided some security. After the fact we now know that the Russians had been very weak in our zone, as their forces had been tied down in Stalingrad and the Red Army leadership didn't believe that we would resolve to undertake a campaign like this into the Caucasus with everything else going on simultaneously. Stalin raged against any kind of retreat, but it was only around the end of the year that he had had sufficient forces from the Zis- and Transcaucasus, who then secured the Russian borders in the south. It took eleven guard divisions defending from south to north in order to finally stop the German advance.

German Intentions and Objectives

The first objective of the Germans was the capture of Caspian Sea oil, which was pumped from the oilfields into the loading harbors on the Black Sea. As this had failed, the focus turned to blocking off the Red Army supply routes that ran through the Caucasus and served as land transportation of goods and weapons for the Russians—courtesy of the Western Allies—originating from locations in Persia. After turning away from the Western Caucasus we set off for the north in a swing-like maneuver on the 15th of August toward open territory and the high plateau of Vorishilovsk (today Stavropol), and began our thrust into the eastern Caucasus. Surely they had in mind the capture of the oilfields near Machatshkala by taking Grosny. On the 28th of August we reached the spearheads of our division at Terek, near Mosdok. Enemy resistance and difficult terrain were becoming more and more problematic. The Russian Air Force had also become much more active during this time. They sent waves of U.S. light bomber "Douglas Bostons" over to harass us after taking off from airfields in Tiflis. On the steppe with no natural cover it was impossible to hide. Severely weakened German formations, which had lost men during the long marches after the crossings of the Terek, were successful in penetrating the narrows at Elchtovo. Here they captured and blocked off the outlet of both Red Army supply routes at Ardon. In the meantime, however, strong, well-trained Russian mountain troops had been led over the passes. Together with the ever-allusive troops from up north they combined to launch an offensive. We did not succeed in taking Ordchonikize. Meanwhile, German mountain troops had climbed the heights of Mt. Elbrus and hoisted the Reich Battle Flag, which was a matter of glory and prestige both for those at home and those fighting on foreign soil. In December came the order to set up our winter positions. Hardly had we initiated preparations when the Russians forced us to retreat. The withdrawal was executed in an orderly manner. It started at Terek on the 30th of December 1942 and ended up in the "Gothic Areas" of Krasnodar, where it halted. When the decision was finally made to take the 13th Panzer Division back into and around Rostow it was already too late. The corridor had been stopped up. The battles at the Kuban bridgehead lasted into the early summer days of 1943. The division was transferred over onto the peninsula of Kertshi. In the middle of December 1942, we of the III./Panzer Regiment 4 were given orders to march back toward the direction of the Reich as a labor unit, as we had been plucked apart pretty badly. We were also very lucky that the railway lines had not yet been interrupted. By way of Prochlanadya, Amavir, Rostow, and Dniepropetrovsk we indeed traveled back "into the Reich."

Country and People

This time we were ready for the campaign. Each soldier had received a so-called "knapsack script" with the title "Caucasus." We could then glean that there were six population groups with about forty tribes. These were then broken down into three religious communities: Russian-Orthodox; Greek-Catholic; and Islamic.

Particularly striking were some of the things we heard from the Cossacks. These were the guys fighting alongside us wearing fur caps and identifiable as follows: Don Cossacks-Red Based Caps; Kuban Cossacks-Blue; and the Terek Cossacks wore yellow-based caps. They told us, which would later be confirmed by reports of the Army order sent down by *Generaloberst* von Kleist to the 1st Panzer Army, that Russian prisoners of war hailing from the Caucasus would be released

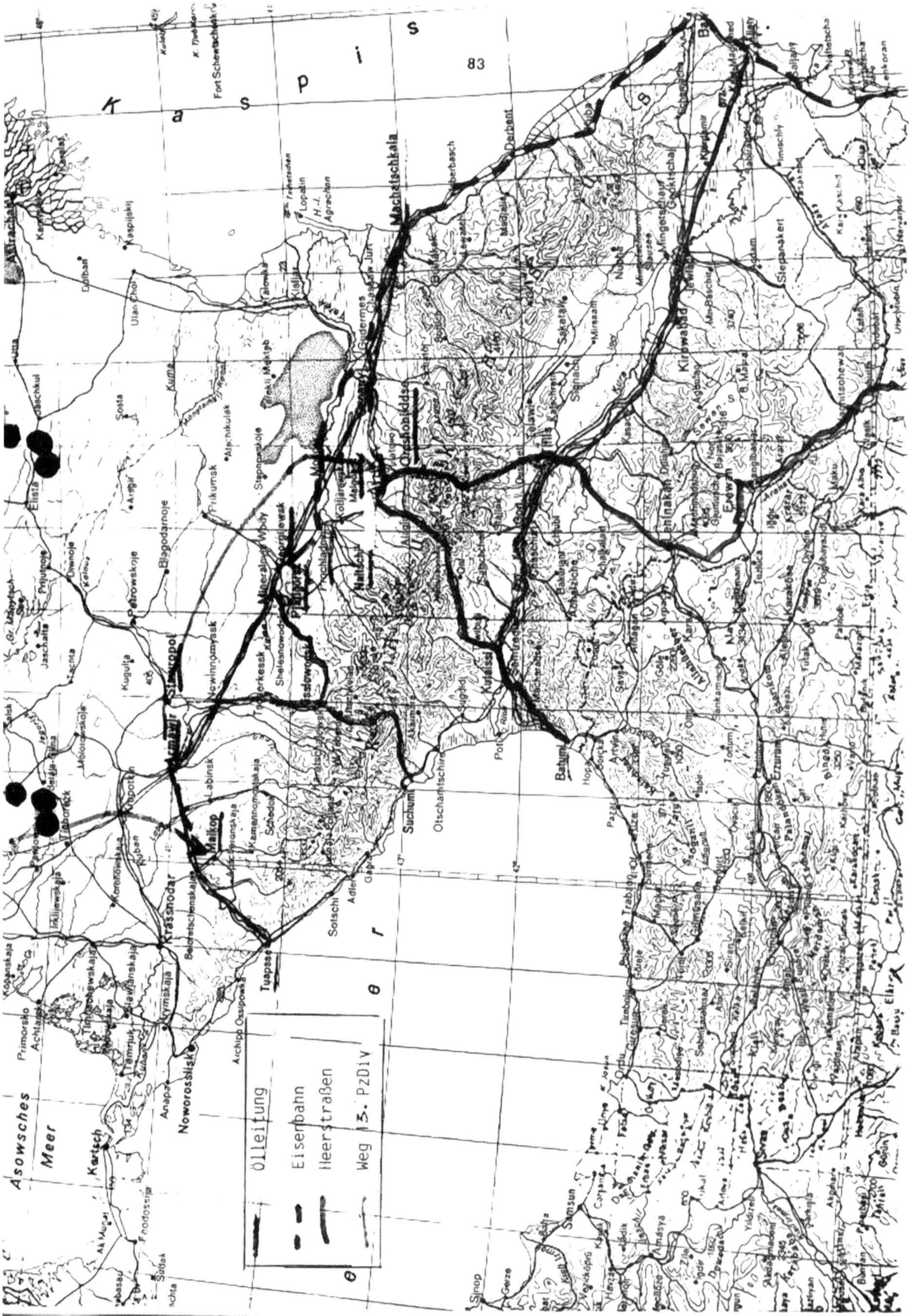
Ölleitung
Eisenbahn
Heerstraßen
Weg 13. PzDiv
Asowsches Meer
Kaspis

to their homeland under the sword. Rules were strictly adhered to, which stipulated that German soldiers could in no way do anything that might do harm to the honor of the Cossacks. The consequence of this line of behavior was that during the course of 1942 there were about fifty Cossack troop detachments that were set up to fight on the side of the Germans. This ranged from the typical Company to the *Kalmücken* Cavalry Corps. These troops, along with their families at that time, had much to fear from the Russians because of their having switched allegiances. Therefore they accompanied our retreat into Austria and Czechoslovakia. After Germany's capitulation the Western Allies inconsiderately delivered them back over to the Russians.

South of the steppe the landscape was favorable due to a mild climate, and thus was quite fruitful. There were huge fields with tomatoes, melons, grapes, vegetable plantations, wheat, and corn. Around Stavropol we ran across herds of horses that were running around freely due to the retreat of the Russians. One day we arrived at a village whose houses appeared quite prosperous. This place was called Gnadenburg, and was inhabited by Swabian speaking people, immigrants who had been brought into the country by Elisabeth. We also remembered that the Russians had had difficulties making their country willingly submit to the regime. In 1922 Stalin, as a first measure of his days as ruler, did everything he could to satisfy the peoples of the Caucasus, as he was himself a Georgian. It was understandable that great hope had been placed on the Germans around here, who were located far away from the area governed by the *Reichscommissar* East, Koch. Here the military wielded a much more sensible occupation policy. However, this policy ultimately failed, as the German contingencies did not suffice to be effective over longer periods of time.

Home to the Reich and Training on the Tiger Tank

The march from Maikop to the eastern Caucasus lasted from the 15th to the 26th of August. This led through the Kalmücken Steppe over the high plateau of Stavropol (Voroshilovsk) and the Elista Steppe. It was the hottest time of year. Drinking water and provisions were very hard to come by at this time. For extended periods of time we had nothing more than oiled sardines and cornbread. Illnesses were becoming more and more prevalent, which is typical for a sub-tropical climate. Malaria, Wolhynishes, Papatatci fever, and lots of cases of jaundice had gripped many of us. I myself became afflicted with malaria and jaundice. For a while I was able to remain with my company while grinning and bearing it. Then I was loaded onto a mass transport into the field hospital for the mildly afflicted at Taganrog on the Azov Sea. I was about the 300th patient of our regiment, which had in fact lost about 1/3 of its personnel to illness. Around this time (the beginning of September), we had overtaken the Terek by Mosdok and were fighting and approaching the key position of Ardon all the while. This was where the Red Army supply routes branched out. I returned to the abteilung in November, and the weather had really cooled off quite a bit. Our Company had sustained very heavy losses of personnel and equipment during the battles for Ordshonikize, near Gisel, and Malgobeck. In the repair facilities I was assigned a shot out tank that had to be onerously refurbished. More than just repairing the damage caused by shelling, we were also responsible for the removal of blood and pieces of the corpses left behind. Then we were sent into laborious small-scale skirmishes near Ardon, Naltshik, Alagir, and Digora. It went well. Around the 15th of December we gave up our piece of equipment. The rest of the II. Abteilung was sent back by train to Germany under the name of "Labor Unit Schober." It was decided that we would be retrained on a new type of tank. On the 23rd of December we were in Berlin, and while underway had been granted a holiday leave for fourteen days at home. On Christmas Eve I was home in Senteinen. This time we had all been given the so-called "Führer Package," consisting of one bottle of sparkling wine, one piece of hard cured sausage, and two cans of meat. On the 10th of January 1943 we were instructed to report to the Panzer Army Gunnery School at Putlos, in Schleswig-Holstein.

Somewhere in October '42 on the Terek. Here was a tank crew with men of the Company Maintenance Corps, 9th Company Panzer Regiment 4.

Heavily camouflaged cover of corn on the steppe near Verchny Kurp in October 1942.

Here we were returning from a firefight. From left to right: *Panzerkommander* Rubbel, *Richtschütze* Utesch, *Ladeschütze* Spallek, *Fahrer* (name forgotten), and *Funker* (name forgotten). In the area of Baslan, December 1942.

Here the above-mentioned crew repairing the drive chain in Ardon, December 1942.

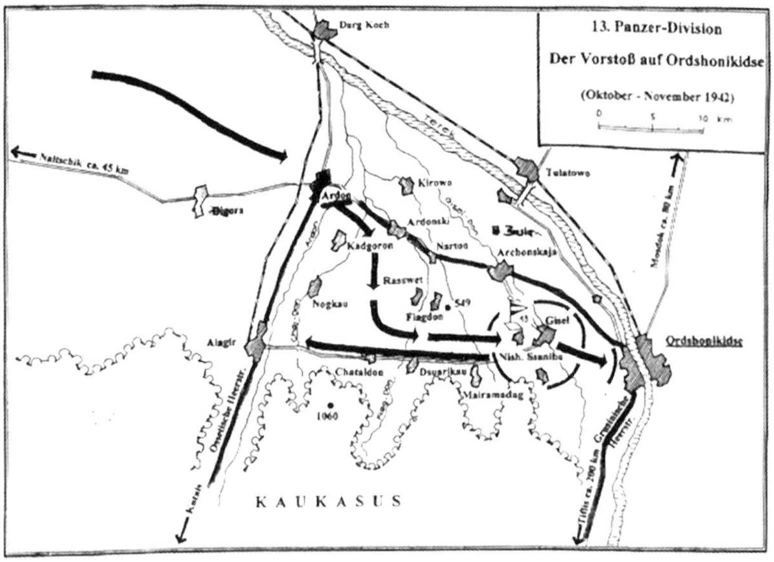

Die Kämpfe der 9. Kp. Pz.Rgt 4 im Kaukasus

Schlacht- und Gefechtskalender
(21. Juli - 14. August 1942)

1. Vorstoß auf Rostow	**21. Juli - 27. Aug. 1942**
- Angriffskämpfe auf Rostow und Straßenkämpfe	21. - 24. Juli 1942
- Brückenkopfbildung über den Don bei Bataisk	23. - 24. Juli 1942
- Sicherungskämpfe in Rostow	25. - 27. Juli 1942
2. Raid zum Kuban	**28. Juli - 6. Aug. 1942**
- Vorstoß zum Kuban und Brückenkopfbildung	28. Juli - 3. Aug. 1942
- Angriff auf Ssalsk und Straßenkämpfe	31. Juli 1942
- Brückenkopfbildung über den Kuban und an der Gorjaka-Einmündung	3. Aug. 1942
- Kämpfe um die Ausweitung des Kuban-Brückenkopfes	4. - 6. Aug. 1942
3. Vorstoß auf Maikop	**7. - 14. Aug. 1942**
- Vorstoß über die Laba nach Maikop	7. - 9. Aug. 1942
- Einnahme von Maikop	9. Aug. 1942
- Säuberungskämpfe in Maikop und Erweiterung des Brückenkopfes	10. - 13. Aug. 1942
- Ablösung in Maikop, Abmarschvorbereitung	14. Aug. 1942

Schlacht- und Gefechtskalender
(15. August - 22. Oktober 1942)

1. Marsch zum Terek	**15. - 26. Aug. 1942**
- Marsch über Armawir bis Raum zwischen Ssablinskoje, Petrowka, Alexandrowskoje	15. - 17. Aug. 1942
- Marschpause für die Masse d. Division bei Ssablinskoje, Petrowka, Alexandrowskoje	18. - 21. Aug. 1942
- Vorstoß zum Kuma und Brückenkopfbildung bei Woronzowo/Alexandrowskoje	18. Aug. 1942
- Vorstoß zum Terek über Miropolskij, Tarskij	22. - 26. Aug. 1942
- Terek erreicht	26. Aug. 1942
2. Kämpfe im Terek-Gebiet	**27. Aug. - 9. Sept. 1942**
- Bereitstellung und Vorbereitung eines Terek-Überganges bei Naurskaja	27. Aug. - 3. Sept. 1942
- Säuberungsgefechte am nördl. Terek-Ufer und neue Bereitstellung zum Terek-Übergang im Raum Mosdok, Kisljar sowie Kämpfe in Brückenköpfen Mosdok u. Kisljar	4. - 9. Sept. 1942
3. Angriffs- und Verteidigungskämpfe im großen Terek-Bogen	**10. Sept. - 22. Okt. 1942**
- Angriff auf Elchotowo	26. Sept. - 3. Okt. 1942
- Stellungskämpfe im Terek-Bogen	4. - 22. Okt. 1942

Schlacht- und Gefechtskalender
(22. Oktober - 12. November)

1. Bereitstellung und Auffrischung rechts der Uruch-Terek-Mündung	**22. - 25. Okt. 1942**
2. Angriffskämpfe auf Naltschik	**26. - 28. Okt. 1942**
3. Vorstoß auf Ordshonikidse	**29. Okt. - 10. Nov. 1942**
- Umgruppierung und Angriffskämpfe im Uruch-Abschnitt	29. - 31. Okt. 1942
- Angriffskämpfe gegen und vor Ordshonikidse	1. - 4. Nov. 1942
- Einnahme von Gisel	2. Nov. 1942
- Verteidigungskämpfe um Gisel/Nish. Ssaniba	5. - 10. Nov. 1942
- Feindliche Angriffe zerschlagen eigene Trosse mit Alarm-Batl. und vollenden d. Einschließung	6. Nov. 1942
4. Ausbruchskämpfe aus dem Kessel Gisel	**11. - 12. Nov. 1942**

Schlacht- und Gefechtskalender
(13. November - 31. Dezember 1942)

1. Sammeln und Bereitstellung	**13. - 15. Nov. 1942**
- Rückverlegung und Auffrischung im Raum Alagir/Ardon	13. - 15. Nov. 1942
- Alarmbataillon bei Kadgoron	13. - 15. Nov. 1942
2. Abwehrkämpfe südlich des Terek-Bogens	**16. Nov. - 31. Dez. 1942**
- Abwehrkämpfe Westufer Fiagdon und Terek bis Darg Koch	16. Nov. - 23. Dez. 1942
- Rückverlegung in die Vierow-Stellung	24. - 25. Dez. 1942
- Abwehrkämpfe in der Vierow-Stellung	25. - 31. Dez. 1942
3. Vorbereitung der Rückzugsbewegung	**30. - 31. Dez. 1942**

Teilnahme der 9. Kp

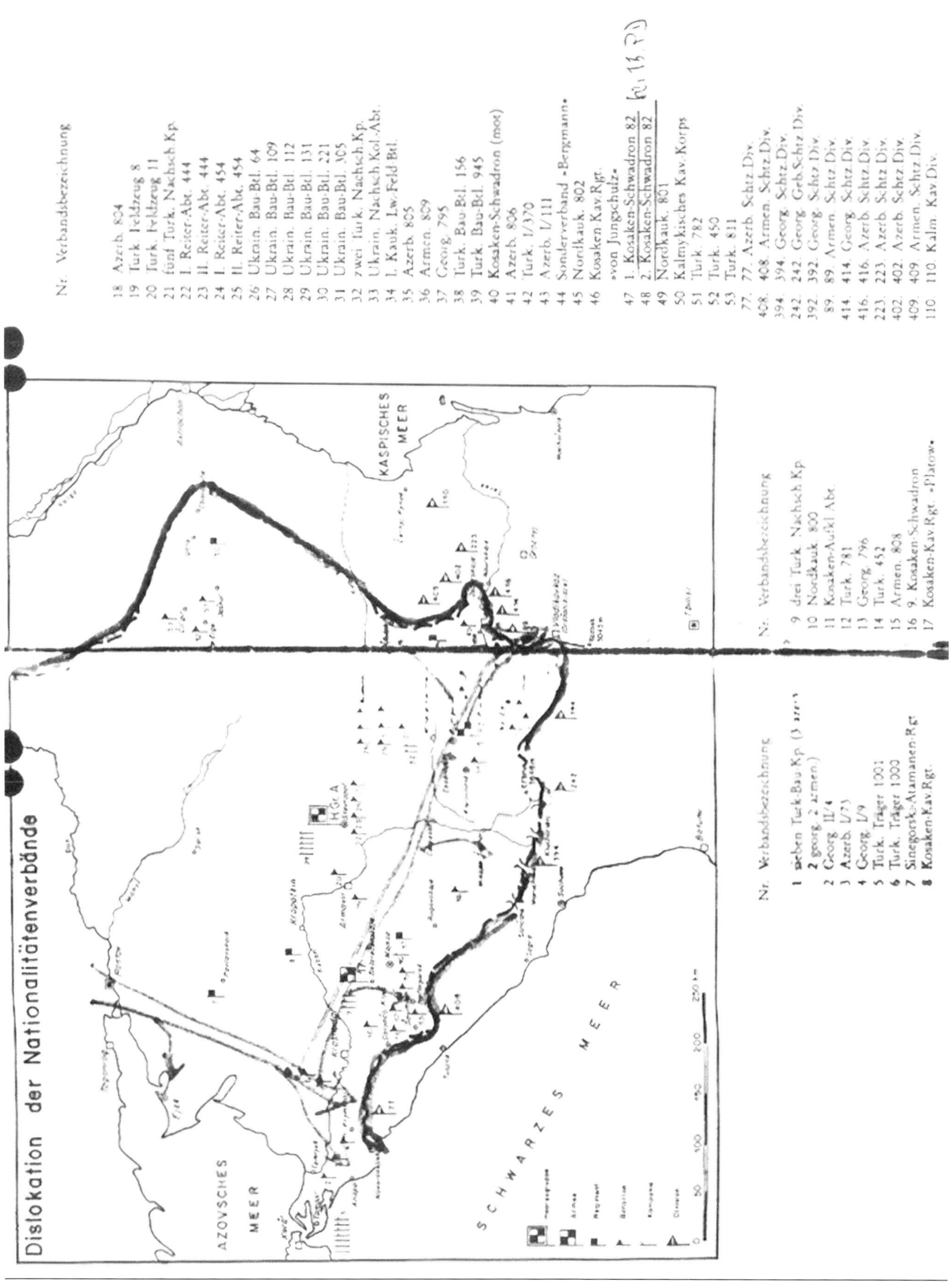
Dislokation der Nationalitätenverbände
AZOVSCHES MEER
SCHWARZES MEER
KASPISCHES MEER
H.Gr.A
0 50 100 150 200 250 km
Nr. Verbandsbezeichnung
1 sieben Turk.Bau-Kp. (3 azer., 2 georg., 2 armen.)
2 Georg. II/4
3 Azerb. I/73
4 Georg. I/9
5 Turk. Träger 1001
6 Turk. Träger 1000
7 Sinegorsk-Atamanen-Rgt.
8 Kosaken-Kav.Rgt.
Nr. Verbandsbezeichnung
9 drei Turk. Nachsch.Kp.
10 Nordkauk. 800
11 Kosaken-Aufkl.Abt.
12 Turk. 781
13 Georg. 796
14 Turk. 452
15 Armen. 808
16 9. Kosaken-Schwadron
17 Kosaken-Kav.Rgt. »Platow«
Nr. Verbandsbezeichnung
18 Azerb. 804
19 Turk. Feldzeug 8
20 Turk. Feldzeug 11
21 fünf Turk. Nachsch.Kp.
22 I. Reiter-Abt. 444
23 II. Reiter-Abt. 444
24 I. Reiter-Abt. 454
25 II. Reiter-Abt. 454
26 Ukrain. Bau-Btl. 64
27 Ukrain. Bau-Btl. 109
28 Ukrain. Bau-Btl. 112
29 Ukrain. Bau-Btl. 131
30 Ukrain. Bau-Btl. 221
31 Ukrain. Bau-Btl. 305
32 zwei Turk. Nachsch.Kp.
33 Ukrain. Nachsch.Kol.Abt.
34 I. Kauk. Lw.Feld-Btl.
35 Azerb. 805
36 Armen. 809
37 Georg. 795
38 Turk. Bau-Btl. 156
39 Turk. Bau-Btl. 945
40 Kosaken-Schwadron (mot)
41 Azerb. 806
42 Turk. I/370
43 Azerb. I/111
44 Sonderverband »Bergmann«
45 Nordkauk. 802
46 Kosaken-Kav.Rgt. »von Jungschulz«
47 1. Kosaken-Schwadron 82
48 2. Kosaken-Schwadron 82
49 Nordkauk. 801
50 Kalmykisches Kav.Korps
51 Turk. 782
52 Turk. 450
53 Turk. 811
77. 77. Azerb. Schtz.Div.
408. 408. Armen. Schtz.Div.
394. 394. Georg. Schtz.Div.
242. 242. Georg. Geb.Schtz.Div.
392. 392. Georg. Schtz.Div.
89. 89. Armen. Schtz.Div.
414. 414. Georg. Schtz.Div.
416. 416. Azerb. Schtz.Div.
223. 223. Azerb. Schtz.Div.
402. 402. Azerb. Schtz.Div.
409. 409. Armen. Schtz.Div.
110. 110. Kalm. Kav.Div.

Stalin's order 227 – Moscow, July 28th, 1942

The Order of the National Commissar for the Defense of the Soviet Union.

July 28 1942, Moscow.

The enemy throws new forces to the front without regard to heavy losses and penetrates deep into the Soviet Union, seizing new regions, destroying our cities and villages, and violating, plundering and killing the Soviet population. Combat goes on in region Voronej, near Don, in the south, and at the gates of the Northern Caucasus. The German invaders penetrate toward Stalingrad, to Volga and want at any cost to trap Kuban and the Northern Caucasus, with their oil and grain. The enemy already has captured Vorochilovgrad, Starobelsk, Rossosh, Kupyansk, Valuyki, Novochercassk, Rostov on Don, half Voronej. Part of the troops of the Southern front, following the panic- mongers, have left Rostov and Novochercassk without severe resistance and without orders from Moscow, covering their banners with shame. The population of our country, who love and respect the Red Army, start to be discouraged in her, and lose faith in the Red Army, and many curse the Red Army for leaving our people under the yoke of the German oppressors, and itself running east. Some stupid people at the front calm themselves with talk that we can retreat further to the east, as we have a lot of territory, a lot of ground, a lot of population and that there will always be much bread for us. They want to justify the infamous behavior at the front. But such talk is falsehood, helpful only to our enemies.

Each commander, Red Army soldier and political commissar should understand that our means are not limitless. The territory of the Soviet state is not a desert, but people - workers, peasants, intelligentsia, our fathers, mothers, wives, brothers, children. The territory of the USSR which the enemy has captured and aims to capture is bread and other products for the army, metal and fuel for industry, factories, plants supplying the army with arms and ammunition, railroads.

After the loss of Ukraine, Byelorussia, Baltic republics, Donetzk, and other areas we have much less territory, much less people, bread, metal, plants and factories. We have lost more than 70 million people, more than 800 million pounds of bread annually and more than 10 million tons of metal annually. Now we do not have predominance over the Germans in human reserves, in reserves of bread. To retreat further - means to waste ourselves and to waste at the same time our Motherland. Therefore it is necessary to eliminate talk that we have the capability endlessly to retreat, that we have a lot of territory, that our country is great and rich, that there is a large population, and that bread always will be abundant. Such talk is false and parasitic, it weakens us and benefits the enemy, if we do not stop retreating we will be without bread, without fuel, without metal, without raw material, without factories and plants, without railroads. This leads to the conclusion, it is time to finish retreating. Not one step back! Such should now be our main slogan.It is necessary to defend each position, each meter of our territory, up to the last drop of blood, to cling for each plot of Soviet land and to defend it as long as possible. Our Motherland is experiencing hard days. We must stop, and then to throw back and smash the enemy regardless of cost. The Germans are not so strong, as it seems to the panic-mongers. They strain their last forces. To withstand their impact now, means to ensure our victory in some months.Can we withstand the impact, and then throw back the enemy to the west? Yes we can, because our factories and plants in the rear are fine and our army receives ever more and more airplanes, tanks, artillery and mortars. What do we lack? There is no order and discipline in companies, battalions, regiments, in tank units and air squadrons. This is our main deficiency. We should establish in our army the most stringent order and solid discipline, if we want to salvage the situation, and to keep our Motherland. It is impossible to tolerate commanders and commissars permitting units to leave their positions. It is impossible to tolerate commanders and commissars who admit that some panic-mongers determined the situation on the field of combat and carried away in departure other soldiers and opened the front to the enemy. The panic-mongers and cowards should be exterminated in place. Henceforth the solid law of discipline for each commander, Red Army soldier, and commissar should be the requirement - not a single step back without order from higher command. Company, battalion, regiment and division - commanders and appropriate commissars, who retreat without orders from higher commanders, are betrayers of the Motherland. These are the orders of our Motherland. To execute this order - means to defend our lands, to save the Motherland, to exterminate and to conquer the hated enemy.

After the winter retreat under pressure of the Red Army, when in German troops discipline became loose, the Germans for recovery of discipline imposed severe measures which resulted in quite good outcomes. They formed 100 penal companies from soldiers who were guilty of breaches of discipline because of cowardice or bewilderment, put them at dangerous sections of the front and commanded them to redeem their sins by blood. They have also formed approximately ten penal battalions from commanders guilty of breaches of discipline through cowardice or bewilderment, deprived them of their decorations, transferred them to even more dangerous sections of the front and commanded them to redeem their sins. Finally, they have formed special squads and put them behind unstable divisions and ordered them to shoot panic-mongers in case of unauthorized retreats or attempted surrender. As we know, these measures were effective, and now German troops fight better than they fought in the winter. And here is the situation, that the German troops have good discipline, though they do not have the high purpose of protection of the Motherland, and have only one extortionate purpose - to subdue another's country, and our troops have the higher purpose of protecting the abused Motherland,and do not have such discipline and so suffer defeat. Is it necessary for us to learn from our enemies, as our grandparents studied their enemies in the past and achieved victory? I think it is necessary.

The Supreme General Headquarters of the Red Army commands:

1. Military councils of the fronts and first of all front commanders should:

a) Unconditionally eliminate retreat moods in the troops and with a firm hand bar propaganda that we can and should retreat further east, and that such retreat will cause no harm;

b) Unconditionally remove from their posts and send to the High Command for court martial those army commanders who have allowed unauthorized troop withdrawals from occupied positions, without the order of the Front command.

c) Form within each Front from one up to three (depending on the situation) penal battalions (800 persons) where commanders and high commanders and appropriate commissars of all service arms who have been guilty of a breach of discipline due to cowardice or bewilderment will be sent, and put them on more difficult sectors of the front to give them an opportunity to redeem by blood their crimes against the Motherland.

2. Military councils of armies and first of all army commanders should;

a) Unconditionally remove from their offices corps and army commanders and commissars who have accepted troop withdrawals from occupied positions without the order of the army command, and route them to the military councils of the fronts for court martial;

b) Form within the limits of each army 3 to 5 well-armed defensive squads (up to 200 persons in each), and put them directly behind unstable divisions and require them in case of panic and scattered withdrawals of elements of the divisions to shoot in place panic-mongers and cowards and thus help the honest soldiers of the division execute their duty to the Motherland;

c) Form within the limits of each army up to ten (depending on the situation) penal companies (from 150 to 200 persons in each) where ordinary soldiers and low ranking commanders who have been guilty of a breach of dicipline due to cowardice or bewilderment will be routed, and put them at difficult sectors of the army to give them an opportunity to redeem by blood their crimes against the Motherland.

3. Commanders and commissars of corps and divisions should;

a) Unconditionally remove from their posts commanders and commissars of regiments and battalions who have accepted unwarranted withdrawal of their troops without the order of the corps or division commander, take from them their orders and medals and route them to military councils of fronts for court martial;

b) Render all help and support to the defensive squads of the army in their business of strengthening order and discipline in the units.

This order is to be read in all companies, cavalry squadrons, batteries, squadrons, commands and headquarters.

The national commissar for defense: J. Stalin.

Order of Battle: 13th Panzer Division 1941/42

Panzer Regiment 4 with three Abteilungs
Panzer Grenadier Regiment 93
Panzer Grenadier Regiment 66
Kradschützen Battalion 43
Panzer Aufklärung Abteilung 13
Panzer Artillerie Regiment 13
Panzer Nachtrichten Abteilung 13
Panzer Jäger Abteilung 13
Panzer Pioneer Battalion 4
Heeres Flak Artillerie Abteilung 271
Division Nachschub Truppe 13

7

Tiger Training in Putlos and Paderborn

First Encounter with the Tiger

We traveled from our holiday back home to Putlos. That which seldom occurred in the army occurred now. They couldn't really employ us at the Panzer Training School. In addition to the school's normal training program they received the order to begin training troops on the Tigers, but there were no Tigers to be had! So they sorted something out next, which only happened with the Panzer troops—they gave us 14 more days holiday. If this had been the infantry, they would have come up with the idea to repeat one's basic training out in the field, or they would have invented some other nonsensical thing with which to indulge oneself. So, once again it was off to Tilsit, which was the deepest point of the communication zone. In Tilsit there were a lot of military personnel; however, my old friends and acquaintances were sorely missing. Only once did I run into an old classmate. Stalingrad hadn't fallen yet, and we were actually allowed to dance again for the time being. I thoroughly seized upon this opportunity, although nobody in my current surroundings wants to believe this. In order to answer the "call of the wild," so to speak, how else were you supposed to meet women?

Out of our circle of comrades of young *Unteroffiziers* there began to emerge a group of friends. Heino Kleiner, Herbert Petzka, Hannes Rippl, and I all came from the same regiment but from different companies. The four of us shared a barracks room in Putlos at the Training Participants Center. Overnight—it must have been around the end of January—everybody arrived. The weather that year was hardly very winter-like in Schleswig-Holstein. At breakfast, the following memorable dialogue had taken place between Heino and me. Heino, I had heard, had seen the Tiger the day before. I said: "Heino, tell me, how did it look?" Heino: "Imagine a very long cannon—

DIE DEUTSCHEN PANZERKAMPFWAGEN (VI) TIGER I

Ausführung:	Tiger I, Ausf. E Sd. Kfz. 181
Hersteller (Endmontage):	Henschel & Sohn
Gefechtsgewicht:	56,9 t
Besatzung:	5 Mann
Bewaffnung (Geschütz, Kaliber, Kaliberlänge, Munition):	1 – 8,8 cm KwK 36 L/56
Turm-MG:	1 MG 34 Kal. 7,92 mm
Bug- (Funker) MG:	1 MG 34 Kal. 7,92 mm
Maschinenpistolen:	1 MP 40 Kal. 9 mm
Mitgeführte Munition:	
Pz.- u. Sprenggranaten:	92
MG-Munition:	3920 – 4500
MP-Munition:	192
Feuerkraft-Durchschlagsl.:	
Pz.-Granate: Gewicht:	10 kg
Mündungsgeschwindigkeit = V°:	810 m/sec.
Durchschlagsleistungen bei	
500 m Entfernung:	140 mm
1000 m Entfernung:	122 mm
1500 m Entfernung	108 mm
2000 m Entfernung	92 mm
2500 m Entfernung:	82 mm
Panzerschutz – Wanne: Bugfr.:	100/66 mm
Fahrerfront:	100/80 mm
Seite unten:	60/90 mm
Seite oben:	80/90 mm
Heck	82/82 mm
Wannendecke:	26 mm
Wannenboden:	26 mm
Panzerschutz – Turm:	
Turmblende:	110/90 mm
Turmseite:	80/90 mm
Turmheck:	80/90 mm
Turmdecke:	26/0 – 9 mm
Höchstgeschwindigkeit:	38 – 45 km/h
Dauergeschwindigkeit:	
Straße:	ca. 20 km/h
in mittlerem Gelände:	ca. 15 km/h
Aktionsradius:	
Straße:	ca. 100 – 110 km
in mittlerem Gelände:	ca. 60 km
Kraftstoffvorrat:	534 l
Kraftstoffverbrauch:	
bei 100 km Straßenfahrt:	ca. 500 – 534 l
bei 100 km Geländefahrt:	ca. 900 – 935 l
Geländeleistung:	
Bodendruck:	1,088 kg/cm²
spez. Leistung: (je nach Motorausführung und U/min)	12,3 PS/t (10,5)

Bodenfreiheit:	47 cm
Grabenüberschreitfähigkeit:	2,30 m
Kletterfähigkeit:	0,80 m
Steigfähigkeit:	35°
Watfähigkeit:	1,20 m*
(* z. T. mit Tauchausrüstung 4 m)	
Längenmaße:	
über alles m. Rohr nach vorn:	8,241 m
über alles m. Rohr nach hinten:	8,350 m
Über alles ohne Rohrüberstand:	6,200 m
Rohrüberstand nach vorn:	2,040 m
Kettenauflagelänge:	3,605 m
Breitenmaße:	
über alles:	3,705 m
über die Ketten:	3,560 m
Spurweite:	2,822 m
Marschketten:	0,725 m
Verladeketten:	0,520 m
lichte Wannenbreite:	1,800 m
lichter Bedienungskreis i. Turm:	1,790 m
Höhenmaße:	
über alles:	2,880 m (3,00 m)
Feuerhöhe:	2,195 m
Motor und Getriebe	Tiger I
Motor (Ottomotor):	Maybach HL 230 P 45
Wagen 1 – 250 m. Motor	Maybach HL 210 P 45
Motorleistung bei:	2500 U/min 600 PS
Motorleistung bei:	3000 U/min 700 PS
Zylinderzahl/Anordnung:	12/V
Hubraum/Kühlung cm³	23,880 (21,353) Wasser
Getriebeart:	Vorwähl-Getriebe Olvar 40 12 16
Anzahl der Gänge:	8 vorw., 4 rückw.

have you done it?" I said "yes." Heino: "Well, this one is much longer!"

Our training was really sluggish, as there was only one Tiger on hand. We had a lot of free time, which we spent in Oldenburg on the Oder in our usual "stomping grounds"—the hotel at the railway station. There we didn't just have the movie theatre at our disposal, but also there were these two daughters!

At some point in February the Panzer Ersatz Abteilung 500, which was responsible for the setting up and training of the Tiger personnel detachments in Paderborn, had established itself in the camp of the 11th Panzer Regiment. We were then transferred there and began a very focused training regimen. Because the armies in Africa were to be strengthened we were examined for possible usefulness in the tropics. We were then supposed to be sent to the 504th Tiger Abteilung, parts of which were already in Sicily. After our training we were sent off to Sennelager, which was the main training area close by. There a Tiger Company was formed and we were introduced to our gadgets—the Tiger tanks. I was the *Panzerkommander*, and I began to put my crew together. The *Richtschütze* was Walter Junge, whom I had known since action at Wolchow. The *Fahrer*

Er hält alles aus....

Dieser Tiger erhielt im Südabschnitt in 6 Stunden:

227 Treffer Panzerbüchse,
14 Treffer 5,2 cm und
11 Treffer 7,62 cm.

Keiner ging durch.

Laufrollen und Verbindungsstücke waren zerschossen,
2 Schwingarme arbeiteten nicht mehr,
mehrere Pak-Treffer saßen genau auf der Kette, und
auf 3 Minen war er gefahren.
Er fuhr mit eigener Kraft noch 60 km Gelände.

4

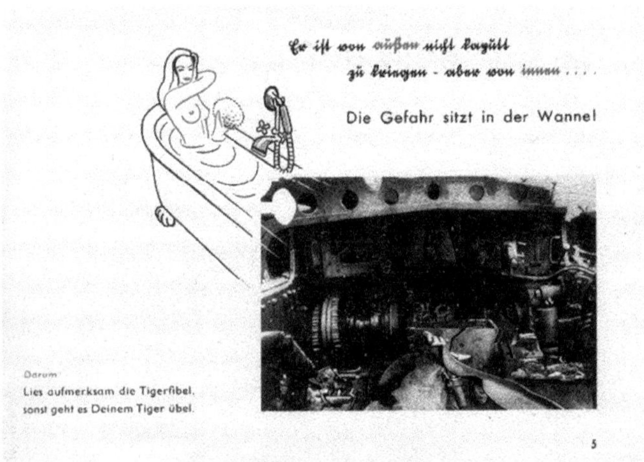
Er ist von außen nicht kaputt
zu kriegen - aber von innen....

Die Gefahr sitzt in der Wanne!

Darum:
Lies aufmerksam die Tigerfibel,
sonst geht es Deinem Tiger übel.

5

was Walter Eschrig, the *Funker* was Alfred Peuker, and the *Ladeschütze* was Johann Strohmer. We had plenty of opportunities to really get to know the tank quite well. We were incredibly proud of this tank, even though I had been somewhat disappointed at first because of its inelegant shape.

At the end of March our Company, which was still led by *Hauptmann* Schober, was ordered to deploy a platoon with four Tigers for action in Russia. Half of the Company consisted of Northern Germans (former troops of the 29th Panzer Regiment), and Austrians & Southern Germans from the 4th Panzer Regiment. The Company was assigned the task of deciding who among us would go to Russia, as we all had eastern front combat experience. There wasn't anything in and of itself which would have attracted any of us back to that theatre of war. We wanted to let fortunes decide who would go where, which meant that we would all be separated from one another. Our platoon leader, the very highly regarded *Oberfeldwebel* Hans Fendesack, made an extraordinary decision for himself. He voluntarily reported for assignment to the eastern front, and his crew was soon to follow. It didn't take long for the rest of the platoon to follow his example. This took place after the Company had formed up, and there wasn't a lot of time wasted agreeing upon this course of action. Fendesack, Petzka, Rippl, Seidel, and I, along with our entire crews made up the *Abgabeelement* (transfer element). It was disclosed to us that we would join the Tiger Abteilung 503, which already was fighting in the area of Rostow. In the middle of March we loaded up at Sennelager and rolled off to the east without any regrets, although we could have spent perhaps a bit more time on holiday at home. The decision was a fateful one; but if one can exert some luck in war, which would later be apparent, it turned out to be a good decision. At the end of March we arrived in

Memorial stone for soldiers killed in training during a diving exercise in the tank on the drill grounds at Putlos.

Memorial stone for the Commander of the Panzer Training Gunnery School Putlos, *Oberstleutnant* Baumgart, who fell at the beginning of the Polish Campaign in 1939.

Bogoduchow, where the 503rd gathered together. The abteilung had to take in a new formation. The mixture of Tigers (Panzer VI's) and light Panzer Type IIIs had proved to be false. The Panzer Company actually consisted of 14 Tigers, 3 platoons of four Tigers, and 2 Tigers to the Company Command. Unfortunately we were then split up. Fendesack, Rippl, and I entered into 1st Company, Petzka into 2nd Company, and Seidel into 3rd Company. We were supposed to belong to these particular detachments all the way to the end. What was to come nobody knew at that time. I was the only commander from our group who survived the war.

In March 1943 in Paderborn. From left to right: Heino Kleiner and Hans Rippl.

Alfred Rubbel.

Excursion to the Hermann Memorial at Detmold. From left to right: Mr. and Mrs. Herbert Rollik, and next to them Heino Kleiner.

Panzer base in Neuruppin 1992, after the withdrawal of the Russians.

Our Tiger, which would become number "114," after loading her up at the Sennelager.

With the 503rd in Bogoduchow, Army Group South, after just having arrived.

Panzer base in Paderborn.

Driburger Street 1942.

With the Panzer Ersatz Abteilung 500, Paderborn

Regimental Commander *Major* Lueder. This Tiger was propelled by propane gas.

Major Lueder at a swearing-in ceremony for recruits.

At the swearing-in ceremony of the Panzer Erstaz Abteilung 500, 1943. These are the first personnel repacements for the Schwere Panzer Abteilung 502.

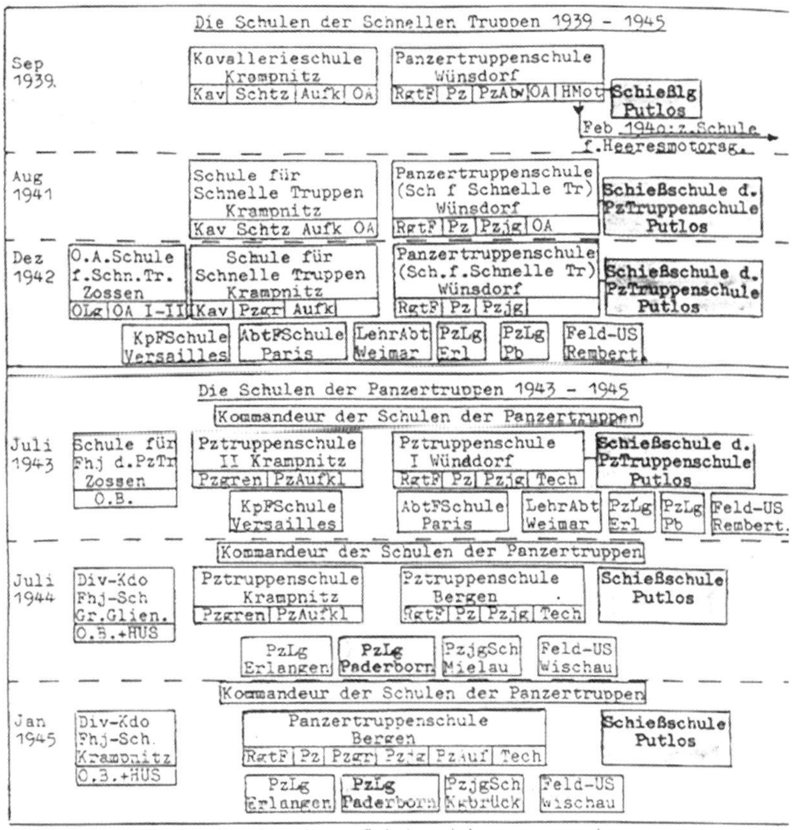

Erklärung: Bei den Schulen deren Lehrbereiche:

Aufk = mot Aufklärer
HMot = Allgemeine Heeresmotorisierung
Kav = Kavallerie = Reiter + Radfahrer
O.A = Offizieranwärter
O.B. = Offizierbewerber (bis z. Leutnant)
Pz = Panzer
Pzgr = Panzergrenadier
Pzjg = Panzerjäger
PzAuf = Panzeraufklärer
Tech = Technische Sonderlehrgänge
Erl = Erlangen
Pb = Paderborn
PzLg = Panzerlehrgänge
Kgbrück = Königsbrück
KpF = Kompanieführer
AbtF = Abteilungsführer
RgtF = Regimentsführer
HUS = Heeres-Unteroffizierschul
Feld-US = Feldunteroffizierschule

8

With the 503rd Tiger Abteilung Army Group South

Integration into 1st Company

We paid a high price. In order to remain together, we voluntarily reported for duty to the eastern front. We also left our crowd behind, in which we knew all the people and all the ropes. We were war veterans and tried and tested Panzer warriors. Of the five commanders, four wore the Iron Cross-First Class. We wondered what it would be like with a new troop detachment that had recently been set up. These were my thoughts as we sat in our train transport and rolled forward from Paderborn to Altenbecken Kassel to Erfurt, Dresden, Breslau, Krakau, and Lemberg. We hadn't even traveled through Lemberg yet when, instead of heading southeast as expected, we headed due east instead. As usual, we knew almost nothing about our new theatre of combat.

This whole deal with transporting the 60-ton Tiger tanks was new to us as well. The Panzer Type IV would be loaded onto a normal, open railway car. With the Tiger there was this special railway car that went by the designation "Symms." Because of the bridges in the east and their limited capacity to bear weight, we had to insert between every two Symms-Railway Cars three Protective Railway Cars, so that the center of weight would be more widely distributed. So our own particular train was made up of five Symms and twelve Protection Railway Cars. On one of them lay the dismantled tank treads. For railway transports the Tiger was outfitted with a smaller tread because of an oversized profile otherwise. As soon as we traveled into the railway areas of the east, two additional Protection Cars were latched onto the front of the locomotive because of the danger of mines.

We became familiar with a new section of the front and with the Ukraine, which was comparable to the center of the eastern front in the areas of Minsk-Smolensk. The weather was appalling, snowy rain, fog, and temperatures just above 0° Celsius. By way of Kiev we arrived at the railway station of Bogoduchow for unloading. There the abteilung gathered together, which partly had been fighting in the lower Don regions. We were designated as army reserves and were supposed to incorporate another formation and begin preparing for the summer offensive, which would be called Operation Kursk-Orel, or "Citadel." Only at that time (March 1943) we weren't aware of this.

Our hope, which as a rule was assumed by many of us in the Panzer Corps, that we would meet up with a proper bunch of troops would soon turn out to be a great disappointment. At least it did with respect to 1st Company, where Fendesack, Rippl, and I had landed. Upon our arrival it was overwhelmingly tangible that this was being handled with the utmost of indifference. There was no proper greeting ceremony, and Company Command saw no reason to be of assistance in our efforts to integrate. We very quickly got to the bottom of just exactly what was wrong with 1st Company. The Company Commander had been sacked during hostilities in the lower Don. The *Spieß*, or "Mother of the Company" so to speak, was pretty much a sadistic acting good-for-nothing. The *Unteroffizier* Corps was a desolated group of guys with no cohesion and was plagued by all manner of insider dealings. The operatives outside of the battle group carried out all these little games. In the *Unteroffizier* Corps there were five *Stabsfeldwebels*, who were all people with over twelve years of military service. With the exception of *Stabsfeldwebel* Ehrentraut, nobody from this military ranking ever sat in the tank. Amongst the common *Unteroffiziers* there were three that had been demoted: they had been penalized and stripped of their *Feldwebel* rankings. This team of rag-tags was a sorry

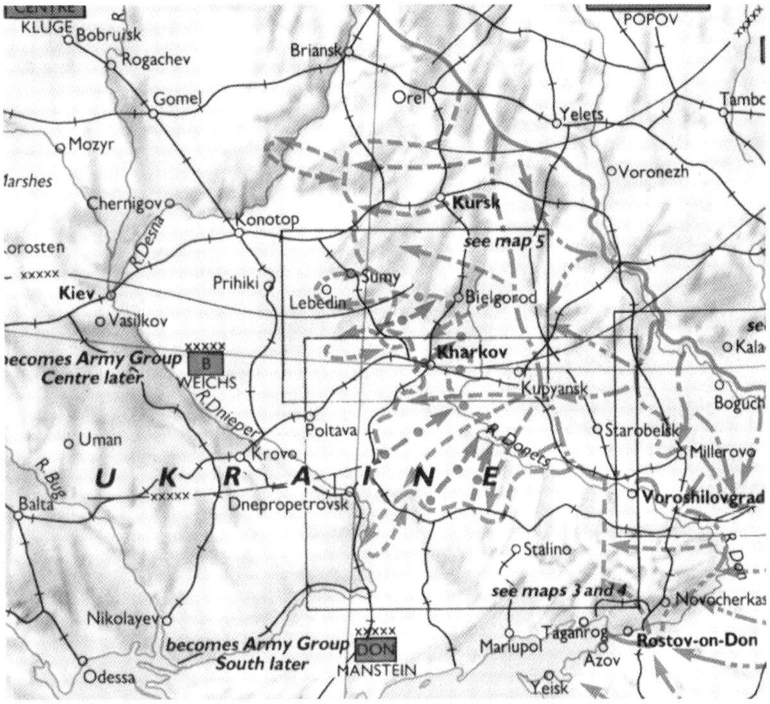

Schwere Panzerabteilung 503 – July 1943

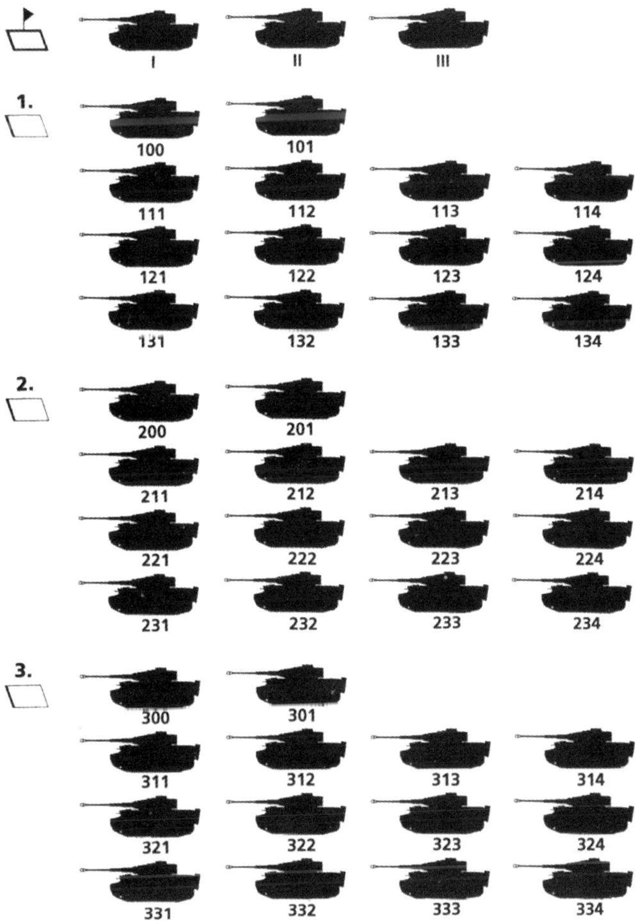

Gliederung 1943/44

Apr. 43 - Frühjahr 45

Abt. 3 Pz VI — 45 Pz VI

St — 1 — 2 — 3 — W — V

Stabs-Zug
N.-Zug
A.-Zug
E.-Zug
Pi.-Zug
Fla.-Zug
San.-Zug

1.Zug (Kette)
2.Zug (Kette)
3.Zug (Rad)
Berge-Zug

<u>Pz.Kp.</u>

Kampfstaffel:

-Kp.Trp.	2 Pz VI
1.-3.Zug	je 4 Pz VI

Räderstaffel:

-Kp.Trp(-)	1 Pkw, gel.	)
	1 B.-Krad	) traten im Gefecht zum Troß I
	3 Solo-Kräder	)
-San.-Dienst)		
-I.-Gruppe)		
-Gef.Troß I)	1 B.-Krad	
-Gef.Troß II)	16 LKw	
-Gepäck-Troß)		

Kampffahrzeuge :	14 Pz VI
Kraftfahrzeuge:	22 Kfz

<u>Personal/Kp.</u>

-Kampfstaffel	7o Soldaten
-Räderstaffel	43 "
davon in I.Gruppe(2o)	
	113

<u>Personal/Abt.</u>

-Offz.	28
-Beamte	7
-Uffz.	274
-Mannsch.	694
-Hiwis	9o
	1o93

old bunch who had all come under fire for the first time on the Kalmücken Steppe. One could count off the number of personnel with any combat experience on one hand. The first measure the *Spieß* tried to take was to separate the *Panzerkommanders* from their crews and to stick us, like all *Unteroffiziers*, into better living quarters. Then I, as the youngest *Panzerkommander* of the bunch, was supposed to cede my tank to an older gentleman for "Probationary Duty at the Front," who'd been recently demoted. Well, that was the last straw! Luckily Fendesack was good friends with the oldest Company officer, who in turn was in tight with Company Command. Fendesack sorted things out so we remained with our crews. This was like a signal to other teams, who cautiously searched contact with us. Dr. Lochmann later described this continuing operation as the "Convalescence" of 1st Company, which really in retrospect turned out to be a pretty good bunch. These sets of circumstances were not to be found amongst 3rd Company, however. We were perplexed because we wondered how we could possibly hand over such valuable, high-performance tanks to such inexperienced and poorly led people. But gradually the positive forces began to win the upper hand. A deep-reaching fallout of personnel laid up in the sick bay also helped. As we relocated to Charkow in the beginning of May and finally received a quality Company Commander, 1st Company was indeed taking on the characteristics of a halfway useful Panzer Company.

Charkow, Summer 1943:
Above and right: Orthodox church underneath multi-story buildings on Red Square, and the circular structure on the exhibition grounds. Both images below:The city was scarcely destroyed, even though it had been twice conquered.

Preparations for the Summer Offensive

Hauptmann Clemens-Heinrich Graf von Kageneck replaced *Oberstleutnant* Hoheisel as abteilung *Kommandeur*. This mastermind and nobleman formed the Officers Corps in his image. This reform process continued on a downward slope with the exception of 2nd Company, which remained a body without a head until war's end. The cause of this was that the Company Commander and the *Spieß* were unsuitable for the job and unfortunately remained in charge.

We enjoyed our time in Charkow. For the first time we were quartered in a relatively unscathed big city. We visited the movies and the theatre; there were sports festivals and Company-sponsored evenings. Our training was conducted in a very targeted fashion. The light Panzer Type IIIs were removed from service. At this time new personnel arrived, many of whom we knew because they originated from our old regiment.

The preparations for the unique offensives of the eastern armies were quite encompassing. The battle for Kursk was supposed to provide for improved operations at the front, as well as extinguish the threat posed to Army Group South. Our abteilung had received the task of supporting the armored troops with air force and live fire in the so-called Turkish area, a large combat area in which we would convince the Turkish General Staff of the "invincibility" of the German army. At the same time, our training was tailored towards the anticipated upcoming skirmishes with the Red Army. Since we hadn't much experience "shooting with the cannon," the Company traveled by itself to positions right on the Donez and shot up enemy targets on the eastern banks.

We left Charkow and moved into our ready positions near Bjelgorod to a place called Tolekonoje. The area we stayed in we named "The Forest of the Nightingales," because the nightingales, or more rightly so the thrush-nightingales, treated us to a never-ending concert. The date to attack was pushed back several times, which gave the Russians (who were fully aware of German intentions) the opportunity to strengthen their defenses on the other side of the Donez.

Freshly imported from home in March 1943, in Bogoduchow, the Tiger had not yet been in combat, and everything was still new and pretty on it. Especially since the *Fahrer* saw to it that we shouldn't do anything to ruin its pristine state. In fact, if it had been up to him, he would have made us climb on board without our boots on. The tank still had no number on the turret; however, it would become "114," which we saw straight through to April 1944, with no harm to its personnel. In fact, it wasn't this tank exactly, but two successors with the same number that we "used up."

From the left:

Funker Alfred Peuker from Silesia, Eule Mountains, born 1923? At that time he was about twenty and had had a commercial career, I believe. His life's maxim was never to voluntarily report himself for any kind of duty. In those days he was quite a "slovenly fellow" and required time and again a firm hand. What was even more astounding was that he was such a finicky old stickler that he actually shrink-wrapped his spare skivvies in a plastic bag! He died in 1998. *Richtschütze* Walter Junge from Luckenwalde near Berlin, or as he would say: "Berlin near Luckenwalde." Born in 1921? He was one of three people that I've encountered in my life who understood me right from the get-go and with whom I was able to get along with virtually no friction. Besides Walter there was the antechamber woman from the tank school at Munster and my grandson Meno. Against resistance from within our Company

Left: The Tiger "114" with its tank crew. We were the 4th tank in the First Platoon of the First Company of the Schwere Panzer Abteilung 503, belonging to the platoon of *Leutnant* Jammerath. We were all about 20 years of age and had, as the decorations suggest—with the exception of Strohmer—all "tasted combat." Right: Arrival at 1st Company 503rd with the "114." Here we were still properly uniformed (left). Soon we would be wearing whatever we pleased or whatever made sense, as the case may be. As a matter of principle, however, we would wear the proper military uniform when we happened to go into battle. If one were taken prisoner wearing leisure clothes, this might have led to that person being hanged on the next tree as a "non-combatant" But, as it would later turn out, this precaution was hardly of any use. Up to the end of 1944 about 90% of all those who fell into captivity with the Red Army were killed.

Tigers arrive from action in the lower Don to Bogoduchow in March 1943.

On the march to Charkow.

A highly visible guidepost in Charkow to our quarters in Plechanovski-Bayon.

Our *Tiger* "114" during training exercises in the quagmire near Charkow in May 1943.

Sharp shooting on enemy targets on the eastern Donez riverbanks.

At the Turkish exercise.

I was able to see to it that he became my *Richtschütze*. Nobody really thought he would be any good at this, but that guy's performance never let me down. He later packed furniture, which was a bit strange for someone his "size." He lived in the GDR (Communist East Germany) and died about twenty years ago (1980s). There's not really much to say about old *Panzerkommander* Rubbel except that he was able to get his crew through thirteen months of combat in Russia safe and sound, which was comprised of (when not in the repair shop) seventy days in action on the battlefield with 57 enemy tank kills. The *Fahrer*, Walter Eschrig from Silesia, was a blacksmith. He was a very skillful tank driver and, like all the others, a good comrade. Quiet, yet self-confident, he went about his job. He also survived the war. Unfortunately we lost track of him after the war; but he died very early. The *Ladeschütze*, Johann Strohmer from Znaim, was a postman. His slowness he surely learned while working in the Czech postal service. He only opened his mouth to eat. How an otherwise slow person could actually load a cannon with heavy 20 kg shells at a pace which could not be surpassed remained a mystery to us. We never knew what became of him after the war.

Generalfeldmarschall von Manstein, Commander-in-Chief of Army Group South during a visit to the 503rd.

December 1942, the lead Panzer "101" on the Kalmücken Steppe. From right to left: *Panzerkommander* (Company Commander): *Hauptmann* Kaphengst (not in the picture), *Richtschütze*: *Unteroffizier* Vogel, *Ladeschütze*: *Gefreiter* Spekin, *Fahrer*: *Feldwebel* Martach, *Funker*: *Gefreiter* Lochmann. This tank had a special searchlight mounted onto the left side of the turret, supposedly to assist in night fighting. The searchlight was not mass-produced.

The "111" on the Kalmücken Steppe in December 1942.

The "101" during the securing of streets in Rostow, February 1943.

The Chief-*Funker*, Franz-Wilhelm Lochmann. He belonged, uninterrupted, to the 1st Company from its formation in May 1942 to the very end in May 1945. He was not only a good and dependable comrade; he was the "benevolent spirit" of the Company.

My *Richtschütze* Walter Junge, who loyally and assiduously performed his duties for over a year.

Above: In the preparation areas near Tolekonoje in the "Forest of the Nightingales." *Richtschütze* and *Panzerkommander* in June 1943. Right: In the preparation area Chief-*Fahrer* Walter Martach (left) and *Unteroffizier* Paul Thome.

Funker of the "114," Alfred Peuker

Above: Portepée-*Unteroffizier* of the 1st Company. From left to right: *Oberfeldwebel* Hörnke; *Oberfeldwebel* Wolff; *Stabsfeldwebel* Ehrentraut; and *Feldwebel* Moscardini. Above right: *Leutnant* Jammerath, still acting Platoon Leader of the Light Platoon with the Panzer Type III. After incorporating "Formation '43" he became my Platoon Leader as leader of 1st Platoon. He fell on the first day of the attack, 4th of July 1943. Right; *Fahrer* of the "114," Walter Eschrig.

This picture shows our position on the left high banks of the Donez River. From here we shelled enemy positions. In the middle of the picture is the Donez River.

Generalfeldmarschall von Manstein.

The *Panzerkommander* of the "114" reposing in the freshness of summer.

Visit of the Turks with Army Group South on the 25th of June 1944 in the area of Charkow. *General der Panzertruppe* Kempf greets the delegation leader, *Generaloberst* Toydemir, on the airfield at Winniza. On the left is *Generalmajor* Dr. Speidel.

Pacing off the formations of an Honor Guard Company on the airfield. Doing the greetings are Kempf and Toydemir.

During battle exercises: *Generaloberst* Toydemir; *Generalmajor* Freiherr von Funk, Commander of the 7th Panzer Division and Director of Military Exercises; *Generalfeldmarschall* von Manstein; and all the way to the right *Oberleutnant* Stahlberg, personal *Ordonnanzoffizier* to von Manstein.

"Turkish Exercises" on the 25th of June 1943 in the area of Byelgorod, Army Group South (von Manstein).

This training exercise and weapons demonstration using live fire in front of a high-ranking delegation of Turkish officers was designed to prove the strength and combat capability of the German *Wehrmacht* in the East. Turkey had been pressured by the Allies to give up their "benevolent" neutrality with respect to the German Reich. This would have meant the end of deliveries of goods and material for war into Germany.

The maneuvers were supposed to demonstrate the successful coordination of armored troops with battle support troops and air forces. They undertook mock battles against field positions that had been built out, and also demonstrated the art

Left: Turkish officers view the Tiger "111." *Leutnant* Jammerath gives the tour. Below: Turkish military mission on the Eastern Front. While the course of battle exercises is being explained, *Generalfeldmarschall* von Manstein follows the operations of the "Tiger" on the scissor- binoculars.
1. *Generaloberst* Toydemir.
2. *Oberleutnant* von Rummel, translator.
3. *Generalmajor* Freiherr von Funk, Commander of the 7th Panzer Division.
4. *Generalmajor* Dr. Speidel, Chief of the General Staff for Army Group Kempf.
5. *Oberleutnant* Lingenthal, Staff Officer with Army Group South.
6. *General der Panzertruppe* Kempf, Commander of Army Group Kempf.
7. *Generalfeldmarschall* von Manstein, Commander of Army Group South.
8. *Oberleutnant* Stahlberg, *Ordonnanzoffizier* to von Manstein.

of the "break-through." The reason for the mock battles was to train the army group for the upcoming attack, Operation Citadel. This exercise was served as both a political demonstration and customized preliminary preparations for the troops.

The "Kings" of the battlefield were supposed to be the new Tiger tanks belonging to Schwere Panzer Abteilung 503 under the direction of *Hauptmann* Clemens Graf von Kageneck, who was a rising star during "Citadel."

This picture that originated from that time was given to Turkey as a gift. In incredible fashion, this layout managed to make it back here after existing in a Turkish office until the summer of 1999.

In Charkow

Charkow was for me the first large city in Russia in which we were quartered. This was from about the end of April 1943 to the middle of June. It was customary to locate the noisy tanker formations out in the forests. Why things were different this time around, I do not know. But this was to be a wonderful time, because the city itself was so congenial, as I am even now able to carry the deepest and most meaningful impressions of these days.

Charkow is not actually a Russian city; rather, a Ukrainian city we would come to learn. The Ukraine had been attempting to assert its independence against greater Russian dominance, yet in the USSR these possibilities were modest at best. It could have been that, under the German occupation, the efforts toward national self-determination had a better chance of success. But we were not sufficiently aware of these issues. One of the first things to strike me was that the national currency had not been the Rubel; rather it was the Chervonez. Additionally, the celebrated Ukrainian national "poet/writer" was Sheftshenkovski. After the German seizure of Charkow in 1942 the city was recaptured by the Russians, and then seized once more by the Germans in the early part of 1943. We had been told that before all this the streetcars of Charkow were running freely and life in the city was quite tolerable. When we finally rolled into town we found it a relatively healthy city, but, as we used to say, we really had nothing against which we could compare. We were then quartered in Plechanovski-Rayon, my tank was on the Starobelsski Uliza; we used to call it "*Ackerstrasse*" (English: field and farming street), and our domicile address was Number 7.

Tankers are, because they are motorized, a mobile set of souls. They are constantly being sent hither and yon. We were stationed in Charkow for an unusually long time and thus have taken with us the most intense and pleasurable impressions. Inside of a corner home plot of land with two houses facing the street and one house in the courtyard we had stationed two or three Tiger tanks. The Panzer crews, in increments of five men each, were supposed to be quartered in the flats normally occupied by its residents. Those of us from the Pz. "114" were supposed to occupy the flat directly right of where one would normally enter through the courtyard gate. How we actually managed all of this, I've no idea; however, I am quite certain that this process did not inspire large amounts of joy amongst the inhabitants. If I remember correctly, there were three rooms and we occupied the first one in front. I am sure we were very careful and cautious all the while during our move-in. We were also very surprised after the inhabitants of the flat began to comply with the unavoidable. The daughter, a very pretty girl who also spoke German, then shockingly began to voice her loudest displeasure over our arrival. I was absolutely amazed at this girl's courage. Supposedly we then went ahead muttering something like "Nitshevo" and simply occupied the room.

It then took a few days until both parties began to get used to each other. At first the parents warmed up a bit, then the daughter Ludmila. This was a very cultivated family, which I noticed after taking the opportunity to glimpse their inventory of books. There were the German classics in the actual German editions and, of course, the Russian classics in voluminous amounts. I already was somewhat familiar with Tolstoy and Dostoyevski from my school days. Now I was just learning about Gogol, Lermontov, Tshechov, and Turgenov, who then, after the war when I became "civilized," became my favorite Russian author with the works of "Fathers and Sons." Ludmila and I became friends. Unending discussions concerning the war would follow, as she always represented a pro-Russian opinion about the whole thing. She placed her trust in me. If I ever betrayed that trust, very unpleasant things could have befallen her. Amongst my tank crew there was always a sixth piece of cooking ware. We survived almost exclusively on grub whipped up in the hotpot. From this sixth piece of cooking ware our Russian co-inhabitants were primarily modestly fed along with us. For my birthday on the 28th of June we were still holed up in Charkow, and my crew and Ludmila's family prepared a little celebration for me, which I by comparison, even under the constrictive conditions imposed by wartime events, never again experienced for all its warmth and sentiment. My crew was only cautiously accepting and understanding of my "fraternization," because none of us had really had opportunity to establish relations, let alone good relations, with members of an enemy nation. I later went with Ludmila and this fox terrier I'd scared up somewhere scampering off in a happy-go-lucky sort of way to this sports festival involving members of the abteilung. Ludmila and I also visited the Shetshenkovski Theatre. I would say that the war was kind of on hold for us. Then the inevitable; we were dispatched into our initial attack positions for Operation "Citadel" near the city of Byelgorod.

I have now needed almost 60 years to bring out that which moved me so much during those days in 1943! I had left my commander's post in the tank and given it over to the *Richtschütze*, Walter Junge. I was then hunched over on the rear of the tank as we were chugging our way to the front, and I was overcome with sadness. For the first time in my life, I was so in love that it actually consumed the substance of my very existence. Thoughts of desertion and high tailing back to my Ludmila even went through my mind! I was able to concoct a scheme to visit her once again under the pretense of having to return to Charkow to have my teeth worked on, all before the front collapsed. It would then lead to a goodbye forever. Because I write this for Ludmila, I have no apprehensions about communicating what happened in the final minute before our eternal parting of ways.

Ludmila kissed me on my eyelids and said: "Good bye, Alfred."

I will until my dying hour always carry this tender and singular memory with me. And my wife, to whom I've been married for the last 54 years, will always maintain an understanding of the fact that I to this day have reserved a special place in my heart for the first love of my life.

In conclusion, I will also add the following, significant because it is almost unbelievable. Ludmila and I never had any type of physical relationship. Not because we were incapable of such, but because we had bonded and were so compatible in the most ideal sort of way, our connections to one another never required any sort of confirmation in the bedroom.

It would be of great joy to me if this text were ever to reach my lovely little Ludmila, who was so affectionately called Luda, or even Mila, by her dear mother. After almost 50 years we were able to establish contact to her through the Red Cross, where we learned that some sort of adventurous little odyssey had swept her off to Kirgisistan somewhere.

Above: Hans Fendesack and Kurt Knispel in September 1943, in Snamenka. Above left and left: In Charkow, June 1943: Ludmila, 20 years old. Alfred, 23 years old.

Kurt Knispel

Fendesack and Knispel in the summer of 1944 on the Army Training Grounds at Ohrdruf.

Abteilung *Kommandeur Hauptmann* Burmester decorates *Oberfeldwebel* Hans Fendesack on the 11th of October 1943 in Snameka with the German Cross in Gold. On the left the abteilung adjutant, *Oberleutnant* Smend. *Courtesy Horst Krönke.*

Scene of battle photographed during "Citadel." Here Martin Burmester of the 2nd Company knocks out two Russian tanks. *Courtesy Martin Burmester.*

Near Merefa/Ukraine in July 1943. 18-ton half-tracks of the Recovery Platoon tow away the "114," which had been damaged by shellfire, during Operation "Citadel." *Panzerkommander Fahnenjunker-Feldwebel* Rubbel off the tank. On the tank were the *Richtschütze* Junge and the *Fahrer* Eschrig with the white canister.

During "Citadel" on the 5th of July 1943. Dissemination of orders amongst 3rd Company. *Oberleutnant* Scherf.

"Citadel" and the Defensive Retreat Battles to the Dnieper

On the 4th of July the difficult assault over the Donez began. The 3rd Panzer Corps, under whose command we were, attacked with the 6th, 7th, and 19th Panzer Divisions after the engineers had built makeshift bridges while suffering heavy losses. The assault was held up in this terrain, which had been fortified with tank traps, field positions, and mine fields. Only after regrouping and a new thrust southward did the assault actually gain some territory. In spite of heavy losses, which occurred amongst the Panzer regiments using the Type IVs, the Corps was successful in accomplishing its task of securing the right flank in an offensive maneuver, which also secured a great amount of real estate. We arrived in the area of Rshavez. To the left of us, near Procharovka, the largest tank battle in history took place. We were lucky to be sent into battle towards the waning days of the conflict, which was broken off on the 12th of July. The "114" sustained a few hits during this time. The left-side transmission (final drive), which sat outside the tank, was demolished, and the bow plate sustained a gash across it. The crew was unscathed. The tank was towed away and sent to Germany for a fundamental overhaul. We quickly received a new Tiger, and we became engaged in tiresome small battles, constantly being switched among assignments to different infantry regiments. After completing a successful withdrawal, which lasted to the 14th of September and ended with the crossing over the Dnieper near Krementshug, the events at that time, as now, seemed impossible to comprehend. The abteilung, which had been scattered over a wide area, gathered up with its remnants in Snamenka, in order to be rejuvenated and revamped into an army reserve unit.

Generalfeldmarschall von Manstein

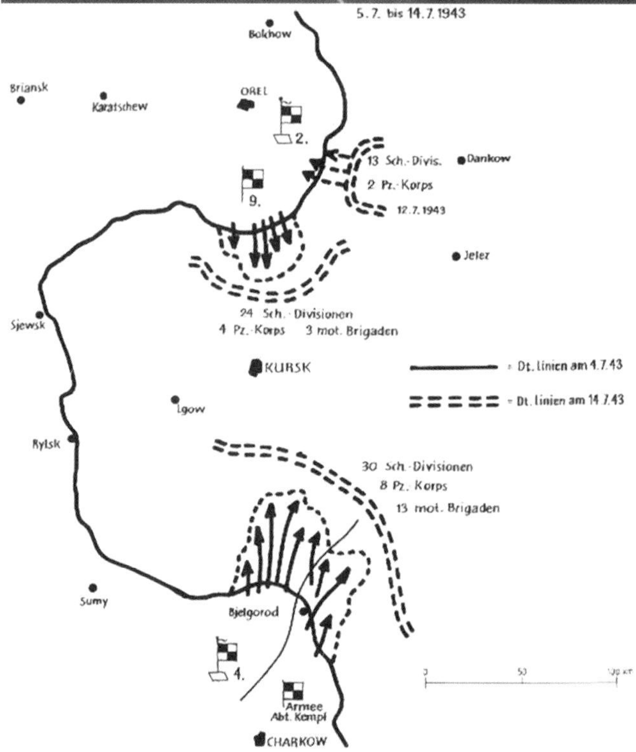

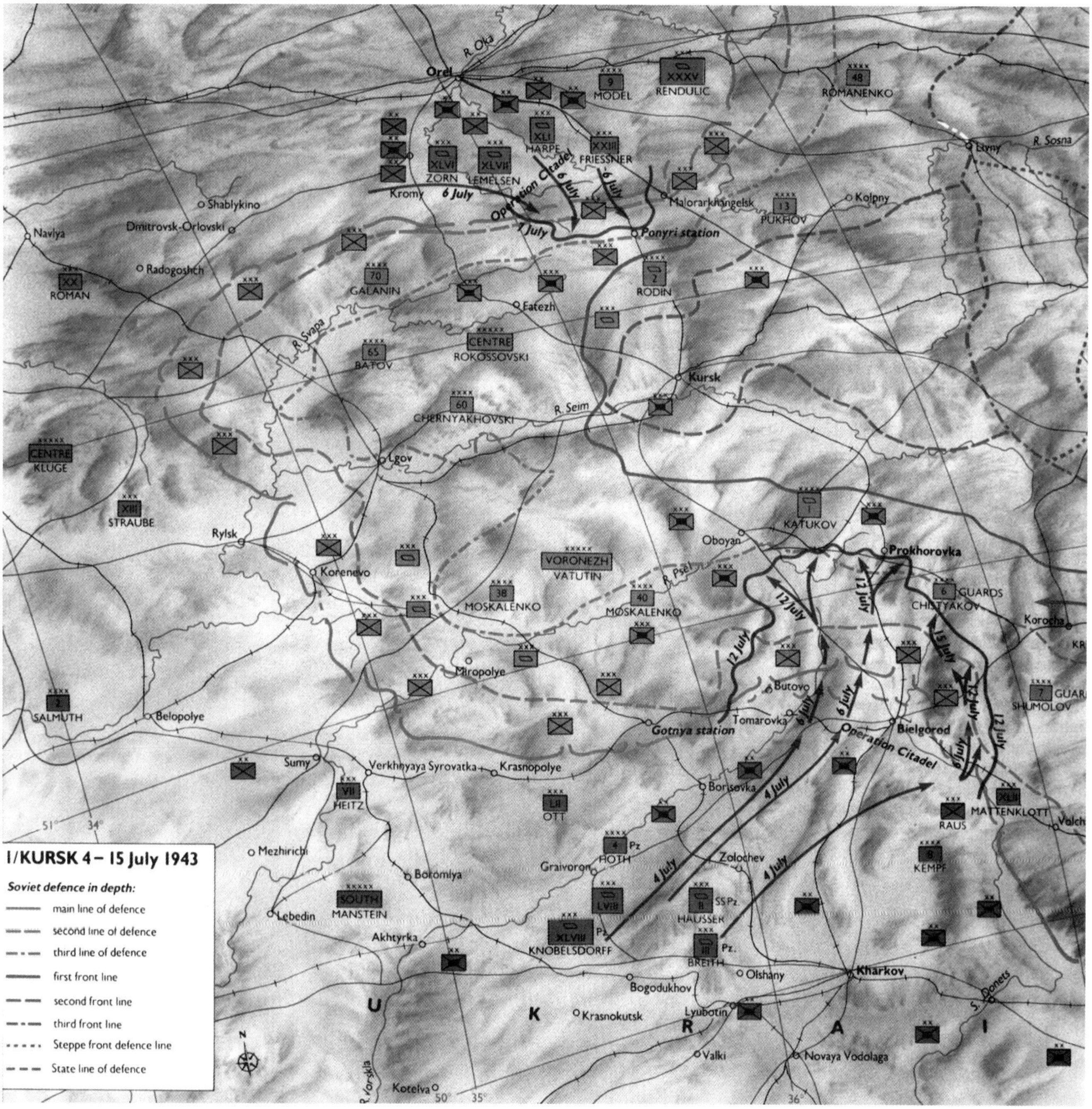

250,000 men fell in the northern areas, as well as 200 tanks and just as many airplanes. On the 10th of July the German attack along the northern salient was brought to a complete standstill. Along the southern salient von Manstein's formations had a bit more luck. They succeeded in breaking through the Soviet defense lines and driving in about forty km, whereby they also sustained losses in the amount of 10,000 men and 350 tanks. When the Soviets brought in reinforcements from the Steppe Front von Manstein's attack was also brought to a halt. Between the 12th and 15th, the Red Army then switched into counterattack mode. On the 20th of July the Germans were in full retreat. Around the 23rd, the Germans were thrown back behind their initial launching positions. Operation "Citadel" had completely failed, and the Soviets pushed ever onward. In the north, Army Group Center was forced to give up Orel and to retreat back to the Hagen Line. In the south, the Voronesh and Steppe fronts converged and attacked the city of Charkow. On the 22nd of August the Germans began to withdraw out of the city, which by the 23rd had completely fallen into Soviet hands. Against Hitler's orders, von Manstein withdrew his troops in an orderly and tactically skillful manner all the way back to the Dnieper.

"Striking with a strong backhand"—the Red Army used its troops, which it gathered together for defensive measures, to launch a far-reaching counterattack that pushed back Army Group South all the way to the Dnieper River. Nowhere did they succeed in encircling or out-flanking us. We were able to evacuate the entire area under the guidance of the civilian population and subsisting on the local crops and cattle. We also destroyed important installations that could have been employed for use in the war effort. Von Manstein had called this his hardest assignment ever.

***Panzerkommanders* of the 1st Company:**

Hannes Rippl (left), Hans Fendesack.

Hans Lewandowski (left).

Feldwebel Wolff (left), Alfred Rubbel.

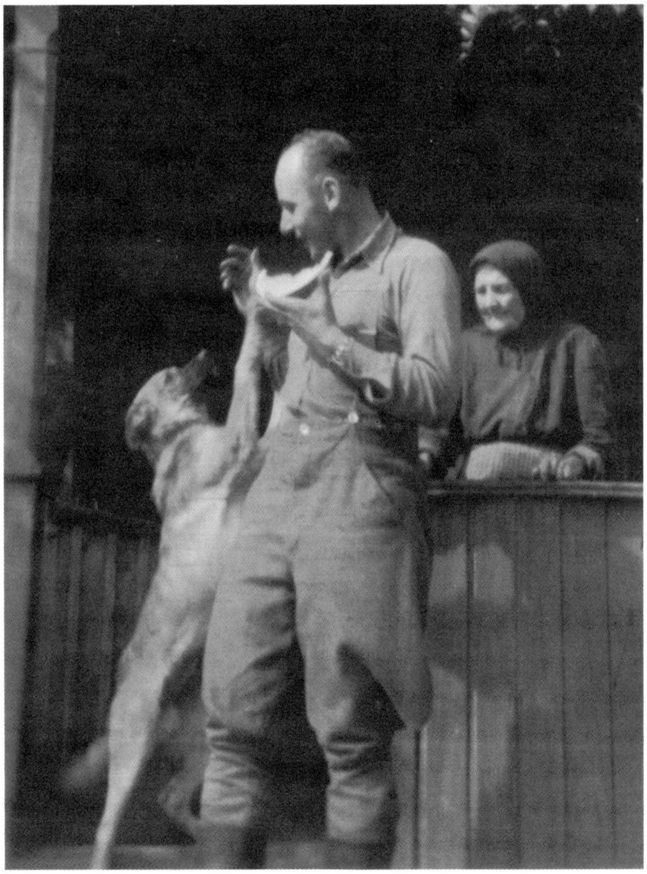

The new *Spieß*, Haase.

Somewhere during the retreat between the Donez and the Dnieper in August 1943. Here was Rippl's Tiger (above), and up front was Helmut Michaelis. These were two officers who avowed the new wonder-tank. Rippl and I with our two Tigers were engaged for a few weeks covering the retreat of the SS Cavalry Division. This division, although commanded by Hitler's brother-in-law Fegelein, was an absolutely desolate bunch. We were glad to be released from these troops.

The Repair Company.

A damaged Tiger getting a tow.

At our quarters in Snamenka. The sisters Hala and Maria, Heino Kleiner, and I.

The *Panzerkommanders* of 1st Company celebrating the occasion of the awarding of the Iron Cross 1st Class to Heino Kleiner, with loads of drink.

In Snamenka. Officer shooting practice. *Hauptmann* Graf von Kageneck tries his hand with a pistol. To the left of him, his adjutant *Oberleutnant* Smend. Partially hidden is the Staff Physician Dr. Schramm.

"Piepel" (nickname) Werner Grasse, *Fahrer*. *Courtesy Horst Krönke.*

The abteilung symbol, which was no longer brandished after 1943 for secretive protective purposes.

Tigers in the Repair Company in Smerinka in December 1943. Here with the brand-new winter paint.

During a friendly parting of ways from 1st Company. Lewandowski and Rubbel were being relocated to a war academy. From left to right: *Oberfeldwebel* (name forgotten), *Oberfeldwebel* (name forgotten), *Fahnenjunker-Feldwebel* Rubbel, *Oberschirrmeister* Wagner, *Oberfeldwebel* Fendesack, *Leutnant* Linsser. End of February 1944.

Rubbel and von Hagemeister deer hunting. Unfortunately, no results.

The best little vehicle which ever laid tracks on this globe of ours—the VW Kübelwagen! Always willing and unpretentious, whether in the blistering sun of Northern Africa or in the bitter cold of Russia. I would bet that this vehicle here, which had been exposed to a deep-freeze during the night, started right up the next morning and ran like a horse.

Tscherkassy

From Snameka the abteilung was engaged in scattered combat across the Ukraine around Kiew, Poltava, Potash, Pawlish, Glinsk, and Chirgrin. Around the turn of the year, 1st Company was situated near Zybulew in the partisan zone. At the beginning of January 1944 the abteilung gathered together at Smerinka in Transistria after long days of action along a fractured front, in order to rejuvenate and reorganize into a battle-ready heavy formation. We also received new Tigers.

The Tscherkassy pocket, which is to say the opening thereof, was the most devastating action yet for the abteilung in terms of losses. I was in the thick of it uninterrupted from the 24th of January to the 25th of February 1944. At the end of fighting the abteilung only had five Tigers left.

In the summer of 1943 I had been promoted to *Fahnenjunker*. In December of 1943 I was promoted to *Fahnenjunker-Feldwebel* and informed that I would be going to the War Academy in early 1944. With Hans von Hagemeister and Hans Lewandoski we were sent off on the march to Paderborn to the Panzer-Ersatz Abteilung 500. I would first see the abteilung again in December 1944.

This picture provides an impressive view of the winter landscape in the early morning dawn, which surely also gripped the men in the Tigers as they rolled onward toward the enemy. Here the Tigers are traveling in a row along each others' tracks because of the danger of mines. Somewhere between Oratoff and Tscherkassy in January 1944.

"*Unteroffizier* Knispel in a schwere Panzer abteilung in the East successfully destroyed 101 tanks in the time between July 1943 to March 1944." This was the official *Wehrmacht* report on the 25th of April 1944. On that same day he was awarded the German Cross in Gold.

Back then and now one might ask, how after such stunning success could somebody be awarded with a rather modest decoration? There are basically two reasons for this: Those in higher places thought the Tiger to be so safe and superior that conducting a tank battle out of one was almost secondary and innocuous. We never fought "at our own risk." We were always attached to higher levels of command, which "booked" our successes as their own and were time and again taking us tank guys on board.

Feldwebel Knispel was severely wounded on the 29th of April 1945, acting as Tiger Commander near Stronsdorf. He died in the main army hospital in Urbau and was entombed in the town cemetery. Knispel was the most successful *Richtschütze* in the German *Wehrmacht*. In March 1945 the abteilung reported his 162nd tank kill to the Panzer Corps FHH (*Feldherrnhalle*—New Designation for the 503rd).

Schwere Panzer-Abteilung 503 with Schwere Panzer-Regiment Bäke from the 21st of January -25th of February 1944

Forward Preparations

January 19th Loading up in Smerinka, Railway Transport
January 20th Unloading in Winniza
January 21st Formation of the Schwere Panzer Regiment Bäke

Assault Medvin

January 22nd Formation of positions for attack in direction of Medvin near Balabanovka
January 23rd Assault on the positions at Bila
January 24th Breakthrough at Bila
January 25th Tank battle at Ssosoff
January 26th Defensive battles at Ssosoff
January 27th Tank battle south of Otcheretnya
January 28th Tank battle and breakthrough near the train station of Oratoff
January 29th Battles near Oratoff
January 30th Defensive battles near Oratoff
January 31st Defensive battles northwest of Oratoff

Assault Tscherkassy

February 1st March to new theatre of action
February 2nd (no action)
February 3rd Assault at Pavlovka
February 4th Breakthrough to Pavlovka
February 5th Assault at Votylevka
February 6th Defensive battles near Votylevka
February 7th Defensive battles near Votylevka
February 8th Assault at Repki
February 9th Battles in the area of Repki

February 10th	Taking up positions for assault on Frankovka
February 11th	Assault and formation of bridgehead at Frankovka
February 12th	Expansion of the bridgehead at Frankovka
February 13th	Tank battle at Chessnovka
February 14th	Defensive battles near Chessnovka
February 15th	Assault and defense south of Dshurshenzy
February 16th	Assault on hill 239
February 17th	Securing of hill 239, picking up of "pocket" troops
February 18th	Securing of hill 239, picking up of "pocket" troops
February 19th	Fighting evasion at the Gnoloi Tikitsh
February 20th	Intervention reserves at Bossovka
February 21st	March to Uman
February 25th	Dissolving of Schwere Panzer Regiment Bäke

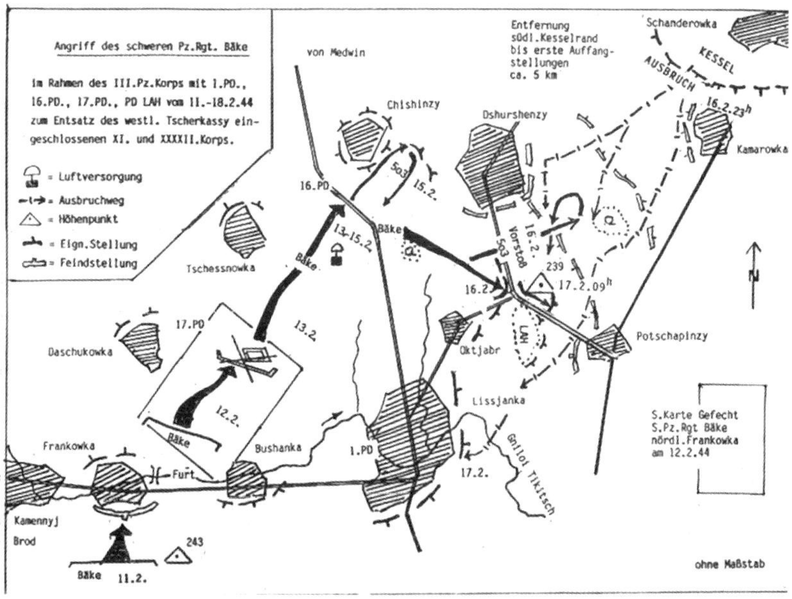

Major Clemens Graf Kageneck, *Abteilungskommandeur* schwere Panzer-Abteilung 503, June 1943-January 1944.

Im Namen des Führers und Obersten Befehlshabers der Wehrmacht

verleihe ich

dem

Unteroffizier Rubbl

1./s.Pz.Abt.503

das

Eiserne Kreuz 1. Klasse

Korps Gef.Std., den 22. Juli 1943

Der Kommandierende General
des III.Panzerkorps

(Dienstsiegel)

General der Panzertruppe

(Dienstgrad und Dienststellung)

2.05/43

Iron Cross First Class

Besitzzeugnis

Dem Fhj. - Feldwebel

Dienstgrad

Alfred Rubbel

Vor- und Familienname

1./ s.Panzer - Abteilung 503

Truppenteil

verleihe ich für tapfere Teilnahme an 25 Einsatztagen

die II. Stufe zum

Panzerkampfabzeichen

in

Silber

O.U., den 20.6.1944

Ort und Datum

Unterschrift

Hauptmann u.Abt.-Kdr.

Dienstgrad und Dienststellung

s. Panz. Abt. 503 Dienststempel 1406

Panzerkampfabzeichen II Stufe 25 Armor Battles

Fahnenjunker-Feldwebel Rubbel, April 1944.

Opposite: *Hauptmann* Rolf Fromme, *Abteilungskommandeur* schwere Panzer-Abteilung 503, February-December 1944.

9

Officers' Training and Education in Ohrdruf and Krampnitz

In Ohrdruf

Our journey went off with no disturbances, although in the beginning of March 1944—the dead of winter—the railway system in the Ukraine had been damaged and hampered by many things. Snow drifts, frozen switches, and detonations of the track by the partisans all contributed to these problems. In the combat areas, railway duty was performed by those in field gray (German military), while in the general provinces (really Poland) this service was performed by blue-uniformed personnel (either German or Polish civilians). Because the personnel cars were not heated, and at this time had no glass in the windows, we traveled along on board the warm locomotive.

In Breslau we visited our commander, Graf Kageneck, who had been severely wounded. Then the three of us took a little side trip to Posen, where Hans von Hagemeister's family lived. Lewandowski and I traveled on further to Berlin where he went to visit his mother. There wasn't enough time for me to travel home to Tilsit; so, I went straight to the Tiger-Ersatz-Abteilung 500 in Paderborn. The *Fahnenjunker* from the Tiger formations were gathered together for a preparation course, which was conducted by the former *Nachtrichtenoffizier* from the 503rd, *Oberleutnant* Reichel. Then we were allowed leave to go home, and then it was off to Ohrdruf. In the meantime, the Panzer armies had suffered a tremendous mishap. The General-Inspector Guderian had been relieved of duty for the second time by Hitler, and since his protective hand was now no longer at play, the enemies of the Panzer armies really started to get into the swing of things. As measured by the declining significance of the Panzer armies, the days of Blitzkrieg were long over; we were supplied in large part with personnel who were missing from the decimated infantry. And so, Hans von Hagemeister was also transferred to the infantry and arrived at the Infantry-*Fahnenjunker*-Academy at Wischau. He had despaired. Lewandowski and I began our training as the 16th Officer Candidate Training Class (Infantry *Anwärter Lehrgang* - O.A.J.), which was supposed to last five months from April until August. Given the situation with the war, this would be sufficient time to properly instruct the combat-experienced "highly ordained" ensigns how to become platoon leaders or rudimentary company commanders. We had a very good tactical instructor, *Hauptmann* Mathias, who also possessed many human qualities. Unfortunately, the malaria that I picked up in the Caucasus caught up with me. I was sent to the hospital and

Oberst Brose, Commander of the *Fahnen-junker* Academy 2 Ohrdruf, 1943-1944.

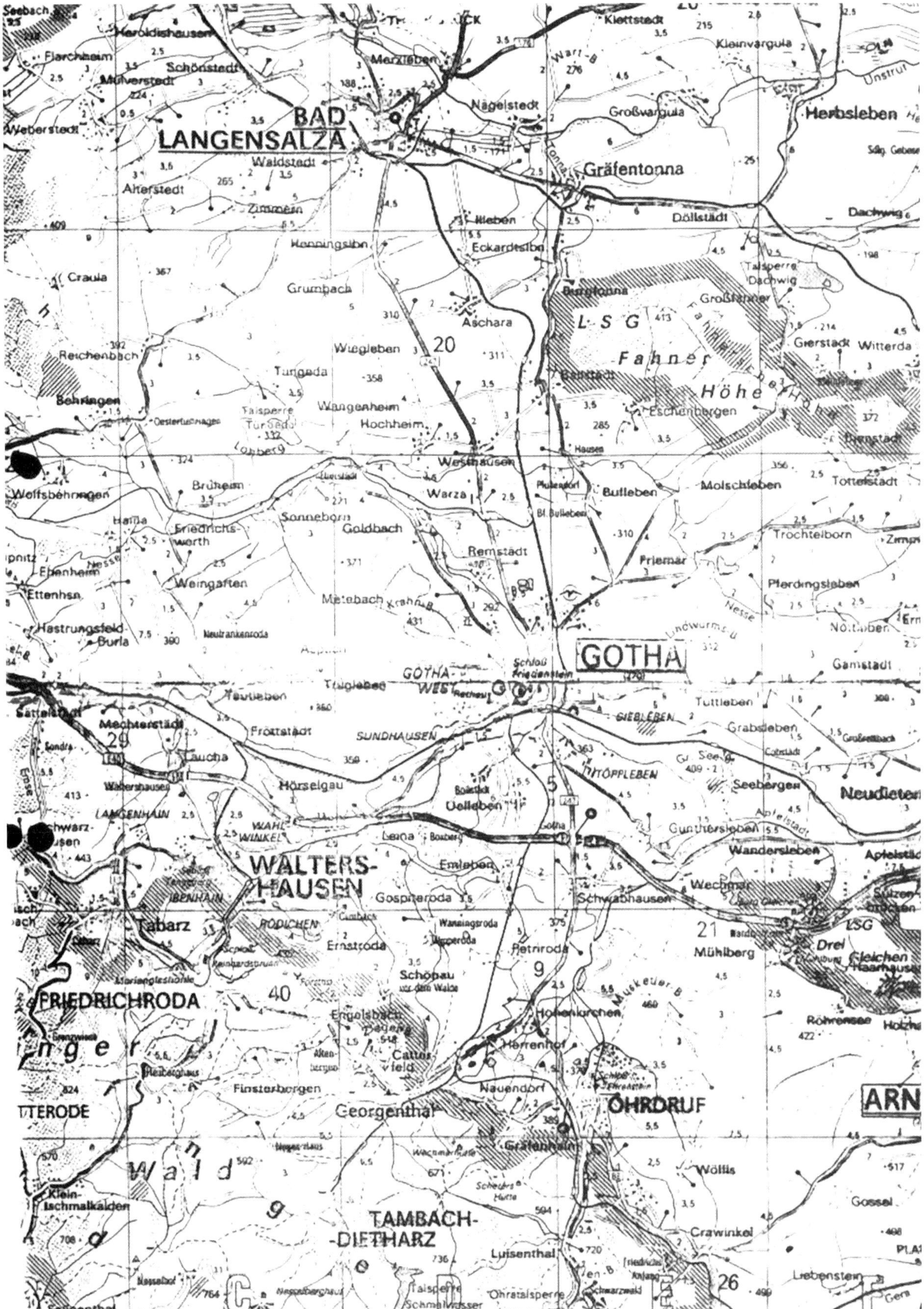
BAD LANGENSALZA
Herbsleben
Gräfentonna
Döllstädt
Nägelstedt
Großwargula
Kleinvargula
Unstrut
Waldstadt
Zimmern
Craula
Grumbach
Aschara
Wiegleben
Eckardtsleben
Reichenbach
Behringen
Wangenheim
Hochheim
Westhausen
Talsperre Dachwig
LSG
Fahner Höhe
Eschenbergen
Gierstädt
Witterda
Wolfsbehringen
Brüheim
Friedrichswerth
Sonneborn
Goldbach
Warza
Bufleben
Molschleben
Tröchtelborn
Remstädt
Weingarten
Ettenhsn.
Hastrungsfeld-Burla
Pferdingsleben
Friemar
GOTHA
Tüttleben
Gamstadt
Mechterstädt
Fröttstädt
Sundhausen
Grabsleben
Seebergen
Laucha
Hörselgau
Uelleben
Siebleben
Neudietendorf
WALTERS-HAUSEN
Leina
Emleben
Wandersleben
Tabarz
Gospiteroda
Schwabhausen
Wechmar
Ernstroda
Petriroda
Mühlberg
FRIEDRICHRODA
Schönau vor dem Walde
Hohenkirchen
Herrenhof
Finsterbergen
Nauendorf
OHRDRUF
Georgenthal
Gräfenhain
Wölfis
TAMBACH-DIETHARZ
Luisenthal
Crawinkel
Gossel
Liebenstein
Frankenhain
ARN

Formation of the 14th *Fahnenjunker* Training Class 2, the Panzer troops, in front of *Oberst* Brose.

then my blood had gotten all mixed up. Were they leukocytes? The result of all this was that after my release from the hospital, I was sent back to the Ersatz Abteilung at Paderborn to take part in the 17th Officer Candidate Training Class, which started after August. This was because I had missed so much time being in the hospital, which really didn't agree with me at all. Academies and courses seemed to me lifelong exercises which, however, were necessary ones. I was layed up in the hospital again and was visited by some comrades from the 503rd. The abteilung, which had last been in action in the area of Tarnopol-Lemberg, had been melded together since Tscherkassy and was transferred to the Troop Training Grounds at Ohrdruf for some freshening up. And there my 1st Company was to be the first troop detachment to receive the legendary King Tigers! The abteilung had time to regenerate from May to July, receive its new equipment, and then be sent into action in France, where the landing of the Western Allies was expected. Had I successfully completed my officer-training course, I could have counted on being sent into action as a *Leutnant* with the abteilung. I was dismayed that this did not happen according to my wishes. I had received permission from the abteilung to return back to them, whereby I then deduced that I was sorely needed at the front.

June 1944, in Ohrdruff. *Generalinspekteur* of all Mobile Troops, *Generaloberst* Guderian, visits the Officer Candidates School 2 and then bestows the first King Tigers on this occasion to the 1st Company, s.Pz.Abt. 503.

One of the three "lookalike" castles belonging to one of the similar Counts in Thüringen, and also (below left) a ruin.

Some comrades of the 1st Company had picked me up from the hospital for a leisure drive. Far right *Obergefreiter* Herrmann Albers, who as leader of the Inst. Troops (Maintenance) of 1st Company got to drive around in a new Volkswagen Kübelwagen.

Also during a leisure drive to Erfurt. From the left: *Leutnant* Bielefeld, *Fahnenjunker-Feldwebel* Rubbel, *Feldwebel* Krönke, and *Oberfunkmeister* (chief radio operator) Endres. *Courtesy Horst Krönke.*

Left and following: In Ohrdruf, Summer 1944. In the hospital; Krönke, Lewandowski, and Rubbel. *Courtesy Horst Krönke.*

That's me in the front, but who the girls are, I really do not know! *Courtesy Horst Krönke.*

Above and following: King Tiger at the Troop Training Grounds in Ohrdruf. This was actually the King Tiger of Horst Krönke, who had joined his brother with our sister Tiger abteilung, schwere Panzer Abteilung 505. Note the "Charging Knight" (Ritter) abteilung emblem on the side of the turret. *Courtesy Horst Krönke.*

In Krampnitz

Back in Paderborn we were allowed convalescence leave to go home. In July 1944 the front had moved dangerously close back to the eastern borders of the Reich due to the collapse of Army Group Center. The new course of instruction took place in Krampnitz near Potsdam at the very beautiful Cavalry Academy. The course was renamed to the (*Oberfähnrich*) Officer Candidates Course, because one would be promoted to this rank upon graduating from the academy. We already enjoyed the rank of *Fahnenjunker*, but not as an officer. Since I was of reserve status I was not a career soldier, because I considered this at the time to be irrelevant; I was not forced to sit for another sequential course of instruction like the "actives" had to. Rather, I would be sent directly to the front as a *Leutnant* der Reserve. After eight months in the homeland I had had quite enough; besides, my homeland was the 503rd Abteilung! The close proximity of Potsdam to Berlin provided this training with some interesting aspects with respect to free time. The State coup on the 20th of July 1944 passed by us without a trace, because the school, as crack troops of the "Valkyries," had had a break from the training program. (Translator's Note: Rubbel is using the Wagner reference to "Ride of the Valkyries,"

Courtesy Horst Krönke.

which symbolizes the final apocalyptic struggle, as a metaphor for they're being sent to the ultimate struggle, and therefore, deserving of a little time off beforehand.) I was made aware of the events in a most unromantic way. At the end of my holiday in late July, I arrived at the Silesian Railway Station in Berlin to change trains and travel with the express to Potsdam. On the platform I had to greet another officer, which I did as usual by placing my hand to my headgear in a normal salute. I did this because I did not know that a.) The "*Reichsheini*" Himmler had become Chief of the Reserve Armies, and b.) The Hitler Greeting had become mandatory for the *Wehrmacht*. The officer I had greeted became very loud! And there would be subsequent relapses into the old style of greeting.

The training program went about as expected; no specific measures or modifications had accompanied the verbal "integration of the *Wehrmacht* into National Socialism." One time we had to sit in on a trial for a so-called "pity-case" at the People's Court. At least the Berliners had named it such a thing, as in "pity that things didn't work out."

It was a wonderful warm summer; in fact, it was downright hot. Because of the blistering mid-day heat the city would take a big break from everything from about noon to 4:00 PM, and in the evenings all services would be open until 8:00 PM. During the afternoons we would lie around at Lake Krampnitz. Toward the end of our courses the Western Allies had crossed the borders of the Reich and taken Aachen. We were witnesses to how a city, seen from today's perspective, undertook the most sensible course of action and flew the white flags. At that time, however, this did not quite dovetail with the political agenda of the day. In the east, the Russians were standing at the East Prussian border. In September I had received a few days' special leave, which I used to be of assistance to my mother in her preparations for her trek. I knew that she was with relatives who were also on the trek to the same places, and before I would step into command on the front—my abteilung was now fighting in Hungary—I wanted to pay her a visit at Braunsberg in East Prussia. When I arrived there on the 24th of December, I was told that she had picked up and left for Saxony. I still managed

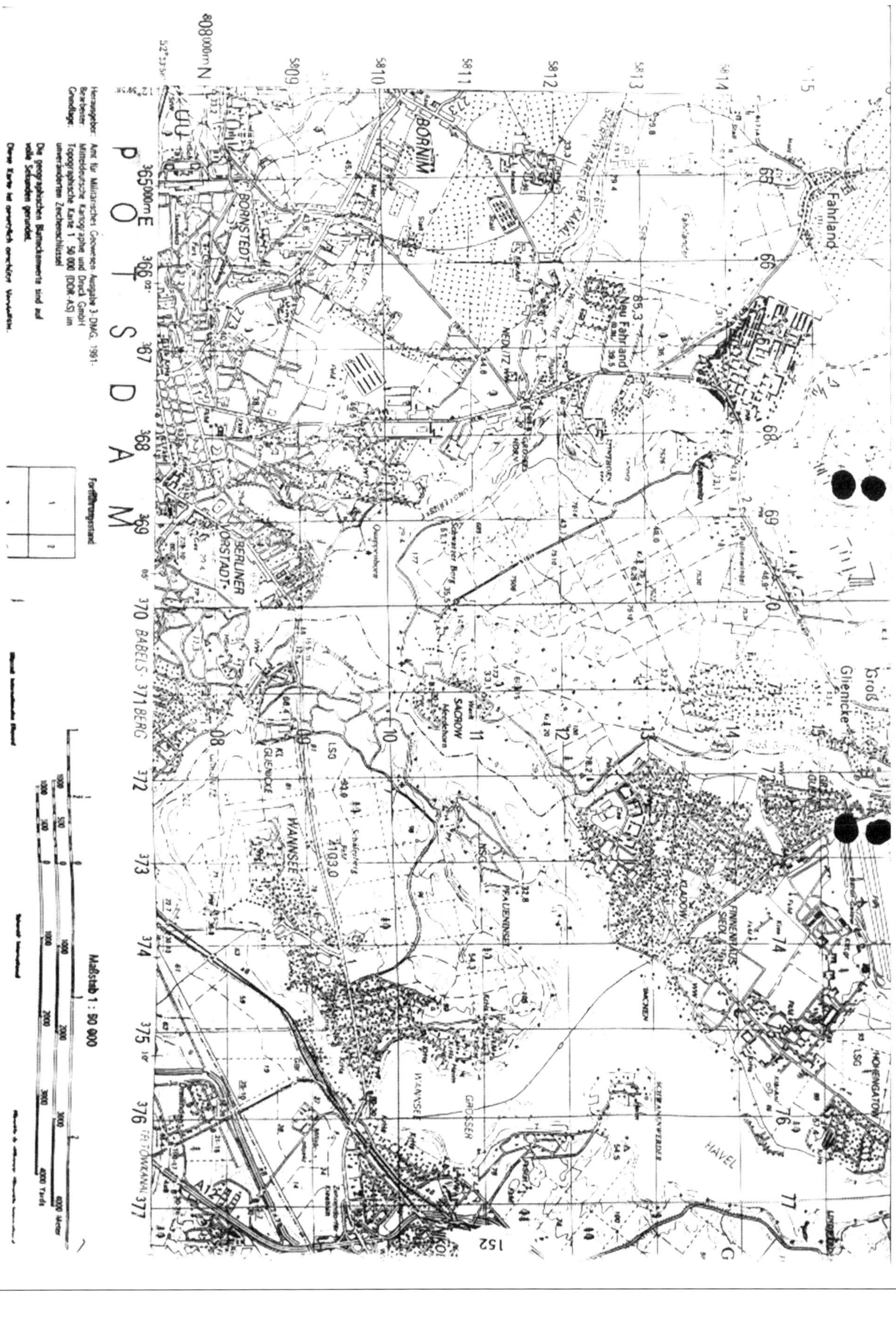
POTSDAM
BORNIM
BORNSTEDT
BERLINER VORSTADT
Fahrland
Neu Fahrland
NEDLITZ
SACROW
KLADOW
WANNSEE
PFAUENINSEL
GROSSER WANNSEE
HAVEL
Groß Glienicke
BABELSBERG
TELTOWKANAL
Maßstab 1 : 50 000

The Tank Camp of Paderborn became the accommodations for the Panzer-Training Programs at Paderborn. Earlier this had been home to the 11th Panzer Regiment.

The Cavalry Academy with the Krampnitz Tower, main gate.

to see her and to celebrate New Year's Eve there. In front of my relatives there and swilling some unfamiliar red wine, I ended up on an absolutely barbaric alcohol bender, which finally died down on the journey to the front control station in Vienna, where I had to report. Vienna, I quickly determined, was not Prussia. We were accommodated in a top-class hotel. Nobody at the control station even knew where the 503rd Tiger Abteilung was. This I'm sure was also due to the fact that, as of the 1st of January 1945, the abteilung no longer went by "the 503rd," rather by the name "*Feldherrenhalle*." I believe today that many things were done in Vienna at that time to destabilize the front. One time I saw a truck from our abteilung on the Ring. I was without regular transportation at that time, so I literally glued myself to the passenger seat in the truck and drove with this guy toward the east. We then arrived in Papateszer to the Maintenance Company, and later I reported to the Commander, *Hauptmann* Dr. von Diest Koerber. I was so happy to be back with this crew again!

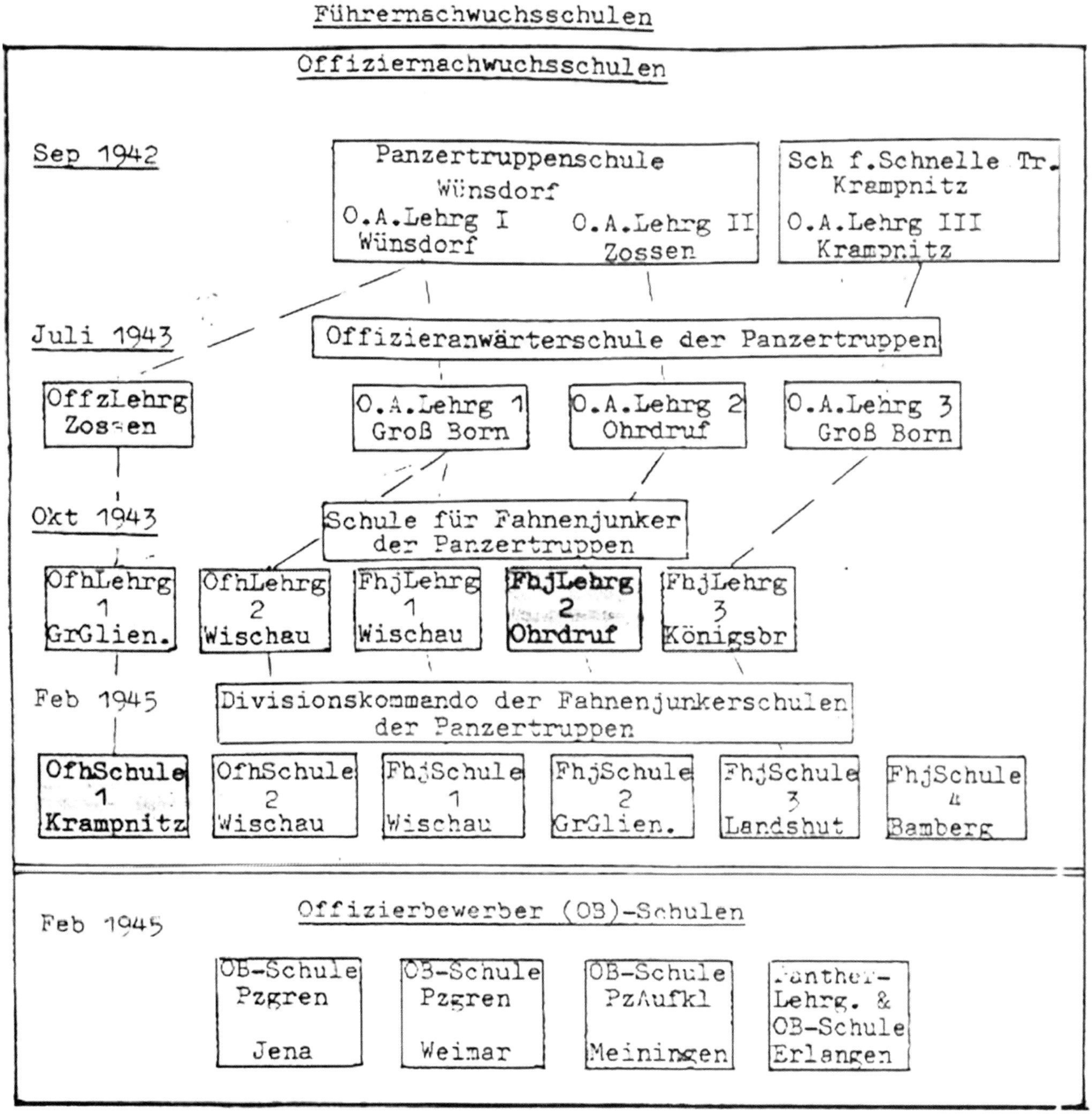

Courtesy Martin Burmeister.

14. Fahnenjunkerschule 1 Gr. Born/Wischau
    Juni 42 - Juli 43 Oberst Schmidhuber, Gerhard
    Sep 43 - Ende 43 Oberst van Nes, Ernst August

15. Fahnenjunkerschule 2, Ohrdruf /Groß Glienicke
    Jan 43 - Apr 43 Oberst Spannenkrebs, Walter
    Apr 43 - Juli 44 Oberst Brose, Otto 16 OAJ [illegible] - Juli 44
    Aug 44 - Okt 44 Oberst Buddee, Walter
    Nov 44 - Ende 44 Obstlt Frhr. von Werthern, Thilo

16. Fahnenjunkerschule 3, Königsbrück / Landshut
    Apr 43 - Nov 44 Oberst Bachmann, Helmut
    Nov 44 - Jan 45 Obstlt von Meyer, Kuno
    Jan 45 - Ende Obstlt Molinari, Karl Theodor

17. Fahnenjunkerschule 4, Bamberg
    Feb 45 - Ende Major Teuber, Johannes (?)

18. Oberfähnrichschule 1, Zossen / Groß Glienicke / Krampnitz
    Apr 43 - Juni 44 Oberst Spannenkrebs, Walter
    Juli 44 - Ende 44 Oberst Wendenburg, Gerhard 17 OAJ Aug - Dez 44

19. Oberfähnrichschule 2, Wischau
    Aug 43 - Sep 44 Oberst Ritter
    Sep 44 - Ende 44 Oberst Jochens, Werner

20. Kdr d. Heeres-Unteroffizierschulen d. PzTr, Krampnitz
    Okt 43 - Juni 44 Oberst Schäfer
    Juli 44 - Ende Oberst von Köppen, Hans Joachim

21. H-Unteroffizierschule d. Schn.Tr. / PzTr., Putlos / Eisenach
    Sep 40 - Sep 43 Oberst Schäfer
    Okt 43 - Apr 44 Oberst Haarde
    Mai 44 - Ende 44 Major Jähde, Willy

22. H-Unteroffizierschule (Panzeraufklärer), Sternberg / Sondershausen
    Sep 41 - März 44 Oberst Stollbrock, Heinrich-Wilh.
    Apr 44 - Jan 45 Major Goder
    Feb 45 - Ende Hptm. Karst, Heinz

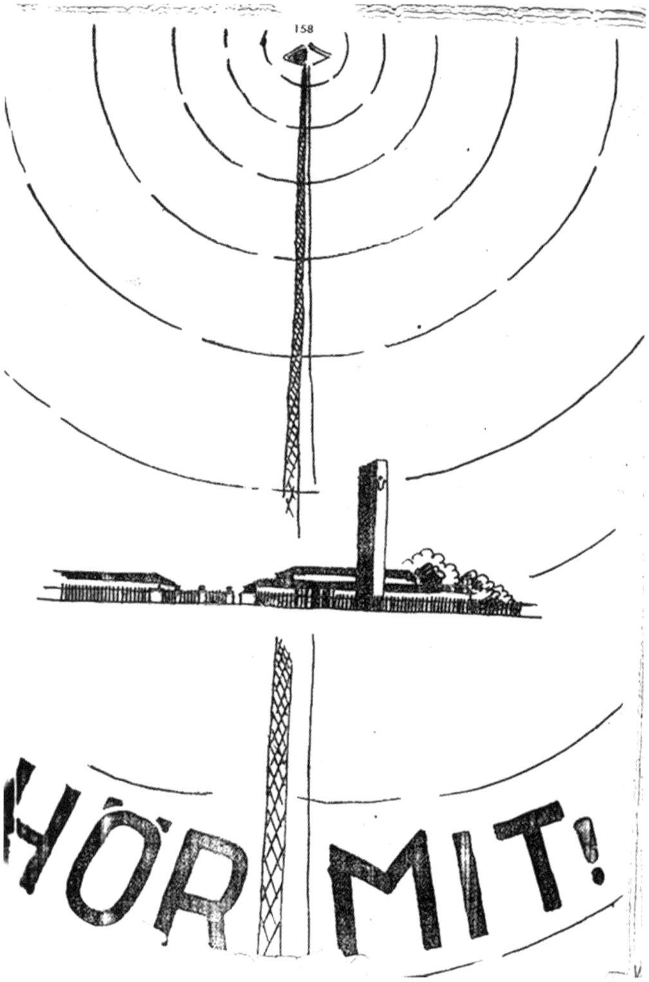

Festprogramm

der

3. Inspektion

21.-22. Dez. 1944

übertragen aus dem grossen Casinosaal
der Oberfähnrichschule 1 der Panzertruppen

Krampnitz

17. OAJ

Inschriften.

Name	Geb.	Anschrift
Behrens, Hinrich	9.4.24	Bremen, Bergerstr. 29/30
Betz, Artur	11.11.23	Herdorf/Sieg Adolf-Hitler-Str. 36
Bichels, Hans	4.12.15	Hamburg-Gr. Flottbek Brinckmanstr. 4
Boehm-Bering, Kurt, von	5. 3.25	Obernigk über Breslau, Trebnitzerstr. 61
Borowski, Kurt	3.10.16	Königsberg, Herbartstr. 2
Degenhardt, Walter	24. 7.23	Görnau b/Litzmannstadt, Rich.-Wagner-Str. 14
Droste, Karl-Heinz	28.11.19	Zittau i. Sa., Löbauer Str. 24
Dunrath, Herm.-Ulrich	24.11.24	Gut Schölich über Stade (Hann.)
Engelhard, Günther	7. 7.23	Hamburg-Poppenbüttel Hummelsbüttlerstr. 67
Engmann, Erwin	24. 8.16	Kiel-Gaarden, Johannesstr. 16
Eversberg, Herm.	18. 9.14	Herdecke/Ruhr, Am Sonnenstein 5
Finkeisen, Fritz	12. 4.22	Essen-Stadtwald, Am Dönhof 12
Fuhrmann, Karl-Heinz	4. 7.25	Allenstein/Ostpr., Liebstädterstr. 45
Gottstein, Hans	29.11.23	Freiburg i. Br., Ad.-Hitlerstr. 331
Graeßner, Klaus-Dieter	27.1.24	Landsberg/Warthe, Kniebelstr. 30a
Gransee, Georg	29. 6.17	Berkenbrügge/Arnswalde
Grimme, Helmut	9.12.19	Berlin SO. 36, Skalitzerstr. 29a
Grubhofer, Karl	11. 7.18	Wien XIX/117, Gebhardtstr. 6/2
Häfner, Paul	6.12.20	Schnait/Waiblingen, Lützestr. 260
Haider, Ernst	19.12.16	Aue/Sa., Schneeberger Str. 132
Häring, Johann	3. 5.24	Gmünd N.D., Adolf Hitler-Platz 13
Hocher, Karl	13. 4.23	Neudorf Kr. Tachau, Nr. 56
Höltmann, Heinz	7. 3.24	Lünen/Westf., Kappenberg 80

Name	Geb.	Anschrift	Note
Hübner, Gerhard	26. 9.24	Troppau/Sud., Olmützerstr. 28	
Immig, Karl	6. 5.26	Paderborn, Bennauserstr. 20	
Jerrentrup, Walter	18. 1.06	Borgholzhausen/Westf. Bielefelder Str. 180	
Keim, Helmut	15.12.21	Waiblingen a.N., Olgastr. 49	
Kloth, Alfred	25. 3.24	Potsdam/Babelsberg, Großbeerenstr.	10
Kohnert-Stavenhagen, Hubertus	5.11.25	Bad Freienwalde/Oder, Eberswalder Str. 54	
Krakow, Willibald	17.11.13	Schwerin/M., Adolf Hitlerstr. 149	503
Kretzschmar, Gotth.	17. 9.22	Dresden-A. 21 Gerader Steg 9	4.G.
Lauer, Wilfried	29. 5.19	Leobersdorf N.D., Siebenhaus Nr. 1	
Lamich, Richard	4. 1.19	Grafenweiler, Krs. Gr.-Strehlitz.	
Larraß, Hans-Jochen	12. 4.24	Neukirch ü/Königsbrück.	
Lehmann, Clemens	6. 1.12	Zaßnitz Nr. 10, Post Rochlitz/Sa.	
Li?v?? ?, Heinrich	8.12.15	Kleve/Rhld., Fra???nstr. 59	506
Lütz, Herbert	17. 3.17	Dattenfeld/Sieg Ad. Hitler Platz	
Malapert, Hans-Heinrich; von	26. 7.11	Darmstadt, Heinrichstr. 14	
Mäusezahl, Wolfgang	13. 5.24	Berlin NW 21, Quitzowstr. 143	
Melsheimer, Werner	27. 3.23	Küstrin-Altstadt, Kommandantenstr. 100b	
Mersmann, Heinrich	20.11.23	Coesfeld/Westf. Borkenerstr. 1	
Moldan, Herbert	12. 7.23	Kuchl b/Salzburg	4 G.
Möller, Adolf	23. 7.21	Ottersberg i. Hann. Ad. Hitlerstraße 208	
Neffgen, Hans	31. 7.15	Bielefeld, Osnabrückerstr. 34	11
Ossenbach, Heinz	10. 2.15	Köln-Lindental, Brahmsstr. 2	
Otto, Martin	23. 7.17	Dörfel 402 Krs. Reichenberg/Sud.	
Peru?h, ??chor	18.10.25	Olbernhau/Sa., Haydnerstr. 3	
Rampelbergh, Karl	28. 1.21	Eupen/Rhld. Paveestr. 35	

Name	Geb.	Anschrift	Note
Reuter, Ernst	6. 3.16	Saulgau, Moosheimerstr. 21	
Roßberg, Walter	1. 8.24	Kulmbach i. Bay., Straße der SA 16	
Rubbel, Alfred	28. 6.21	Tilsit Hoh?nzollernstr. 31	583
Rüsen, Hanswalter	16. 5.19	Seestadt Wismar, Klüßer Damm 62	100,07
Sandkuhl, Hermann	17. 3.15	Potsdam, Augustastr. 41	
Schabbel, Hans-Günter	5.10.17	Eisenach, Frankfurterstr. 77	
Schick, Günter	9. 7.24	Offenburg/Baden, Okenstr. 49	
Schnell, Nikolaus	7. 7.12	München 2, Arnulfstr. 112/3	
Schulz, Joachim	15.11.17	Berlin-Charlottenburg, Pestalozzistr. 33	
Schulze, Bernhard	30. 5.14	Weimar, Schützengasse 12	
Sch[illegible], [illegible]	10.10.24	Cottbus, Bonna?kenstr. 10	
Sch[illegible]ger, Toni	8. 6.18		
Uebersc[illegible]t, [illegible]rich	12.11.22	Berlin O 112, Samariterstr. 27	
We[illegible], [illegible]	4.10.18	Mainburg/Ndb., Adolf Wagnerstr. 265	
Wie[illegible], [illegible]; von	9. 1.24	Neuhof b/Ingramsdorf	
Wo[illegible]jew, Georg	21. 1.16	Bremen, Schleifmühle 17	

199? entdeckte ich als damaligen Angehörigen des Lehrgangs Kurt Böhm-Berg[illegible] beim Offz Kurs [illegible]

10

With the 503rd Tiger Abteilung Until War's End

With 3rd Company

Things at first did not go well at all. I had reported back to the Abteilung Staff to officers whom I did not know and who did not know me. These were the new Abteilung *Kommandeur*, *Hauptmann* Dr. Nordewin von Diest-Koerber, and the adjutant, *Oberleutnant* Heerlein. They then sent me to 3rd Company, which didn't sit well with me because I had been expecting to return to "my" old 1st Company! *Oberleutnant* Richard Freiherr von Rosen commanded the 3rd Company, and the company officers were the *Leutnants* Koppe and Rambow, all of whom I did not know in the slightest. I noticed how the faces of all personnel had changed in the eight months since April 1944, and through my long absence I had sort of become a "nobody." I then traveled to the Company, which was situated in a small place called Borbaly Puszta. I had no tank and sat around in the ruins of some barn, which clearly showed the markings of battle the Company had been engaged in. I also got the feeling that the Commander of this Company was not exactly thrilled with my arrival here. 3rd Company had been a very opinionated club since 1942, which preferred to move about on the fringes of the Abteilung and couldn't get over the fact that it had been outsourced from the 502nd Abteilung and incorporated into the 503rd. Also, there had been a continuous struggle against the 1st Company as to whom the better company really was. And so, in their opinion, nothing good could come out of 1st Company! After two days of sitting around things had really gone too far. I kept getting the feeling that those in the 3rd Company were purposely trying to put in my face the fact that they could easily get on without me. I went to the Commander, von Rosen, and told him that they should either assign me something—which meant letting me actually get into a tank—or I would go back to the baggage Company behind the lines. I had more months in combat to my name than all the other officers. To be subjected to constant displays of callous behavior aimed my way specifically was really pretty demeaning, because it would do nothing to further my reputation within the company. Von Rosen, a gentleman, appreciated this dilemma and ended the situation which, according to my estimations, had been staged by the *Spieß*, the *Feldwebel*, and also the Company Officers. But also with the baggage Company, the people were not exactly too accommodating. I found myself there resisting against un-comrade like behavior all the time. I admit that I could not settle in with the 3rd Company. In fact, I didn't even want to, and it only pushed me further in the direction of wanting to return to 1st Company. But, as it happens, I wouldn't be sent there either out of fear that certain disciplinary complications might ensue because I would be reunited with certain comrades, who had been of the same rank when I left and over whom I would now be a superior officer. This was highly visible. Since the strength of the Panzer armies had shrunk so significantly the normal Company boundaries had blurred; so that when assembled into battle groups, one now had free contact to those in all three Panzer companies. The mutual aversion between 3rd Company and myself continued—even to this day! About ten years ago I decided to break away from the veteran's circle. In the history of the 503rd Abteilung, which I had composed, they were of the opinion that I hadn't accurately described the 3rd Company in a manner inherent to them. Conversely, Von Rosen had been a good comrade to me; in fact, we remained good friends through the end of the war and into our days in the Bundeswehr, and even today remain very close.

I had become Platoon Commander of 3rd Platoon and found myself involved in action many times around the area of Samoly, which demanded a lot from me. Eventually I was

Church in Verebely, a town in Hungary. This is where our abteilung was in March 1945.

becoming the sort of person whom I really was: an experienced and recognized *Panzerkommander*.

With the Abteilung Staff

In our *Kommandeur* we had a thoughtful and responsible officer. Because I was one of the people in the abteilung with the most tank experience, the *Kommandeur* switched the *Ordonnanzoffizier*, *Leutnant* Rollik, out into the combat echelons and put me in his place. Staff service wasn't exactly my favorite thing; but as an *Ordonnanzoffizier* I was at the same time the Commander of the 3rd Staff-Tank, Commander of the "III." So, I was then able to see even more combat. One thing that was downright exasperating was continuation of the *Kriegstagebuches* (KTB - war diary). Every evening the Ia. Writer, *Oberfeldwebel* Hugo Weber, would come up to the front lines where combat was taking place, and I would report to him about that day's events. Weber would then make a clean copy of it "at home," and then would bring it back with him the next evening for review and a signature. Because I would always accompany the *Kommandeur* to meetings and issuing of orders and because I, as a liaison officer, would be dispatched to various posts occupied by superior officers, I was able to become fully aware of proceedings within the abteilung, including the history of its days in combat. This had put me in a position almost half a century later to issue a written history of the abteilung.

The End

That the end of the war would come in the form of unconditional capitulation was evident beyond a doubt. How, when, and where this would occur remained the only big questions. All considerations with respect to these questions led us to the firm determination that capture by the Red Army was absolutely out of the question. The long, drawn-out advance of the Americans in Southern Germany and their halt at the Bohemian Forest moved all German troops in the vicinity to slowly ease their way to this area, all the while putting up resistance, in order to allow the civilian population to reach the U.S. lines before the Russians, who were certain to exact incomprehensible revenge. We, too, would then allow ourselves to be captured by the Americans. What we didn't know was the agreement the Americans had to transfer the 6th and 8th Armies over to the Russians. Our wishful thinking then resulted in about half of our soldiers—maybe 500 or so—actually ending

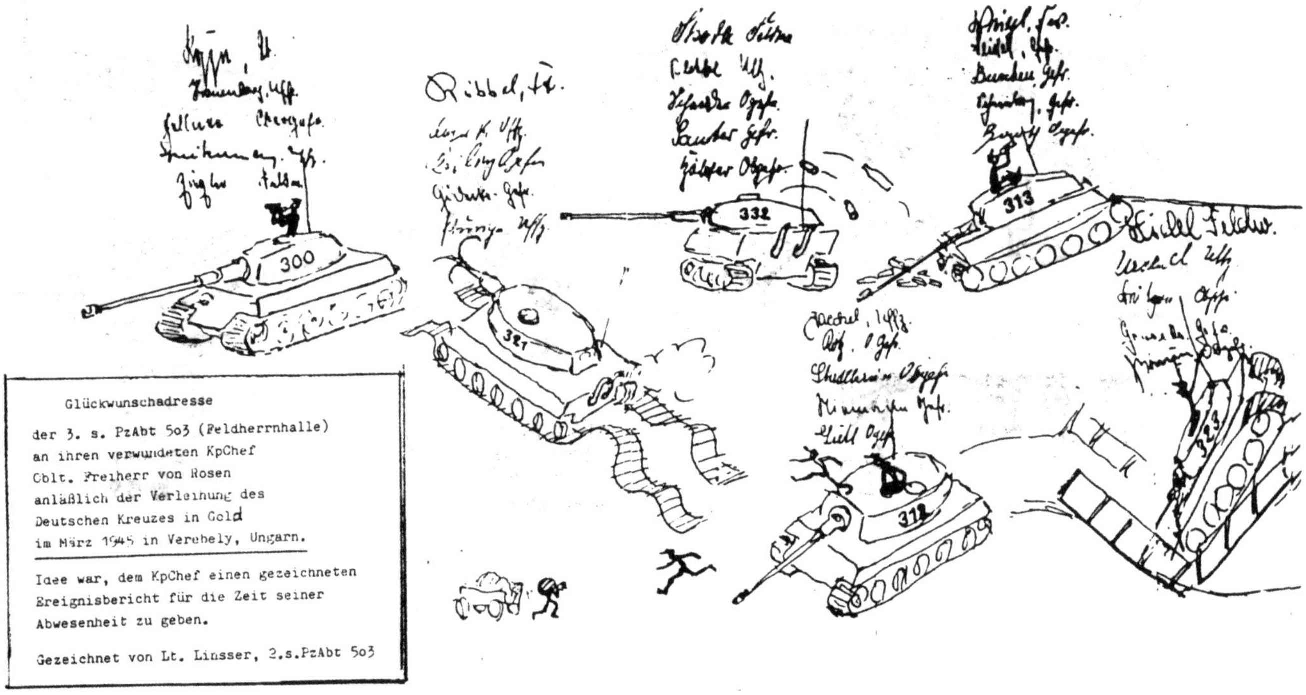

Glückwunschadresse

der 3. s. PzAbt 5o3 (Feldherrnhalle)
an ihren verwundeten KpChef
Oblt. Freiherr von Rosen
anläßlich der Verleihung des
Deutschen Kreuzes in Gold
im März 1945 in Verebely, Ungarn.

Idee war, dem KpChef einen gezeichneten
Ereignisbericht für die Zeit seiner
Abwesenheit zu geben.

Gezeichnet von Lt. Linsser, 2.s.PzAbt 5o3

Best wishes from the 3rd Company schwere Panzer Abteilung 503 (*Feldherrnhalle*) to our wounded Company Commander, *Oberleutnant* Freiherr von Rosen, in celebration of the awarding of the German Cross in Gold in March 1945 in Verebely, Hungary. The idea was to provide a brief overview of what the company experienced during the commander's absence. Drawing by *Leutnant* Linsser, 2nd Company schwere Panzer Abteilung 503.

The *Instandsetzungs-Truppe* (maintenance section) of the 1st Company schwere Panzer Abteilung 503/*Feldherrnhalle* with their vehicle, a *Zugkraftwagen* 1, in March/April 1945.

up in Soviet captivity anyway. To this day it is not really known how many of them survived. We guessed that maybe half never saw home again. I was lucky, or shall I say, I did everything in my power to make sure that I was never captured. In this manner, with the exception of the few days I spent in a U.S. discharge camp, I arrived unscathed into freedom.

I intentionally have left out an exhaustive description of my time with the 503rd schwere Panzer Abteilung, which can be read in detail in our chronicle.

The Abteilung *Kommandeur Hauptmann* Dr. Nordewin von Diest-Koerber in Spring 1945.

Leutnant Alfred Rubbel, the last *Ordonnanzoffizier* of schwere Panzer Abteilung 503/*Feldherrnhalle*, Nikolsburg, March 1945.

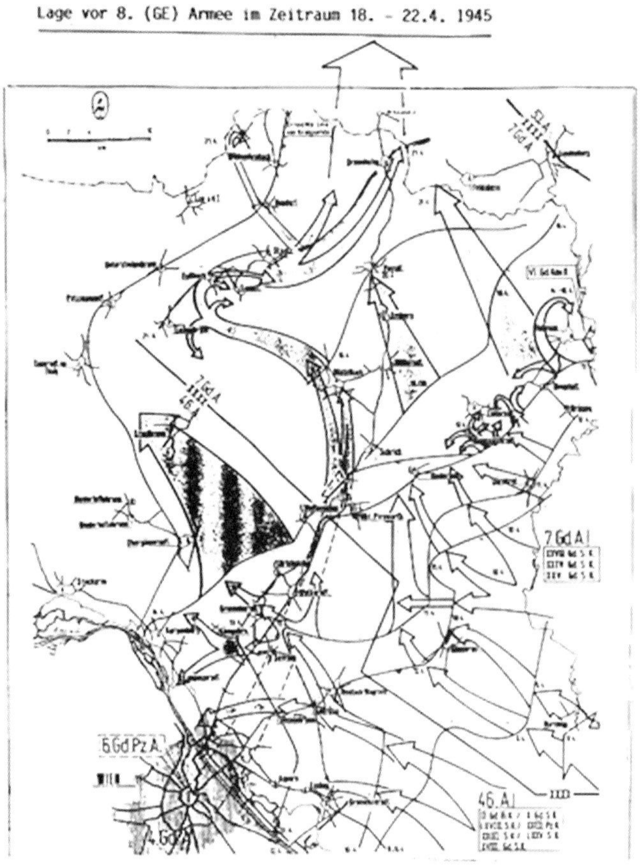

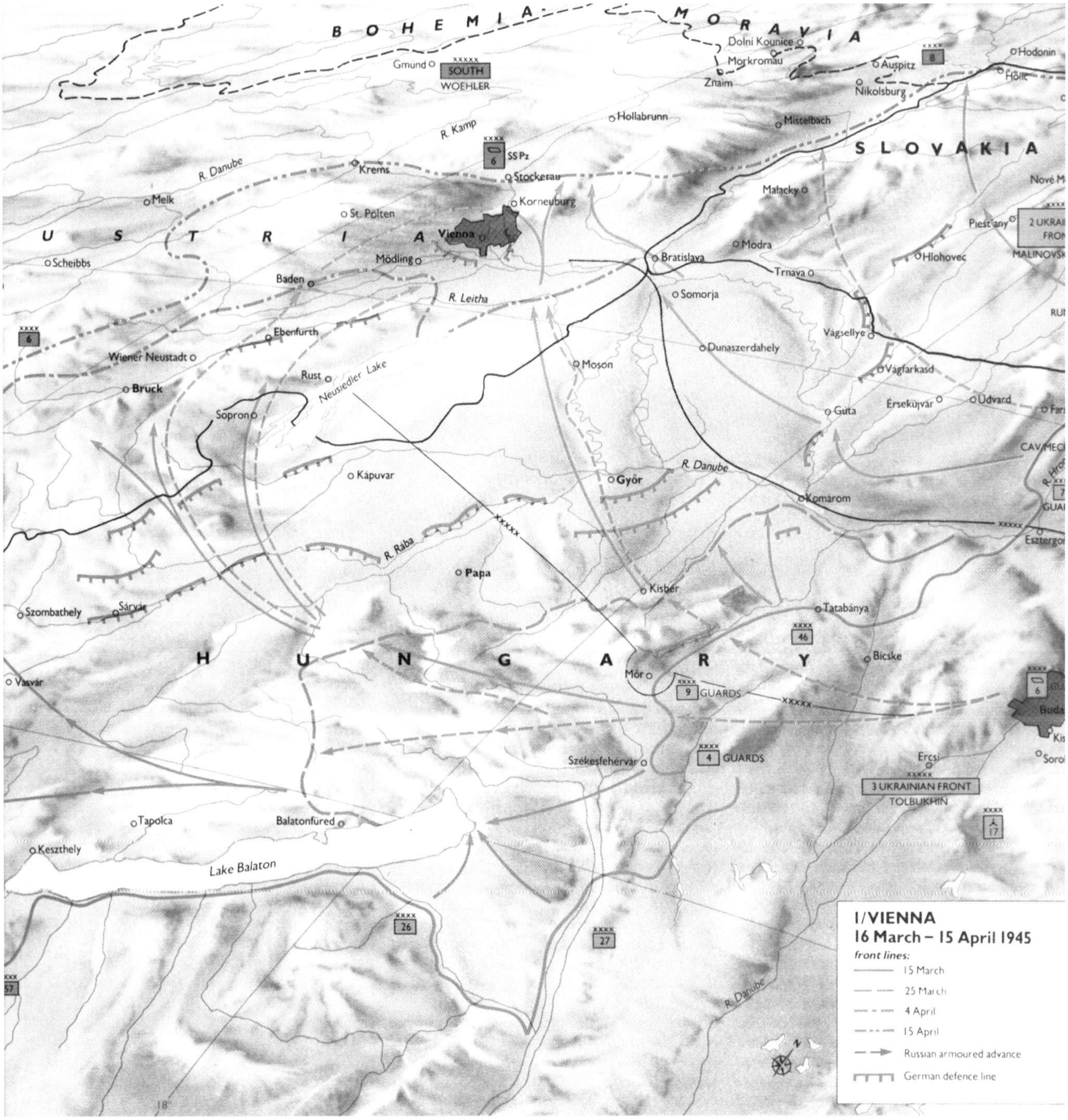
I/VIENNA
16 March – 15 April 1945
front lines:
15 March
25 March
4 April
15 April
Russian armoured advance
German defence line
BOHEMIA
MORAVIA
SLOVAKIA
HUNGARY
SOUTH
WOEHLER
SS Pz
2 UKRAINIAN FRONT
MALINOVSKY
3 UKRAINIAN FRONT
TOLBUKHIN
9 GUARDS
4 GUARDS
Gmund
Dolni Kounice
Morkromau
Znaim
Auspitz
Nikolsburg
Hodonin
Hollabrunn
Mistelbach
R. Kamp
R. Danube
Krems
Stockerau
Korneuburg
Melk
St. Pölten
Vienna
Mödling
Scheibbs
Baden
R. Leitha
Bratislava
Modra
Malacky
Piešťany
Hlohovec
Trnava
Somorja
Ebenfurth
Wiener Neustadt
Bruck
Rust
Neusiedler Lake
Moson
Dunaszerdahely
Vágsellye
Vágfarkasd
Guta
Érsekújvár
Udvard
Sopron
Kapuvar
Győr
Komárom
Esztergom
R. Rába
Papa
Kisbér
Tatabánya
Szombathely
Sárvár
Bicske
Vasvár
Mór
Székesfehérvár
Ercsi
Buda
Tapolca
Balatonfüred
Keszthely
Lake Balaton

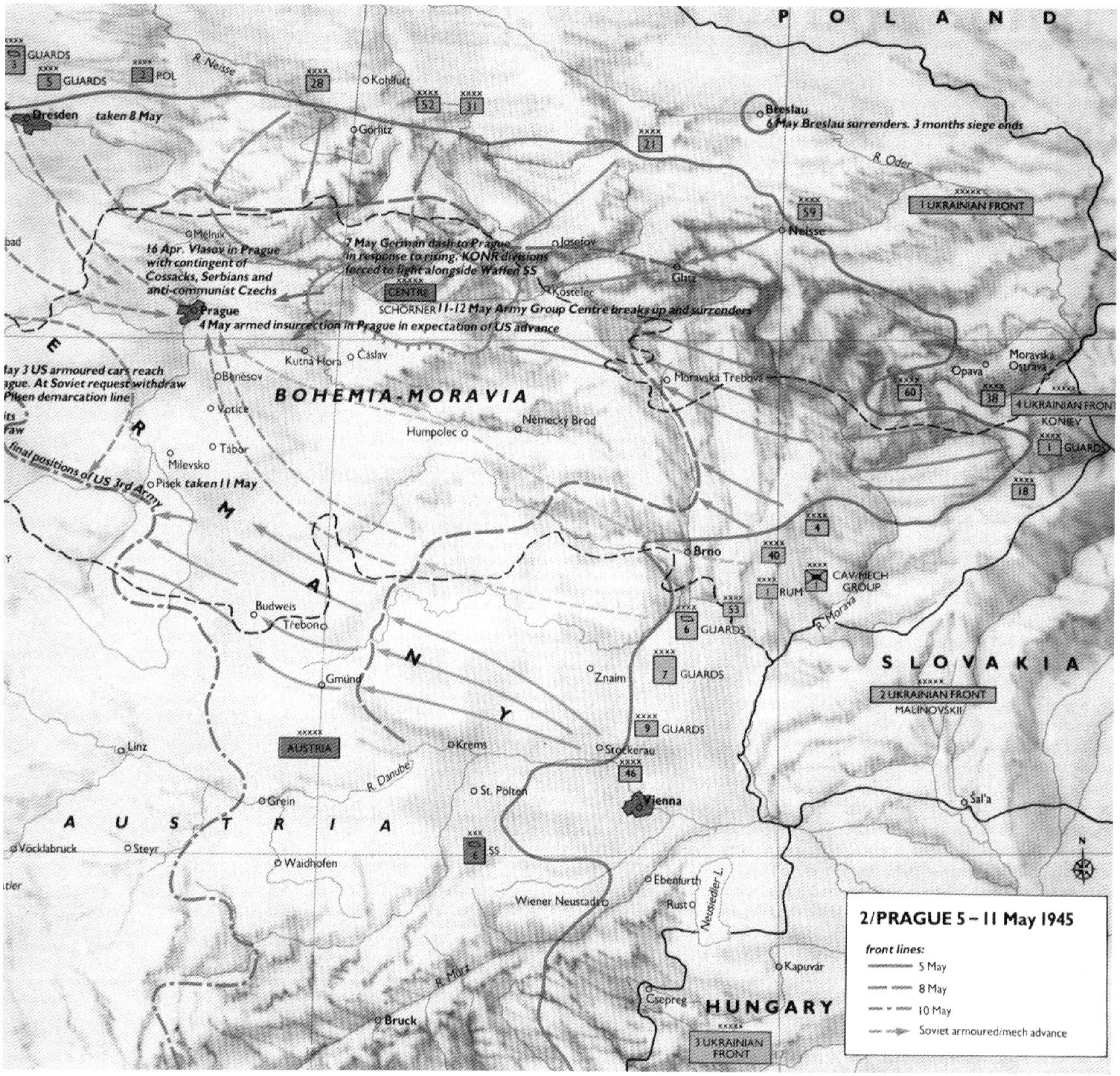

Opposite: *Leutnant* Alfred Rubbel, *Ordonnanzoffizier*, schwere Panzer Abteilung 503, December 1944.

11

The War is Over, What Now?

By Way of the Bohemian Forest to the West

On the afternoon of the tenth of May, the forest meadow near the village of Dobrusch was emptied. After our Commander's last role call and our subsequent releases each and every one of us was now left to our own devices. Owing to the instructions afforded us to attempt to traverse the American lines in front of us in small groups, it then became advisable that we actually would begin marching by foot. This, in spite of the prevalent slogan that the tankers on such a journey would have to forfeit much in the area of self-confidence corresponding to the mandatory distances made to cover by foot. Unfortunately, many amongst us did not behave according to this directive and ended up traveling west by machine, and were later snapped up by the Americans in the complicated mountainous regions; they then subsequently paid the price for their levity by being handed over to the Russians as prisoners. With a small group of soldiers I then got under way on foot. I was equipped with marching provisions, a set of binoculars, a map, a compass, and a pistol as my only luggage, and therefore I was easily mobile. Around evening time—it was still light out—we reached the first of the American lines, which ran up and down in a North-South direction along the road running from Prachatitz to Christianberg. We waited for nightfall in the cemetery of Oberhaid and attempted all the while to ascertain the numbers and positions of the sentry posts. The "Amis" (German slang abbreviation for Americans) made it easy for us. They conducted their patrols in their jeeps with all lights blazing. At their guard posts they also carried on talking and gossiping profusely. We starting creeping by in our best soldiers' habit—surrounded by riflemen—all the way to the road embankment, which unfortunately ran along a terrace. The about one meter high obstruction we overcame with a cohesive jump, which also wasn't the quietest of endeavors, and in so doing almost ran a complete circle around one of the American guards. In his astonishment he let out a grumble, and after some time of fumbling about he finally found the trigger on his machine gun and uselessly emptied his entire magazine shooting at us. So, the first step into freedom had been traversed. Unfortunately, I then got myself so hung up in the crotch of some tree branch along the embankment in all this darkness that my provisions and my binoculars were lost as a result of my efforts to extricate myself. Also, our little group was now no longer together. The only guy left with me was a chap named "Bubi" Böhler from 3rd Company, nicknamed such because of his youthful appearance. We then spent that night under a canopy of fir trees, and it was bitter cold! Beside our stone-gray light Panzer uniforms we had no warm clothing. During days of respite in Socherl I had read a few things in Stifter's "High Forest." I now had all day to acquaint myself with the book's depictions of various landmarks and objects in the Bohemian Forest and to recognize them by sight. We crossed the mountain range of the Kubany at an elevation of 1100 meters, at times wading through slush and snow. Here in the forests we were safe. The Americans did not ever like to leave their jeeps, or the roads for that matter. Our stomachs at this time really began to grumble. Now and again we would bump into these little forlorn inns and pubs along the way, where we were then modestly fed. One day we descended into a civilian area and landed near the town of Zwiesel in Buchenau.

After marching by foot for a good 100 km, almost exclusively through forest trails and such, we as a group, which had swelled in ranks through the addition of some stray soldiers who possessed maps and compasses, were in much need of significant rest. The little village was teeming with refugees, which allowed us to blend in amongst the crowds without standing out. In the castle of the Count Ex we then devised a military-like routine in a civilized manner. When the Americans would come to patrol the village, we would retreat back into the forest utilizing our alarm system.

It was probably about the middle of May now, and it was time for us to move on. In order to "travel" legally, one needed an Allied discharge certificate stating that one was now a demobilized soldier. This was to avoid the danger of falling into enemy captivity. My goal was Hanover.

Because the group was now too large and too frivolous, we headed out toward the West in the direction of Regensburg. Böhler wanted to travel to see his parents in Schwetzingen. Somewhere along the way we bumped into a group of "terrain-savvy" students with their hiking coach. Because "Bubi" Böhler would fit right in with the shorts he had on, I convinced him to ally himself with this nomadic bunch, especially because they were humping it along the same exact trail as ourselves. This he did, although somewhat against his will, and he then landed safe and sound at the end of June back at home. There he was assisted greatly by a document provided him by a sympathetic and reasonable mayor.

My next goal was Staffelstein. This is where the family of Hans von Hagemeister had gone. I hoped then to meet him there, and therefore commenced the next phase of my sojourn by myself.

One problem I now had was my provisions. The areas between the Bavarian Alps, the Donau, and Regen, in which I had taken up a westerly course, was also completely overflowing with former *Wehrmacht* soldiers, refugees, and D.P.s ("Displaced Persons"—expelled and released prisoners of war from the East). All these peoples were very hungry. The D.P.s were well provisioned by either the U.S. Army or from the U.N.R.A., a U.N. organization. The two remaining groups, the German soldiers and the civilians, were then reliant upon the mercy and generosity of the indigenous peoples of the area. I must now emphasize that I received tremendous help from these people during these weeks. Also from the "traveling folk" we could obtain ration stickers from the community administrations, which were always valid for one day and then allowed one to go shopping. The only people for whom it was not allowed to assign ration stamps were those without one of these now famous "release documents". One also needed money and I, to be frank, no longer remember if I had any. So, my system for obtaining rations then became one where I would politely request the same type of meal as friendly as possible.

And so, on that second Whitsunday, this is how a luscious meal at a well-to-do farmhouse at "Gauboden," near Nittenau, "almost" turned into a fatal disaster. I was thoroughly satisfied with my meal. We had had roast pork with dumplings, and for dessert enjoyed confected plums. I then set out into the forest, zigzagging about without really paying the proper amount of attention. Suddenly, as if appearing out of thin air, there stood an American jeep five meters in front of me with soldiers on board. They signaled to me to approach them, screaming "come on" and waving me toward them. My leap over a ditch and subsequent disappearance into the underbrush happened so fast that it came as a total surprise to the Amis. They didn't even have time to reach for their weapons. I was now safe. However, as well as the day had begun, it would end just as badly.

As I found out later, because of a lack of opportunities for many U.S. combat units to prove themselves under fire, these men then became insanely competitive in the sport of capturing German stragglers now that the war was over. This would be their only chance to taste real combat. And, to this effect, they went all out!

Somewhere the forest came to an end at a sloping meadow, which was covered with erratic rocks and blocks and such. I would have to slip across this meadow and then vanish once more into the next patch of forest. To the right and behind me in a valley at a distance of about 200-300 meters there was a road. As I was about 100 meters away from reaching the next tree line I heard the sound of a motor and a whistle. Yes indeed, there they were again...my American friends from a short while back. They were now waving at me again, this time much more intensely. In the meantime they had loaded onto the jeep 2 soldiers. But what was now of even greater concern was the fact that they had loaded onto a gun carriage a heavy machine gun, caliber 12,4, and they had this thing aiming right at me! Just as I started "trotting away" in the direction of the forest I heard reports and bullet strikes pelting everything around me. These bandits were firing with explosive ammunition, and suddenly a piece of shrapnel ripped right through my left earlobe! At some point thereafter I had taken cover and was bandaging my wounded ear with the only belonging I had left, my "all-purpose cloth rag" (handkerchief, hand towel, scarf, protective cover from gnats and other bugs, sunshield—and now it was band aid material!). I now came to the extraordinary conclusion that this simply could not go on in such a way. After surviving almost six years of intense combat, I was not about to become a moving target for some trigger happy Americans. A new "strategy" was desperately called for!

In Weiden, Amberg, and Grafenwöhr the U.S. Army had set up these so called "discharge camps." After delivery of the soldiers of the remaining 6th and 8th Armies was over (they'd been snapped up near the border) they then went about registering the captured troops. As long as nothing too damning was detected, such as having belonged to the SS, holding a high-ranking Party office, or of being an officer of superior rank, one would then receive his "discharge certificate." At first I was not sure how my belonging to an outfit called "*Feldherrenhalle*" would be evaluated. After questioning several soldiers who'd received their discharges, I made the decision to voluntarily give myself up at the camp in Weiden. My judgment had been sound; after four days I had my "papers"—now the war was definitely at an end for me!

Where to then?

The war was over. During the combat years we had become hardened to the risking of life and limb and being taken prisoner, both of which were a constant threat 365 days a year. Now this was all over. We were consumed with sudden and euphoric feelings of joy and happiness. You made it through alive! You are healthy; everything that awaits you now can only be better than before! Both this feeling and that somewhat lowbrow sensation of being a 24 year old, someone from whom the lion's share of all major decisions had been stripped away for over 6 years, had combined to form the very essence of what I was at that time. Like a fallow deer living its young life sequestered and penned in somewhere, this was my experience in the military. Now, I was to be set free into the wilderness for the first time without the desired supervision or orientation.

The enemy now occupied my hometown of Tilsit in East Prussia. The population had fled, been driven out, or killed. One heard the most atrocious, unimaginable stories told of the Red Army and their behavior there. The possibility of returning home was basically blocked off for me, which I thought at that time to be forever. My immediate family, of which there was now only my mother, I knew had gone off to Saxony just at the right moment. Whether she had actually survived the end of the war, I did not know. I also didn't know if either American or Soviet troops were there in the area where I thought my mother had fled to. Germany was recognizably completely occupied by enemy forces. The first thing I planned to do was search for my mother and visit with her, if possible. It had been supposed by some soldiers I encountered that perhaps she might be at another port-of-call, to which many of the younger females had gone. I was familiar with the place they were referring to, but this scenario didn't apply, as she had headed elsewhere.

During our "dissolution roll call" on the 10th of May we exchanged addresses with those of our comrades who still had homes. A few of these actually became ports-of-call, so to speak. The question, then, is why? Wandering hordes of displaced persons in a magnitude hardly imaginable today overflowed the country in the first months after the war, especially in those areas not under control of the Red Army. There were literally millions of refugees from the East who were streaming into the Western Allied Occupied Zones: released soldiers, who either had a destination or were searching for one; prisoners of war taken by the Eastern or Western enemy forces, who only in part wanted to return home; foreign workers who didn't know where to go, as things in the East were also very unstable and uncertain; German evacuees from the bombed out big cities on the prowl for a new place outside of the city to call home; and the usual movement of men and material of occupation forces all combined to make Germany a crawling mass of displaced and confused humanity. Although the German State and its administration of orderly affairs had completely collapsed, the Occupation Forces, with the exception of the French, whose rigorous behavior outdid even that of the Russians, were able to secure and stabilize the country with their armies so that on a basic community level the German population was provided the elementary necessities to get by, and the foreigners who happened to be in Germany were also fairly well-respected and looked after. Security, nourishment, living space, information, traffic, and administration were all up and running in an amazingly short amount of time, starting in about the late summer of 1945.

Against this backdrop, there I was with my U.S. papers ("Certificate of Discharge"), and I knew that I was indeed no longer a soldier. My belongings consisted of a stone gray Panzer summer uniform, a toothbrush that had been gifted to me, and a large *Wehrmacht* handkerchief. I had no money, nor possessions of any value. I had left my *Wehrmacht* watch by the banks of the Moldau River after bathing in it; but I was still happy and unencumbered. It must have been about the beginning of June '45 when I began to "do the waltz!"

What skills did I have? A modest school education, a career education in the area of administration that was also just as modest, and which had been interrupted by the war, and a basic understanding of certain operating procedures related to farming from my days as a work hand at home. Along with this, I enjoyed a thorough smattering of knowledge in the following insubstantial areas:

> From my home life with my parents: a sense of obligation, modesty, and an appreciation of family;
> From school: an appreciation of social tolerance and the ability to think;
> And from the *Wehrmacht*, an understanding of the necessities of discipline and order.

I slowly began to realize that I now had to walk on my own two feet. My friend and comrade from the war, Walter Wegmann, who had been severely wounded in 1941 and never deemed fit for service again, had an important position in Oldenburg in business administration. He granted me a position as "quality control manager for fruits and vegetables," although in reality I could hardly distinguish the difference between a pear and a carrot. Because of this—although this was just a temporary position—it became increasingly evident where my journeys needed to take me. Many thanks to Walter Wegmann.

Now even this next incident depicts the situation in Germany at the time. While searching for those responsible for the lost war, the Germans themselves, not our former enemies, came across the idea that this must also include officers who had been in the *Wehrmacht*. So, in order to atone for all this, I was sent to mandatory labor in a mine in the Ruhr valley. It is not difficult to understand that I tried with all my power to escape this situation, which I did by accepting a teaching contract in the farming industry, which then sprung me from the mines. This career choice was not only a good way to dodge the awful former position; it really turned out to be a wise move. I happened to meet my wife while doing this, which was an incredibly lucky sequence of events. I can only afford her an unending amount of gratitude for the fact that she had accepted me, an unknown quantity with no possessions or tangible skills, and against the misgivings of her family.

In conclusion, the following: The most difficult and uncertain phase of my life was trying to find a sphere of order, where I could actually fit in. Many people did not have such luck. With that I will finally end the story of "My War" and its respective direct consequences.

A Bit More on von Hagemeister

The year 1943 brought us "Citadel" and the defensive retreat to the Dnieper; 1944, with the encirclement at Tscherkassy, had brought us many uncomfortable and dangerous months. Hans had been transferred to the Staff Company and assigned to the Recon Platoon, probably because he possessed tremendous reading and writing skills. He was excellent at reading maps and could also speak Russian. His former life was a very unusual one. He hailed from Estonia and was a son of powerful money, as had been formulated by Schiller in *Wallenstein's Camp*. Supposedly he had been chosen to take over the family manor of Pavekül near Reval. Until then he would cut his teeth while serving in the Estonian army. As the Ribbentrop-Molotov agreement, which included re-incorporating the three Baltic States into the USSR, became reality, Hans was a *Fähnrich* with an Estonian tank division and had, as he put it himself, not really learned much of anything besides how to dance. Because they were of Germanic heritage, the Hagemeisters' lives were spared by the Soviets. Instead, in 1939 they resettled into the Reich in the Posen District, which after the Polish Campaign had gone to Germany. The *Fähnrich* von Hagemeister took yet another detour; he was supposed to become a Russian Junior Lieutenant first before he could be released to go to Germany. Provided now with his German citizenship, his 3rd round of military service now waited for him, an opportunity he happily seized upon! And so, in 1941, he became a Panzer soldier in Neuruppin with the objective of becoming an officer.

In April 1944 he, the *Fahnenjunker-Feldwebel* Hans Lewandowski, and I were all transferred to the Panzer Replacement Abteilung 500 in Paderborn, and from there we were commanded to go to the Officers' Training Program in Ohrdruf. Hans von Hagemeister was now befallen with a bit of bad luck. He had been deemed an "inexperienced" Panzer Soldier (the official qualifications criterion was EK I), and thus was transferred into the infantry because they were in desperate need of leadership due to heavy losses amongst the officer corps. Hans was deeply upset about this. His mood during the day had settled down between outright anger and deep depression. But, as luck would have it for the Panzer troops, Guderian had been rehabilitated and named to the General Supervisors position of the Panzer Armies. One of the first measures he took was to bring back personnel who had been dealt off to the infantry. Hans was once again amongst the Blackshirts. With me everything was taking much longer than normal, as I had fallen ill with malaria and, as a result, had to repeat the Officers' Training Program in Krampnitz. In the meantime, Hans had become a *Leutnant* in August 1944 and was sent into Normandy with the Abteilung. I did not return to the Abteilung until January 1945 when I was sent to Hungary. It was here that I finally bumped into Hans again, who since July 1943 had been in action and made it through unscathed. Since we were now both working at Abteilung Staff we saw each other frequently. Although our character makeup was really quite different, we became good friends. Hans, who was three years older than I, was in contrast to myself very ambitious and also somewhat meticulous and finicky. I had inherited the optimistic side of my father, and therefore I always seemed to exhibit the baffling feature of finding something good even in the most wretched of things. Hans, on the other hand, could display these boundless fits of anger and rage, while I laboriously kept my "mean-streak" in check.

On the 9th of May 1945 we were in the area of Brünn, and the war was over for us. Before this, on the 2nd of May in a place called Socherl—which was in Czechoslovakia, very close to the border of lower Austria—we had celebrated Hans' birthday in a massive way! We were all quite aware that we were being unceremoniously hurled into a catastrophe the likes of which had never before been witnessed in history. The last military assessment of the situation was the following: neither the *Wehrmacht*, nor the Abteilung, nor the individual has in any way the capacity to do anything whatsoever to avert the outcome of the war. We still didn't know what that outcome would be exactly, either. We held on to the hope that we would eventually have a little luck handed our way, and why not? Maybe there would be some mercy shown to those, especially those like us, who had remained in the land of the living and remained faithful for the entire duration of the war. Only one absolute remained in my mind: I would in no way entertain any ideas of being taken prisoner by the Russians.

Because Panzer people generally lose a lot of dignity when having to cover any sort of distances by foot, Hans and I jumped into one of those VW-Kübelwagens I've spoken about with a driver and baggage for our getaway, and then we made off ASAP to the border of the Reich, which lay between the Bavarian and Bohemian Forests. My Königstiger, the "III," I gave up just west of Brünn after a short firefight with Czech guerillas at the Moldau Bridge, who tried to stop us and our trek out of there. Also, in the ever-more difficult mountain terrain of the Bohemian Forest, a light bridge called a halt to our use of heavy armor. So, we let our tank crash into a gully and it was off in the VW. On the 10th of May 1945, after the dissolution of the rest of the Abteilung at Dobrusch, we approached the American blockade lines, whose position we were familiar with. Hans insisted on going further; I objected because the danger of being snapped up by the Americans off the streets was too large in my estimation. The Americans, as far as we observed, would only go where their jeeps would take them, which meant they stayed out of the forests. This was the opportunity to get into Bavaria. Hans and I left each other because each of us thought that he had the better solution. We exchanged addresses. Hans knew that his family, wife, daughter, and mother were staying in Bavaria in the vicinity of Staffelstein at Schloss Oberau (?).

Hans soon had to give up the Kübelwagen and progressed unscathed through the barricades and found his family. I, on the other hand, had some difficulties. First through the dirty, slushy snow of the high forest at 1,200 meters, then constantly bumping into Americans, then shot at near Deggendorf while fleeing (right ear shot through). I finally was able to slowly make my way forwards. It became clear to me that I definitely required having discharge papers from the Americans. So, I needed to research how to do this! Near the border the captured soldiers (it was now June) were still being delivered over to the Russians. The prisoner camp at Grafenwöhr had a mean S-O-B American Commander by the name of Kahlscheren running the place. Hunger and beatings were on the daily agenda. In Weiden, however, things were in comparison supposedly quite humane. There apparently was some sort of "De-mobilization and Discharge Camp" there; so, that's where I traveled to, and after five days I had my discharge papers and could now move about freely. I even had some stamps for food and provisions, which meant I no longer had to beg for every meal! At that time I experienced a tremendous willingness to help from the Bavarian population. Refugees, DPs (displaced persons, foreigners), prisoners-of-war, and German soldiers—yes, everybody seemed to be on the move. I then marched to Oberau to see Hans, who had already been there about four weeks!

Somehow, we needed to get the ball rolling with our new situation. After five years of constant regulation as to our existence and whereabouts at all times under Army Command now one had to plan for himself, which meant having to actually set near-term goals and then executing them. With Hans it was plainly evident that he felt more compelled than I to actively take life into his own hands. It was more than just the necessity to provide for his family. He put a lot of energy into actually establishing a real existence, which he had no intention of being meager about. This pretty much remained a distinguishing feature of his entire life. And in so doing, he certainly didn't make life for himself or anyone near him very easy. He was successful and always seemed able to surmount any difficulties. *Laissez-faire*, which I often leaned towards, was totally foreign to him. He was always very active in determining his life's course. He only allowed himself to be happy for certain fleeting moments, and so he always drove himself and those around him ever forwards, whether they liked it or not. He was a person who loved routine and order, and was never lax in business or private affairs. One could almost say he was restless.

We decided at this time to go to Hanover, which wasn't as easy as it sounds, as the transgression from the U.S. to the British zone of occupation was almost an illegal act. Anyhow, Hans wanted to head in that direction because he surmised that he had a cousin there, from whom he might derive some valuable advice. This is where his marked sense of family really began to shine, which probably developed over the centuries and was passed on from generation to generation, as the Hagemeister clan had to fend for itself in a foreign territory. His cousin,

Hauptmann Botsch, had spent a lot of time in the service in the area of Hanover-Celle and therefore knew, as Hans had rightly guessed, the surrounding area well, and also knew just how to get on. It was not yet clear to me that one would actually have to stand up on his own two feet, so I traveled with him mostly out of curiosity; but also because I really hadn't much else better to do. Hans developed all sorts of plans, for me as well, with which one could actually get by. As a farm boy, I figured I would find accommodation somewhere in the agricultural industry, as I knew the business modestly well and I knew there would definitely be things to eat. The first job Hans picked up was as an interpreter at Hannomag in Hanover between the Russian guest workers and the labor contract providers. It was clear to him that this would only be a temporary gig. He then recalled his dancing capabilities, and soon he was acting as an assistant at the Meseke School of Dance in Hanover. He almost seemed to me like a man possessed, who spared nothing of himself. He was absolutely full of ideas. Soon, however, he had a massive rout with his boss, Ms. Helga Meseke, and so decided to do this on his own. He went on to actually become one of the most recognized professionals of this art in all of Germany. He gradually had less and less time for his family and for his friends. But, with all that, he still managed to seize the opportunity to make it to our Tiger-Abteilung reunions and meetings. He died, as one would say, "in harness" of a heart attack. It must have been 1975. Along with our friendship, which was an inseparable bond between us, came also that amongst our wives and families. This connection will survive until our last days. Of this I am certain. I never knew anybody who had more earned the title of comrade or friend, and to whom such enduring, deep, and sometimes strained ties existed. Maybe the aforementioned title concerning the "somewhat difficult friendship" is very illuminating, because this friendship was no simple matter of course—we really had to work at it. There were no superficialities, and it never required needy little affirmations of our loyalty, which is today so often the case. There is this one statement he made that I will never forget, as we were arguing amongst a circle of our comrades during the war about our respective eastern heritage. He stated in his most beautiful Baltic tone of voice: " The further east one goes, the smaller the wash bowels become and the larger the drinking vessels become. And at that point where they are exactly the same size, is where you are from." The somewhat larger distances to the West, in his case, probably led to, admittedly to me, the tipping of the scales in favor of over dimensioned drinking vessels. But he never really developed a true affection for these!

Left: Hagemeister in a motorcycle sidecar of the Recon Abteilung in summer 1943. Right: Hans had become a *Fahnenjunker-Feldwebel*, got married, and let himself be photographed on the 20th of February 1944.

Hagemeister appraises a letter from a bride written to Hannes Kück. In this house, Hagemeister celebrated his birthday on June 2nd, 1945, in true Russian Bojaren manner in Socherl. There we enjoyed practically uninterrupted peace until May 7th, 1945, when the Russian storm broke loose, against which we had nothing left with which to fight.

Appendices

My Medals

From left above: Iron Cross, 2nd Class (EK 2); Iron Cross, 1st Class (EK 1); *Panzerkampfabzeichen*, Silver (Tank Combat Badge) for 3 engagements, Stufe 1 (level 1); *Panzerkampfabzeichen*, Silver for 25 engagements, Stufe 2 (level 2); *Panzerkampfabzeichen*, Silver for 50 engagements, Stufe 3 (level 3); *Verwundetenabzeichen Schwarz* (Wound Badge black); *Winterkampfabzeichen* (Eastern Front 1941-42); *Flutmedaille* Hamburg; Bismarkmedaille.

Award Dates and Promotions

Award	Date	Assigned Unit
Panzerkampfabzeichen Silver (3 engagements)	July 21st, 1941 Regiment 29	9th Company, Panzer
Eiserne Kreuz II	April 5th, 1942	“ ”
Eiserne Kreuz I	July 22nd, 1943	1st Company, schwere Panzer Abteilung 503
Verwundeten Abzeichen Black	June 3rd, 1943	“ ”
Panzerkampfabzeichen Level II (25 engagements)	June 20th, 1944	“ ”
Panzerkampfabzeichen Level III (50 engagements)	ca. February 1st, 1945	3rd Company, schwere Panzer Abteilung 503

Promotions

Born: June 28th, 1921

Service Ranks	Date of Promotion	Unit of Assignment
Enlistment	December 5th, 1939	14th Panzer Abweh*r* Company, Infantry Ersatz Regiment 21
Oberschütze	June 1st, 1940	“ ”
Gefreiter	December 1st, 1940	9th Company, Panzer Regiment 29
Obergefreiter	January 1st, 1942	3rd Company, Panzer Regiment 29
Unteroffizier	April 1st, 1942	“ ”
Fahnenjunker	September 1st, 1943	1st Company, schwere Panzer Abteilung 503
Feldwebel (*Fahnenjunker*)	March 1st, 1943	“ ”
Oberfähnrich	October 1st, 1944	*Oberfähnrichschule* 1
Leutnant der Reserve	December 1st, 1944	Panzer Ersatz Abteilung 500

Dates of My Service in the *Wehrmacht*

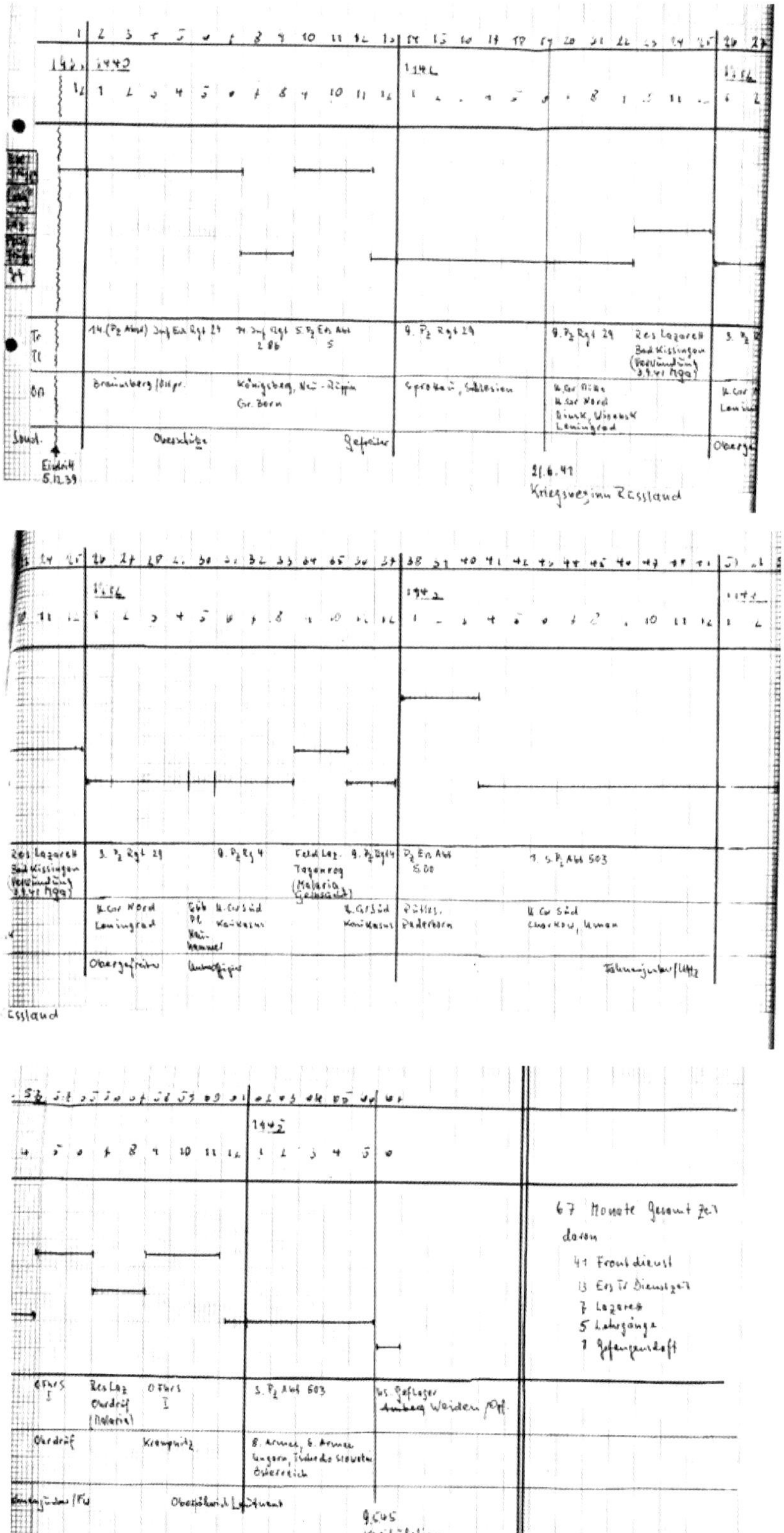

Personal Combat Log with 503

Personal Combat days from January 1st – May 10th, 1945 for:

Panzerkampfabzeichen Level IV (75)
Panzerkampfabzeichen - Silver - Level I (3) -July 21st, 1941
Panzerkampfabzeichen - Level II (25) - June 20th, 1944
Panzerkampfabzeichen - Level III (50) - February 1st, 1945

Prepared: December 24th, 1953

Combat day	Date	Town/Area	Battle Action
1.	early January	Borbala Puszta	recapture of Stuhlweissenberg
2.	"	"	Stuhlweissenberg
3.	"	"	Scalla advance to Venlence-Lake
4.	mid-January	?	
5.	early February	Samoly	attack east of Samoly
6.	"	"	" "
7.	mid February	Borbala Major	
8.	" "	Udvard	loaded onto trains in Mor, unloaded
	to end February	in Udvard	
9.	early March	Kür	attack along railline Pressburg-Budapest
10.	"	"	Pressburg-Budapest
11.	" "		
12.	" "	Essergoml	
13.	" "		night attack on Essergoml
14.	" "	Udvard/Verbely	loaded onto trains in Udvard,
	to end March		unloaded in Verbely
15.	23rd March	Nagy Kalna	forcing of the Gran-bridgehead from the north
16.	24th March	Kis Kalna	
17.	25th March	Verbely	fighting withdrawal towards Verbely
18.	26th March	Verbely	night battle
19.	27th March	Verbely	
20.	28th March	near Neutra	retreat towards Neutra
21.	29th March	"	"
22.	early April	Holic	
23.	early April	Holic	Russian breakthrough cleaned up
24.	early April	Laa/Thaya	adjustment of lines
25.	21st April	Mitterhof	
26.	"	"	Mitterhof night mission
27.	Easter	Erddorf	taking of Erddorf
28.	"	"	Maustrech
29.	early May	south of Brünn	retreat in the direction of Budweis
30.	8-10 May	Budweis	retreat towards Moldau
31.	"	"	Moldau River

Unit attached to	special events	combat leader
1. 1st Hungarian Panzer Division (?)		3rd Co. – von Rosen
2. "	"	" "
3. ? Panzer Grenadier Division		
4.	- through town of Fehervasurgo	3rd Co. - Rubbel
5. *Schützen* Regiment 5	- drove on a mine, lost both tracks	1st Co. - Beyer
6. " "	- penetration hit near driver, Beyer went running from enemy	" "
7.	- difficult salvage, 5 panzers lost, among them Heino	1st Co. - Fürlinger
8.		
9.		3rd Co. – von Rosen
10.		
11.		
12.	- von Rosen wounded	
13. 12th SS-Panzer Division	Hitler Jugend"	3rd Co. - Wiegand
14. " "	" "	
15.		Abteilung *Kommandeur*
16.		
17.		1st Co. - Fürlinger
18.		
19.	- Fürlinger killed	3rd Co. - Rubbel
20.		3rd Co. - Wiegand
21.		
22. ? Infantry Division		3rd Co. - Rubbel
23.		
24.	- crossing the original Reich border	
25.	- tank hunt behind front lines, 10 destroyed	Rubbel, Piepgras Abteilung *Kommandeur*
26.	- Linkenbach wounded	Linkenbach
27.		
28.	- combat in the oilfields	
29.	- rearguard actions . protecting westward withdrawal	local commanders
30.		
31.		

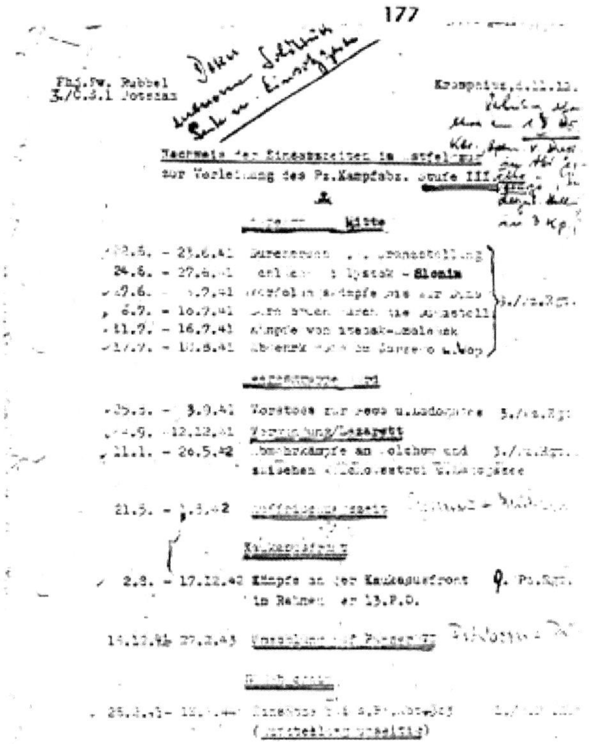
177

Fhj.Fw. Rubbel
3./O.S.1 Potsdam

Krampnitz, 1.12.44

Nachweis der Einsatzzeiten im Ostfeldzug zur Verleihung des Pz.Kampfabz. Stufe III.

Mitte

Kaukasusfront

2.8. - 17.12.42 Kämpfe an der Kaukasusfront 9. Pz.Rgt. im Rahmen der 13.P.D.

Bei der Oberfähnrich-Schule 1 in Potsdam wurde aufgrund neuer Bestimmung für die Verleihung der höheren Stufen des Panzer-Kampfabzeichens Antrag für die III. Stufe = 50 Panzer-Kampftage gestellt. Es wurden für mindestens 9 Monate Panzereinsatz 25 Kampftage angerechnet.

Die Aushändigung erfolgetwa am 1.2.1945 bei der s.Pz.Abt 503/FHH in Fehervasurgo/Ungarn. Die Urkunde ist verlorengegangen, im Besitz sind die Anträge vom 1.12.44

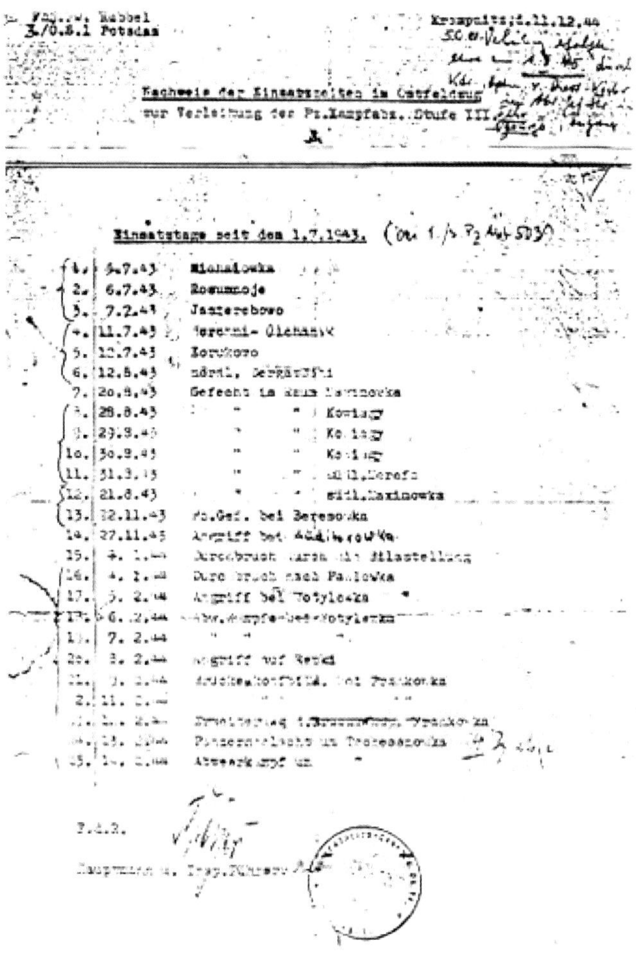
Fhj.Fw. Rubbel
3./O.S.1 Potsdam

Krampnitz, 1.12.44

Nachweis der Einsatzzeiten im Ostfeldzug zur Verleihung des Pz.Kampfabz. Stufe III.

Einsatztage seit dem 1.7.1943.

1. 5.7.43 Michailowka
2. 6.7.43 Rosumnoje
3. 7.7.43 Jasterebowo
7. 20.8.43 Gefecht im Raum Iswinowka
13. 22.11.43 Pz.Gef. bei Beresowka
20. 8. 2.44 Angriff auf Wereki

F.d.R.

Hauptmann u. Insp.Führer

Battle Near Mitterhof

In 1993, members of the Austrian Federal Army, through their military historical research that was aimed at reconstructing the battles that took place near their garrisons, described the engagement which took place near Mitterhof on the 21st of April 1945. Through all this they were made aware of us.

The last Abteilung *Kommandeur*, Dr. von Diest-Koerber, reported on page 323 of our "503" book on the events which took place during that engagement. The noteworthiness of the fighting and shelling, which took place in an especially indirect manner coming at us from all sides, had disappeared from my memory, as it had been 50 years since that time. The events during the last weeks of the war rushed by at a frenzied pace. It wasn't until the detailed research conducted by the Austrians into the events of that engagement had taken place that my memory was jogged and I once again was aware of probably the most noteworthy of all Panzer skirmishes that I ever experienced during the war.

The map that was put together by the Austrians detailing the hostilities at Mitterhof was published in the Austrian Military Newspaper *Pallasch* in issue 3 in the year 1998.

Oberfeldwebel Heino Kleiner, the "artistic *Richtschütze*" who, in not normal fashion for him, had actually knocked out a T 34/85. Pictured here in his private quarters in March 1945, in Verebely/ Hungary.

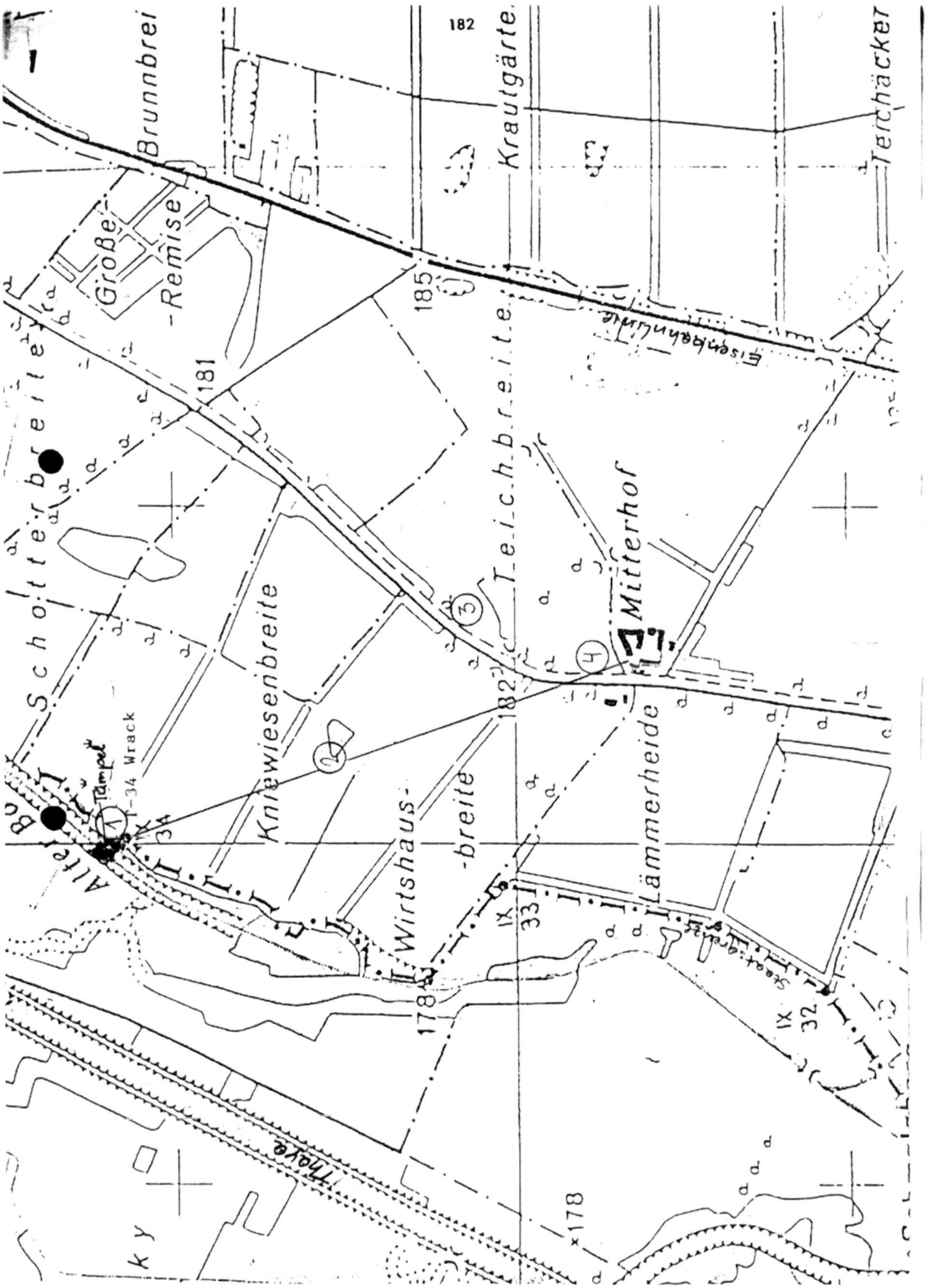
Brunnbrei
Große
-Remise
Krautgärte
Teichäcker
Eisenbahnlinie
Schotterbreite
Teichbreite
Mitterhof
Kniewiesenbreite
Wirtshaus-
-breite
Lämmerheide
Alte B
T-34 Wrack
Thaya
182
185
181
178
IX 33
IX 32

Mitterhof, on the border of Austria and the Czech Republic on the 15th of August 1995. Fifty years later eyewitnesses gathered together at the site of the wreck, which served as a reminder of the heavy fighting in April 1945. From left to right: Dr. Schuler (Austria), who as a child had lived in the area and was a witness to the fighting. Alfred Rubbel (Germany), who as a *Leutnant* had led three Tigers into combat at Mitterhof on the 21st of April 1945.

A Somewhat Difficult Friendship

In May of 1943, we were in the city of Charkow. Our Company (the 1st) was situated in the Plechanovski District. Plechanovski was a model Soviet figure of the day. On the Uliza Starobelska, we said to ourselves, why not just call it "*Ackerstrasse*" (field or farmland street)? The 1st and 2nd Platoons were situated in such a way that the Tigers standing on the street were practically leaning up against the houses, and the tank crews were now living peacefully amongst the Russian, or more accurately, the Ukrainian citizens. The weather was beautiful, our duties never got in the way of our free time activities, and the war, initially, was quite far away—at least fifty km!

The Company was in this area at that time to take on our new "Formation 1943," which included fourteen Tiger tanks, as well as new personnel. Naturally we were curious to see whom we would be bringing on board to go into battle with. The social procedures had now leveled off to a point where everyone was pretty much comfortable with them. The axiom for this was that new personnel would report to their superior officers, and amongst those equal in rank there were no rules. One day during a Company roll call it was read aloud that a certain *Fahnenjunker-Unteroffizier* named von Hagemeister would be joining our Company. Were we then to become some sort of Nobleman-type outfit? We already had a von Borries amongst us! Our Commander was a *Graf* (Count), and in 3rd Company there was a *Freiherr* (Baron).

After the Company roll call everybody would then engage in doing whatever felt right or comfortable, which we had actually been ordered to do. One can be of the opinion that the roots were laid for what is today still a "Society of Amusement" amongst us. When I set my crew of the "114" about working, one must imagine what they were actually doing. This usually meant that the *Fahrer* Walter Eschrig was feverishly toiling away, demanding inspections ten times over and asking for a helping hand. The *Richtschütze* Walter Junge, always a friendly chap, would often lend a hand. It was only the *Funker*, Alfred Peuker, who would constantly question the necessity of such things. I was certain, though, that the process of this "duty" would eventually work itself out, and so I set about paying some visits to other Panzers in the locality. There was always the possibility that at some neighboring tank there might be something to drink, maybe something along the lines of vodka. Just behind the yard gate of Ackerstrasse Number 7—our Tiger was standing in the yard—I saw near a neighboring tank (turret number and name of *Panzerkommander* now forgotten) and a group of men gathered together looking at something. They were eyeballing the new addition to our family, Hans von Hagemeister. What he was actually assigned to do with this tank, I no longer remember. It was either in the capacity of *Panzerkommander* or *Richtschütze*. The only thing for certain was that he hadn't the slightest trace of combat experience.

Now, at this point I would like to communicate the fact that the reader needs to do away with the false notion that a tank is mainly a combat vehicle only. A tank is also a home where one lives, sleeps, is looked after, and recovers from a hard day's work. It is also a means of transportation and, most

Previous page and above: These are the so-called "Company Gatherings" on the Tigers. The picture on the previous page probably depicts the allotment of canteen items, usually a modest amount of alcohol and cigarettes. The picture above depicts thirteen men who have all decided to camp out on the "122." This means that eight men are visitors. What they're all doing; well, they had a lot to talk about those days in the 1st Platoon of 1st Company. One could hardly find better documented the disposition of the men in August 1943.

of all, an element of protection. Also, in comparison to the lower species of military personnel—like the infantry, among others—there is a certain feeling of prestige to go along with it. And, if unavoidable, the tank can also guarantee a first class burial in fire! As such, we absolutely loved this "vehicle" and were tremendously thankful to the constructors over at Henschel for having designed these things with so much room to gather about on the turret and on the rear. In and around the Hagemeister tank just such a gathering was taking place. As a rule, this was a reason to go fraternize amongst your comrades. This noble surname allowed slightly for some memories of dance lessons or something, and then this chap stepped up and introduced himself as the one who would be joining us. I then climbed up on the tank and headed for the new guy. I told him my name; he told me his while dropping the "von" from it, which I actually found quite likable. We shook hands, and then from morning to lunch we sat around bantering about, whereby Hagemeister, as I observed him, was very reserved and barely spoke a word. I knew next to nothing about this fellow.

CONTROL FORM D.2
Kontrollblatt D.2

CERTIFICATE OF DISCHARGE
Entlassungschein

ALL ENTRIES WILL BE MADE IN BLOCK LATIN CAPITALS AND WILL BE MADE IN INK OR TYPESCRIPT.

I
PERSONAL PARTICULARS
Personalbeschreibung

Dieses Blatt muss in folgender weise ausgefüllt werden:
1. In lateinischer Druckschrift und in grossen Buchstaben.
2. Mit Tinte oder mit Schreibmaschine.

SURNAME OF HOLDER RUBBEL
Familienname des Inhabers

CHRISTIAN NAMES ALFRED
Vornamen des Inhabers

CIVIL OCCUPATION LANDWIRT
Beruf oder Beschäftigung

HOME ADDRESS Strasse NR. 5
Heimatanschrift Ort CANTRUP
Kreis DIEPHOLZ
Regierungsbezirk/Land HANNOVER

~~DATE OF~~ BIRTH 28. 6. 21.
~~Geburtsdatum~~ (DAY/MONTH/YEAR Tag/Monat/Jahr)

PLACE OF BIRTH SENTEPNEL
Geburtsort

FAMILY STATUS—SINGLE † Ledig
Familienstand ~~MARRIED~~ ~~Verheiratet~~
~~WIDOW(ER)~~ ~~Verwitwet~~
~~DIVORCED~~ ~~Geschieden~~

NUMBER OF CHILDREN WHO ARE MINORS
Zahl der minderjährigen Kinder —

I HEREBY CERTIFY THAT TO THE BEST OF MY KNOWLEDGE AND BELIEF THE PARTICULARS GIVEN ABOVE ARE TRUE.
I ALSO CERTIFY THAT I HAVE READ AND UNDERSTOOD THE "INSTRUCTIONS TO PERSONNEL ON DISCHARGE" (CONTROL FORM D.1).

Ich erkläre hiermit, nach bestem Wissen und Gewissen, dass die obigen Angaben wahr sind. ~~Ich bestätige ausserdem dass ich die "Anweisung~~ für Soldaten und Angehörige Militär-ähnlicher Organisationen" u.s.w. (Kontrollblatt D.1) gelesen und verstanden habe.

SIGNATURE OF HOLDER Alfred Rubbel
Unterschrift des Inhabers

II
MEDICAL CERTIFICATE
Ärztlicher Befund

DISTINGUISHING MARKS NARBE LI. HAND
Besondere Kennzeichen

DISABILITY, WITH DESCRIPTION —
Dienstunfähigkeit, mit Beschreibung

MEDICAL CATEGORY FIT.
Tauglichkeitsgrad

I CERTIFY THAT TO THE BEST OF MY KNOWLEDGE AND BELIEF THE ABOVE PARTICULARS RELATING TO THE HOLDER ARE TRUE AND THAT HE IS NOT VERMINOUS OR SUFFERING FROM ANY INFECTIOUS OR CONTAGIOUS DISEASE.

Ich erkläre hiermit, nach bestem Wissen und Gewissen, dass die obigen Angaben wahr sind, dass der Inhaber ungezieferfrei ist und dass er keinerlei ansteckende oder übertragbare Krankheit hat.

SIGNATURE OF MEDICAL OFFICER Dr. Schinke
Unterschrift des Sanitätsoffiziers

NAME AND RANK OF MEDICAL OFFICER IN BLOCK LATIN CAPITALS DR: MARTIN SCHINKE ASS: ARZT
Zuname Vorname Dienstgrad des Sanitätsoffiziers
(In lateinischer Druckschrift und in grossen Buchstaben)

P.T.O.
Bitte wenden

† DELETE THAT WHICH IS INAPPLICABLE
Nichtzutreffendes durchstreichen

PRS 2334 6.45 500m

III
PARTICULARS OF DISCHARGE
Entlassungsvermerk

THE PERSON TO WHOM THE ABOVE PARTICULARS REFER
Die Person auf die sich obige Angaben beziehen

WAS DISCHARGED ON (Date) 21. März 1946 . FROM THE* HEER
wurde am (Datum der Entlassung) vom/~~von der~~* entlassen

No 27 DIS... CONTROL UNIT

RIGHT THUMBPRINT Abdruck des rechten Daumens

CERTIFIED BY .... OFFICIAL EMBOSSED SEAL
Beglaubigt durch

NAME, RANK AND APPOINTMENT OF ALLIED DISCHARGING OFFICER IN BLOCK CAPITALS MAJOR ... R.A. Amtlicher Einprägestempel

* INSERT "ARMY", "NAVY", "AIR FORCE", "VOLKSSTURM", OR PARA-MILITARY ORGANIZATION, e.g. "R.A.D.", "N.S.F.K.", ETC.
Wehrmachtteil oder Gliederung der die Einheit angehört, z.B. "Heer", "Kriegsmarine", "Luftwaffe", "Volkssturm", "Waffen SS", oder "R.A.D.", "N.S.F.K.", u.s.w.

MILITARY GOVERNMENT OF GERMANY

TEMPORARY REGISTRATION — Zeitweilige Registrierungskarte

Name / Name: R u b b e l , Alfred — Alter / Age: 24 — Geschlecht / Sex: männl.

Ständige Adresse / Permanent Address: Grettewitz Kr. Grimma — Beruf / Occupation: Bauer

Jetzige Adresse / Present Address: Trebsen Ortst. Pauschwitz, Hindenburgstr. 54

Der Inhaber dieser Karte ist als Einwohner der Stadt Trebsen/Sachsen vorschriftsmässig registriert, und es ist ihm oder ihr strengstens verboten, sich von diesem Platz zu entfernen. Zuwiderhandlung dieser Massnahme führt zu sofortigem Arrest. Der Inhaber dieses Scheines muss diesen Ausweis stets bei sich führen.

The holder of this card is duly registered as a resident of the town of Trebsen/Sachsen and is prohibited from leaving the place designated. Violation of this restriction will lead to immediate arrest. Registrant will at all times have this paper on his person.

Entlassungsschein

Legitimations-Nummer / Identity Card-Number

Unterschrift des Inhabers / Signature of Holder

Right Index Finger

H. PETERSON Captain

Name and Rank — Mil Gov Officer, U.S. Army

18. Juni 1945 — Datum der Ausstellung / Date of Issue

(Dies ist kein Personal-Ausweis und erlaubt keine Vorrechte.)
(This is not an identity document and allows no privileges.)

Reiseurlauberkarten von ... bis ... erhalten

Mit Lebensmittelkarten versorgt bis

Ernährungsamt der Stadt Bad Kissingen

Gemeinde Oberdellmar

23. Juli 1945

Deutsches Rotes Kreuz Kreisstelle Kassel-Stadt

Kartoffelschein

Frischmilchschein

Ernährungsamt Abt. B

Urlauberkarten vom ... bis ...

The Panzer Replacement and Training Abteilung 500, Paderborn

With the introduction of the Kampfpanzer (battle tank) Type VI, the Tiger Tank, it became necessary to form a "Tiger Center" that provided education, formation of troops, area for replacement personnel to report for duty, evaluation of combat experiences, and further development of the weapons systems. The ten Army Heavy Panzer Abteilungs, which were under the command of Army High Command, were assigned in the aforementioned areas to Paderborn. Other detachments that had Tiger tanks, for example the three Heavy SS-Panzer Abteilung*s*, were professionally supported.

The first three Tiger Abteilungs, 501, 502, and 503, were set up in May 1942 in different locations under the direction of the Panzer Supervision Office at Army High Command, and consisted of Panzer-Replacement Abteilungs. On the 20th of December 1942, this Supervision Office (S.O. 6) ordered the formation of the Panzer-Replacement Abteilung 500 through the Defense District X (Hamburg) at the Panzer Army Gunnery School at Putlos in Schleswig-Holstein. On the 22nd of February 1943 the abteilung was transferred to the barracks of the 11th Panzer Regiment in Paderborn on Driburger Street and was initially designated the "Staff/Panzer Training - Tiger and Panzer Replacement Abteilung 500." In the meantime, the Tiger Abteilungs 504, 505, 506, 507, 508, and 509 had been formed, and on the first of August 1943 the department was divided up because of proliferating assignments. This was now called "Tank Command Training - Tiger/Panzer Replacement and Training Abteilung 500." The troops were officially subordinate to the Commander of the Panzer Army Schools and territorially to the Defense District VI (Münster). The Commander had the status and authority of a regimental commander. In February 1945 there was again another new structural modification, in which the Panzer Training and the Replacement and Education Abteilungs, as well as the Technical Training Group, were melded together and became known as the "Panzer Replacement and Training Abteilung - Tiger" (no number). Towards the end of the war in April 1945, in the Westphalia area, additional parts of the abteilung were split up and sent into action without any real results worth speaking of. The British occupation forces moved into the barracks on Driburger Street.

The Commanders were:
April 1943- July 1943:
Major Hannibal von Lüttichau
July 1943- June 1944:
Oberstleutnant Hans-Georg Lüder
July 1944- December 1944:
Oberstleutnant Erich Hoheisel
December 1944- April 1945:
Major Werner Freiherr von Beschwitz

The location of Paderborn had been selected because:

Sennelager (Camp Senne) lay directly north of the city and offered ample space and opportunities to undertake such things as testing, shooting, driver's school, and mobility in water.
The restricted area secured its privacy and secrecy.
Its proximity to the Henschel Tiger Production Works at Kassel meant it was a short drive from one location to the other.

Training in the following areas meant an almost obligatory road through Paderborn:

Tank Driver
Tank Repair (with Industry-Command)
Richtschützen (gunnery)

The entire replacement abteilungs and the recovering wounded returning to their field abteilungs were sent here for training or further education. The troops in the field could assume then, that the personnel who were trained here, mostly those from the rank and file, were well trained and educated. This was also valid as a rule for the *Panzerkommanders* (Tank Commanders), *Feldwebels* (Sergeants), and *Unterofficiers* (Junior Officers). Unfortunately the officers, platoon leaders, and company commanders generally weren't too intimate with the technical aspects of the Tiger because the Replacement and Training Abteilung either did not have the sufficient capacity to individually train these officers, or they were of the false opinion that most officers did not feel it necessary to involve themselves in such weapons and equipment studies. All in all the training in Paderborn remained excellent all the way to the end of the war because experienced front-line Tiger veterans provided this training. About 16 field detachments with Tigers, to which around 16,000 tank professionals belonged, were, next to their normal training, also supported by educational and tactical written texts, or "Paderborner Pages," which was a sort of "re-printing" style, as we used to appraise such things in the Bundeswehr during the early regulation-free days. Paderborn is sure to have its fair mention in any sort of "Tiger primer."

In order not to travel to the drill grounds at the Sennelager through the city, Schloß Neuhaus, or Schlagen, near the mill located on the pond there was an equipment park. Located there also was the diving basin, which allowed for diving depths of up to four meters. Gunnery practice was held on the "Bismarck" firing range, and the drivers' school was located north of the troop camp. Because of limited fuel supplies a few Tigers were outfitted with four large fuel cans, or with a propane gas generator. It could not be avoided that these tanks would grind to a halt in inconvenient areas and at inconvenient times.

Paderborn was sufficiently large enough that it could assimilate the many soldiers—an estimated 2,000 tank personnel and the soldiers at the air base—which allowed for the general population and military personnel to get on quite nicely. The charming surroundings, the Teutoburg Forest, the Egge Mountains, and other areas were all easily accessible through use of the well established tramway network, with which one could travel as far as Detmold. The nice thing was that in the city and surrounding areas there never developed that primitive "German Soldier-Ambiance" with all its arcane little pubs scattered around.

In all the extensive Tiger literature out there, one normally only sees the Field Units ever written about. Up to now there has never really been anything written about the Replacement- and Educational Training Abteilungs. These people, who also were very much a part of the Panzer troops attending these schools and about whose significance the subject has never been appropriately treated, have truly been passed over and undeservedly so.

Rubbel, June 1995

Above: *Major* Werner Freiherr von Beschwitz. Right: *Major* Hannibal von Lüttichau

The German Soldier as Viewed by His Former Adversaries

In war a soldier enjoys a certain ability to have trained and learned well, in order to carry large amounts of responsibility. In our Western ideas of man, which are Christian in their origins, the overall concept of "Miles Christanium"—the Christian Knight—has been revered and exalted throughout the centuries. The soldier should defer to the moral court of higher instance in times where orders and their execution are strongly called into question. Because these lofty ideals very often do not actually function in reality it gives rise to the need to adhere to them even more. We Germans, in our divided homeland, had the greatest opportunity to observe the conflicting worldviews first hand and to remark on their influence on the common soldier. The soldiers of the National Peoples' Army (East Germany) were indoctrinated with the theory of the Western foe and the "enemy of the classes," which in turn inculcated them with a certain hatred of this enemy as a consequence. The soldiers of the *Bundeswehr* (West Germany) were mainly concerned with the defense of their country, and their educational concepts were focused on certain traditional values, such as loyalty, bravery, camaraderie, and humanity. These were not discoveries of late, rather, these were virtues that were never lost even in the worst of all wars ever witnessed, the Second World War.

The war in Russia took on a hard, even gruesome form. It was forced on us by our opponent. The German soldier was brave and self-sacrificing. He fought hard if it had to be that way. That the boundaries of international military law were crossed is not denied; it was the exception, however, and never the rule.

There were two reasons for that. Germans in general, and thus the German soldier as well, are normally disciplined and humane. Goebbels complained in his diary that the German soldier of the Eastern Front treated the civilian populace too humanely and circumspectly. The other reason takes on a more pragmatic form. German military leadership ensured until the end of the war that law and discipline prevailed. Whenever necessary it enforced this with punishment. A "wild" troop element, a band of ill-disciplined soldiers, is almost impossible to lead.

There are abuses and crimes in every war; we cannot pronounce our opponents non-guilty in that respect either. Take the unbelievable brutality of the Red Army, for example. One allowed it or, indeed, even encouraged it to take "revenge." That had, as a consequence, the fact that almost all units of the Red Army had become ill-disciplined after the end of the war. They had fought their way to Berlin, but had also murdered, plundered, and raped along the way. As a result, they had to be exchanged with other elements.

Our former opponents have evaluated the *Wehrmacht* as follows:

General George C. Marshall (USA):

> The Germans are natural fighters. You have to admit that...born soldiers. And they were trained magnificently...their discipline was unshakeable.

Field Marshall Lord Alexander (Great Britain):

> I doubt whether there is another soldier in the world who could survive that and continue to fight with the same cohesiveness. (Monte Cassino)

Marshall Lattre de Tassingny (France):

> In our times there have been a few major accomplishments ... the Germans at Stalingrad, for example. They carried out an illogical order. But what they accomplished is exemplary.

Marshall Zhukov (Soviet Union):

> The fighting capabilities of the German soldiers and officers and their professional and tactical training reached a high level, especially in the *Luftwaffe* and among the armor units. The German soldier knew his responsibilities in battle and in the field, and he was persistent, self-continent, and disciplined.

The tragedy of the German soldier was as follows:

- He believed he had to fight bravely in a cause for his fatherland.
- Four and one half million young men died in the war—approximately one third of those who were called to service between the ages of 18 and 40.
- His fatherland allows "know-it-alls" who weren't even born then to label those surviving and the dead—who can't even defend themselves anymore—potential criminals.

The heads of state of former enemy nations will speak to soldiers from the war, even if German heads of state are silent. French President Mitterand said the following on 8 May 1995:

> I have discovered what virtue, what courage the German people possess. When I think of the German soldiers who died in such large numbers I no longer think of the uniform, nor of the ides that motivated them. They were courageous. They had set out in that storm and risked their lives. They gave up their lives for something bad, but how they did it had nothing to do with that which was bad. They were people who loved their fatherland – and one must not forget that.

The Fallen and Survivors

"The Fallen" of the schwere Panzer-Abteilung 503

The Survivors of the schwere Panzer-Abteilung 503 "TIGER" Commemorate their Comrades who fell during the 2nd World War from 1942-1945

They died on the battlefields
In Russia, in the Ukraine, in Poland,
In France, in Hungary, in Austria,
In Czechoslovakia

The War, which they did not want, took from them their young lives. Their Fatherland, for which they died in good faith, today admits, that its honor may be challenged, for their obligation to stand as soldiers, it may be dammed as personally guilty.

The combat deaths from the 1st *Panzerkompanie*

80 Comrades

7 *Offiziere*, 27 *Unteroffiziere*, 46 *Soldaten*

Adamek, Barton, Bausinger, Beyer, Bleß, Bobsin, Böhm, Böhme, Bohn, von Borries, Brück, Bürger, Buck, Dankert, Djuba, Dunkel, Dürrlich, Erdmann, Fendesack, Fürlinger, Gehrke, Griewald, Großmann, Gronau, Gükl, Grütter, Heider, Höppner, Hornberger, Jammerath, Jokwer, Knake, von Koerber, Knispel, Krause, Krüger, Kubin, Kukla, Lehmann, Leitzke, Marat, Markus, Mau, Meß, Meller, Mink, Minek, Mundry, Neumann, Öls, Oelsner, Oppe, Rauschenberger, Reutermann, Rippl, Ritscher, Scheele, Schielke, Schiekarski, Schmähl, Schmidt, Schneider, Schröder, Schult-Dargen, Schulz, Schulze, Schütze, Spatke, Thome, Vogt, Vorderbrügge, Vorreith, Wagner, Walter, Wedler, Werner, Wiesenfarth, Woisin, Wollmann, Zimmermann.

The combat deaths from the 2nd *Panzerkompanie*

68 Comrades

3 *Offiziere*, 22 *Unteroffiziere*, 43 *Soldaten*

Bartsch, Bähr, Beck, Becker, Beckmann, Behrens, Beringer, Bendler, Behn, Besenhardt, Bielfeldt, Billy, Blank, Böge, Bohn, Braatz, Cüsow, Damlaks, Dähne, Degelow, Drücker, Fink, Gergens, Golder, Golz, Hammrich, Heckmann, Hein, Heinl, Hennig, Hüneken, Keller, Klatt, Klein, Knapp, König, Kutzner, Lebert, Messer, Meyer, Mühl, Nachbaur, Nowacki, Paech, Panknin, Paulsen, Pausewein, Pitz, Plum, Porsch, Pörwol, Rabe, Ramp, Reich, Rohlfs, Ruffert, Schellicke, Schlorke, Schmidt, Schröder, Siebert, Stober, Streetz, Tettenborn, Utesch, Wahl, Williard, Zabel.

The combat deaths from the 3rd *Panzerkompanie*

59 Comrades

2 *Offiziere*, 22 *Unteroffiziere*, 35 *Soldaten*

Angerer, Baschek, Bierig, Blunk, Böttcher, Bornschier, Bormann, Brendecke, Brunswik, Clas, Dolk, Ebert, Essler, Fuhrmeister, Gärtner, Gerrels, Hinterpichler, Höhn, Jäger, Jürgensen, Kunze, Legath, Liebscher, Matthes, Meinert, Miederer, Mühling, Peters, Petzka, Pichler, Pukwnik, Roth, Radestock, Rahn, Rauh, Ricke, Riedel, Rieschel, Rothermann, Rummel, Sauerbier, Schilling, Schmidt, Schulte, Schubert, Schuster, Skoda, Steininger, Stühler, Taubert, Thon, Tröger, Wehrheim, Weiland, Weinert, Westerhausen, Will, Wunderlich, Zäh, Zahn.

We only know the names of the 201 soldiers from the three Panzer Companies who fell. There are neither numbers nor names from the other Companies in our Abteilung:

The Staff Company,
The Supply Company,
The Maintenance Company,

We commemorate these loyal and selfless auxiliaries of the Panzer Companies.

By War's end, an estimated 300 soldiers of our abteilung had fallen into Soviet captivity, and only a fraction of them are known by name. And to this day it is not known who amongst them passed away there. We commemorate our Comrades who were taken prisoner and who perished. We mourn with the relatives of the dead and missing, whose fates remain forever shrouded in darkness.

The list of those from 2nd Company who fell was only kept until December 31st, 1945; the list from 3rd Company is not complete because of missing sources.

From the time of formation (May 4th, 1942) to capitulation (May 9th, 1945), the abteilung had personnel losses of the following percentages:

Out of 28 Officers	14 fell = 50%
Out of 279 Junior Officers	72 fell = 26%
Out of 598 common soldiers	148 fell = 24%

Mainly the three Panzer Companies suffered these documented losses. The losses suffered by the Staff-Company, the Supply Company, and the Maintenance Company, with a total personnel population of 646 soldiers, can only be estimated. If the numbers from the German Red Cross form a basis that 28% of all German soldiers died in war and captivity, then the abteilung may interpolate 180 more deaths. In total: 234 in the battle squadrons and 180 in the mobile (wheeled) squadrons = 414.

Barely half of all soldiers from our abteilung were killed. Of noteworthiness is the high number of officers who fell in combat and the many who perished in Russian captivity, which by early 1945 amounted to about 90%.

About half of our soldiers, measured against a personnel population of 910 men, perished in the war. An estimated 300-400 soldiers fell into Soviet captivity by war's end. We do not know their names. How high the death rate is amongst these comrades nobody knows, because the *Wehrmacht* Information Office and the Red Cross did not register the names of the troops who had died in captivity back to their actual detachments.

Der letzte Wehrmachtbericht

Seit Mitternacht ſchweigen nun an allen Fronten die Waffen.

Auf Befehl des Großadmirals hat die Wehrmacht den auſſichtslos gewordenen Kampf eingeſtellt. Damit iſt das faſt ſechsjährige heldenhafte Ringen zu Ende. Es hat uns große Siege, aber auch ſchwere Niederlagen gebracht. Die deutſche Wehrmacht iſt am Ende einer gewaltigen Übermacht ehrenvoll unterlegen.

Der deutſche Soldat hat, getreu ſeinem Eid, im höchſten Einſatz für ſein Volk, für immer Unvergeßliches geleiſtet.

Die einmalige Leiſtung von Front und Heimat wird in einem ſpäteren gerechten Urteil der Geſchichte ihre endgültige Würdigung finden.

Den Leiſtungen und Opfern der deutſchen Soldaten zu Lande, zu Waſſer und in der Luft wird auch der Gegner die Achtung nicht verſagen. Jeder Soldat kann deshalb die Waffe aufrecht und ſtolz aus der Hand legen und in den ſchwerſten Stunden unſerer Geſchichte tapfer und zuverſichtlich an die Arbeit gehen für das ewige Leben unſeres Volkes.

Die Wehrmacht gedenkt in dieſer Stunde ihrer vor dem Feind gebliebenen Kameraden.

Die Toten verpflichten zu bedingungsloſer Treue, zu Gehorſam und Diſziplin gegenüber dem aus zahlloſen Wunden blutenden Vaterland.

Losses of the German *Wehrmacht* in WW II:

5,318,000 dead (fallen, missing, perished in captivity)
Every 8th male German died in the war.
Of those born in1920, 41% had died in the war.
28% of Wehrmacht soldiers and 34% of Waffen-SS soldiers died in the war.

Of those soldiers who fell into Russian captivity by the end of 1944, 95% were either killed when taken prisoner or later perished in captivity.

The losses suffered in the war by the schwere Panzer Abteilung 503, with personnel strength of almost 1,000 men, including Hiwi: The numbers that fell were:

Offiziere:	*50% (14 out of 28)*
Unteroffiziere:	*26% (72 out of 279)*
Soldaten:	*24% (148 out of 598)*

That was 234 out of a total of 905.

In the 3 Panzer Companies with target personnel strengths of 88 men, the numbers who died in battle were:

1st Company:
7 Offiziere, 27 Unteroffiziere, 46 Soldaten = 80, of which there were 4 Company Commanders

2nd Company:
3 Offiziere, 22 Unteroffiziere, 43 Soldaten = 68

3rd Company:
2 Offiziere, 22 Unteroffiziere, 35 Soldaten = 59

Total: 207

The numbers of dead from the Staff, Maintenance, and Supply Companies could not be ascertained, as there are no complete lists of such. Their personnel strength was that of 633 men, of which we estimate about 200 perished in combat. Out of the 500 or so who fell into Russian captivity by war's end, according to official estimates, about 30% passed away, and we assume perhaps as many as 170 more may have died. So the amount of those belonging to our abteilung who died in combat is around 580.

Newspaper Article :

Panzer Soldiers Hold Meeting

eg Bassum, The desire to stage a reunion of former comrades of the schwere Panzer Abteilung 503 finally took place right here in Bassum after a lot of preliminary work (out of 1,000 veterans, only the addresses of 80 were known). During the course of that Saturday about 40 of them got together, among them the former Abteilung Kommandeur, thanks to the warm reception afforded them by TSV Bassum, who allowed them to meet at the Sporting Academy. The maintenance of tradition and camaraderie, clarification of the fates of those still missing, collection of more addresses of former comrades and strengthened continuance of research in favor of the 16 vets still in captivity were, next to the exchanging of stories, the themes of the meeting. On Sunday the group attended a wreath laying ceremony in front of the war memorial. "We want to strive", so said their Kommandeur, "among other things, to show ourselves worthy of the sacrifices they made." The participants left Bassum imparting a special thanks to the TSV for their hospitality shown them at their Sporting Academy, whose facilities garnered much admiration and recognition.

Abteilung Reunion from 12-14th August 1955: Upper row (from left to right): Hans Kück (1st Company), Fritz Riemer (1st Company), Otto Mewes (1st Company), Helmut Vogel (1st Company), Günter Piepgras (1st Company), Hans von Hagemeister (Staff Company), Fritz Plenge (Staff Company), Dr. Walter Barkhausen (Maintenance Company), Dr. Franz-Wilhelm Lochmann (1st Company), and Walter Laden (Maintenance Company) Middle row: Alfred Rubbel (1st Company), Hans-Martin Müller-Nobiling (1st Company), Richard Freiherr von Rosen (3rd Company), unknown, Heine Rondorf (3rd Company), unknown, Martin Burmester (2nd Company), Rathje (Maintenance Company), Holger Wiegand (Supply Company), and Dr. Nordewin von Diest-Koerber (Abteilung Kommandeur). Bottom row: Eberhard Lange (3rd Company), Hermann Albers (1st Company), unknown, Hans-Jürgen Burmester (1st Company), unknown, Dr. Helmut Linsser (1st Company), Gerhard Niemann (3rd Company), and Ludwig Werkmeister (3rd Company).

Bibliography

Errinerungen an die Tiger-Abteilung 503, 1942-1945

The Combat History of schwere Panzer Abteilung 503: In Action in the East and West with the Tiger I and Tiger II

Tscherkassy: die Kämpfe der s.Pz.Abt. 503 vom 19.1.1944-25.2.1944

Putlos, Schleswig-Holstein: Panzertruppen-Schießschule: Truppenunterkunft: Truppenübungsplatz, in der Zeit 1935-2000: Eine Quellensammlung

Nehring:
The History of German Armored Warfare 1916- 1945
Rittgen: Die Schulen der Panzertruppen des Heeres, 1918 bis zum Aufbau der Bundeswehr.
Tessin: Formations of the German Wehrmacht and Waffen SS, volumes 10/11.
AG 503: Memoirs of the 503rd Tiger-Abteilung 1942-1945

A Word from Alfred Rubbel

To the book title...

This book took rise slowly, over a two-year period, because of all the memories of events and people who had played a major role in my experiences.

It was not only about the recollections of events and training, although there were many such experiences.

By far the most significant, highest valued, and longest lasting impressions from the war was the comradeship. Because of those feelings, I gave this book the title:

Five Comrades

...and I dedicate this book to my panzer crew, the five soldiers who crewed Tiger panzer "114".
They were:

- the Richtschütze (gunner) Walter Junge fom Berlin, always a helpful and happy comrade who performed his duties well and was highly decorated
- the Ladeschütze (loader) Johann Strohmer from Bohemia who worked quietly and efficiently
- the Panzerfahrer (tank driver) Walter Eschrig from Silesia who was brilliant with the technicalities of the panzer
- the Panzerfunker (tank radio-operator) Alfred Peucker also from Silesia, who in his secondary function - acquiring the on-board provisions - always kept the crew content

We all returned home from the war with our lives but not without our share of wounds.

My four comrades have all since passed away and their remembrance is left to me. The idea of comradeship has always been held in high-esteem in the German Army.

From shared experiences developed a strong understanding, a thorough bond and personal acceptance of each other. We all looked out for each other and were willing to make the ultimate sacrifice for our comrades, our lives.

The special conditions in a panzer, in which everyone had to give their best within the confines of a narrow space, formed us into an ever-strengthening proficient and efficient panzer crew.

Our crew remained together for more than a year and through many battles across the Ukraine successfully proving ourselves time and again.

The panzer was not only our transport full of munitions into battle; it was our living quarters for weeks and months at a time. It provided us a place to sleep and lasting protection, not only against the enemy, but also against the weather.

Fellowship, Esprit 'de Corps of the Panzertruppe and the combat life together in a panzer yielded a unique and good reputation for the German Panzertruppe.

We, the "Five Comrades" from "114", contributed to that spirit. Our black uniforms and the deaths-head badges on our collars separated us from the gray masses of the Army; we wore them with pride.

During my five war years, I met many soldiers who I also was proud to consider as good comrades. We five of Tiger "114" became and remained an unbreakable group of comrades long after the war had passed.